A BOOK OF

BUILDING CONSTRUCTION AND MATERIALS

FOR

SEMESTER - III

SECOND YEAR DEGREE COURSE IN CIVIL ENGINEERING
ACCORDING TO NEW REVISED SYLLABUS OF
SHIVAJI UNIVERSITY, KOLHAPUR
(JUNE 2014)

V. R. Phadke
M. E. (Civil)
Professor, Civil Engineering Deptt.,
Rajarshi Shahu College of Engineering
Tathwade, **PUNE.**

Mrs. V. S. Limaye
M. Tech. (Civil - TP) M.P.M.
Assistant Professor, Civil Engineering Deptt.,
Sinhgad College of Engineering,
Vadgaon (Bk), **PUNE.**

M. V. Jadhav
M. E. (Civil)
Professor, Civil Engineering Deptt.,
Sanjivani College of Engineering,
Kopargaon, **AHMEDNAGAR.**

U. S. Patil
B.E. Civil, M. Tech (Construction Management),
Associate Professor, Civil Engg. Deptt.,
Bharati Vidyapeeth's Group of Institutes Technical Campus,
College of Engineering, Lavale, PUNE - 43

BUILDING CONSTRUCTION AND MATERIALS (S.E. CIVIL Semester - III)

First Edition : September, 2014

ISBN: 978-93-5164-231-2

© : **Authors**

The text of this publication, or any part thereof, should not be reproduced or transmitted in any form or stored in any computer storage system or device for distribution including photocopy, recording, taping or information retrieval system or reproduced on any disc, tape, perforated media or other information storage device etc., without the written permission of Authors with whom the rights are reserved. Breach of this condition is liable for legal action.

Every effort has been made to avoid errors or omissions in this publication. In spite of this, errors may have crept in. Any mistake, error or discrepancy so noted and shall be brought to our notice shall be taken care of in the next edition. It is notified that neither the publisher nor the authors or seller shall be responsible for any damage or loss of action to any one, of any kind, in any manner, therefrom.

Published By :
NIRALI PRAKASHAN
Abhyudaya Pragati, 1312, Shivaji Nagar,
Off J.M. Road, PUNE – 411005
Tel - (020) 25512336/37/39, Fax - (020) 25511379
Email : niralipune@pragationline.com

Printed at
Repro Knowledgecast Limited
India

DISTRIBUTION CENTRES
PUNE

Nirali Prakashan
119, Budhwar Peth, Jogeshwari Mandir Lane
Pune 411002, Maharashtra
Tel : (020) 2445 2044, 66022708, Fax : (020) 2445 1538
Email : bookorder@pragationline.com

Nirali Prakashan
S. No. 28/25, Dhyari,
Near Pari Company, Pune 411041
Tel : (022) 24690204 Fax : (020) 24690316
Email : dhyari@pragationline.com
bookorder@pragationline.com

MUMBAI
Nirali Prakashan
385, S.V.P. Road, Rasdhara Co-op. Hsg. Society Ltd.,
Girgaum, Mumbai 400004, Maharashtra
Tel : (022) 2385 6339 / 2386 9976, Fax : (022) 2386 9976
Email : niralimumbai@pragationline.com

DISTRIBUTION BRANCHES

NAGPUR
Pratibha Book Distributors
Above Maratha Mandir, Shop No. 3, First Floor,
Rani Jhanshi Square, Sitabuldi, Nagpur 440012,
Maharashtra, Tel : (0712) 254 7129

BENGALURU
Pragati Book House
House No. 1, Sanjeevappa Lane, Avenue Road Cross,
Opp. Rice Church, Bengaluru – 560002.
Tel : (080) 64513344, 64513355,
Mob : 9880582331, 9845021552
Email:bharatsavla@yahoo.com

JALGAON
Nirali Prakashan
34, V. V. Golani Market, Navi Peth, Jalgaon 425001,
Maharashtra, Tel : (0257) 222 0395
Mob : 94234 91860

KOLHAPUR
Nirali Prakashan
New Mahadvar Road,
Kedar Plaza, 1st Floor Opp. IDBI Bank
Kolhapur 416 012, Maharashtra. Mob : 9855046155

CHENNAI
Pragati Books
9/1, Montieth Road, Behind Taas Mahal, Egmore,
Chennai 600008 Tamil Nadu, Tel : (044) 6518 3535,
Mob : 94440 01782 / 98450 21552 / 98805 82331, Email : bharatsavla@yahoo.com

RETAIL OUTLETS
PUNE

Pragati Book Centre
157, Budhwar Peth, Opp. Ratan Talkies,
Pune 411002, Maharashtra
Tel : (020) 2445 8887 / 6602 2707, Fax : (020) 2445 8887
Pragati Book Centre
Amber Chamber, 28/A, Budhwar Peth,
Appa Balwant Chowk, Pune : 411002, Maharashtra,
Tel : (020) 20240335 / 66281669
Email : pbcpune@pragationline.com

Pragati Book Centre
676/B, Budhwar Peth, Opp. Jogeshwari Mandir,
Pune 411002, Maharashtra
Tel : (020) 6601 7784 / 6602 0855
PBC Book Sellers & Stationers
152, Budhwar Peth, Pune 411002, Maharashtra
Tel : (020) 2445 2254 / 6609 2463

MUMBAI
Pragati Book Corner
Indira Niwas, 111 - A, Bhavani Shankar Road, Dadar (W), Mumbai 400028, Maharashtra
Tel : (022) 2422 3526 / 6662 5254, Email : pbcmumbai@pragationline.com

PREFACE

It gives us great pleasure in presenting this book on **"Building Construction and Materials"** for the Second Year Degree Course in Civil Engineering students of Shivaji University, Kolhapur. It is strictly as per the New Revised Syllabus (2014).

The book has been written in simple language to understand. It explains the theory as well as the applications of various topics step by step so that the students can understand the logic behind the topic.

Our sincere thanks to **Shri. Dineshbhai Furia, Shri. Jignesh Furia, Shri. M. P. Munde** of Nirali Prakashan for publishing our book in time.

We are also thankful to staff members of Nirali Prakashan who have worked hard in bringing out this book.

We are also thankful to **Mr. Virdhaval Shinde**, Branch Manager, Kolhapur Office and **Mr. Ashok Nanaware**, Branch Manager, Sangli District for their valuable help and efforts for promotion of our book.

Our special thanks to our family members, students and all those who directly or indirectly supported us in this project.

Any suggestions and feedback shall be appreciated and acknowledged.

September 2014   **Authors**
Pune

SYLLABUS

SECTION - I

Unit - I (08 Hours)

Engineering properties and uses of following materials.

Stones – Requirements of good building stone, Uses of building stones.

Bricks – Manufacturing, Types (clay bricks, fly ash, cellular light weight concrete brick, aerated cement concrete brick or autoclave brick) and Engineering properties.

Aggregates - Fine aggregates and Coarse aggregates - Origin, types, particle size and shape, mechanical and physical properties, artificial sand.

Timber – Natural and Artificial wood and their applications in Civil Engineering.

Steel – Standard structural sections, steel as reinforcement. High yield strength steel and high tensile steel, Uses of steel in Building Construction.

Cement - Types.

Tiles - Ceramic, Vitrified, Natural Stone, Paving Blocks etc.

Miscellaneous – Aluminium, Glass, Plastic, Admixtures: chemical (plasticiser and super plasticisers), Minerals (fly ash, microcilica).

Unit - II (06 Hours)

Basic requirements of a building as a whole: Strength and stability, Dimensional stability, Comfort and convenience, Damp prevention, Water-proofing techniques, Heat insulation, Day lighting and ventilation, Sound insulation and anti-termite treatment.

Building components and their basic requirements : Foundations, plinth walls and columns in superstructure, floors, doors and windows, sills, lintels and weather sheds, roofs, steps and stairs, utility fixtures.

Formwork: Materials (wooden, steel and aluminium).

Foundations: Types and their suitability (Stepped, isolated, combined, strip, raft, strap or cantilever, pile).

Unit - III (04 Hours)

Stone masonry – Random Rubble, Uncoursed Rubble, Coursed Rubble and Ashlar Masonry.

Brickwork and Brick Bonds - English, Flemish, Rat trap bond (one brick thick).

Composite masonry, Various partition walls, Brick, aluminium and timber.

SECTION - II

Unit - IV (06 Hours)

Arches: Arches and their stability consideration, Technical terms in arches, Types of arches, Methods of construction.

Lintels: Necessity, Materials: wood, stone, brick, steel, R.C.C. and reinforced brick lintels.

Doors: Classification, T.W. Paneled Door, Flush Door, Aluminium Glazed Doors, Steel Doors, Fixtures and fastening.

Windows: Classification, T.W. Glazed Windows, Aluminium Glazed Windows, Steel Windows, Fixtures and fastening.

Unit - V (05 Hours)

Stairs: Technical terms, Requirements of a good stair, Uses, Types, Materials for construction. Design of stairs (Dog Legged, quarter turn and open well), Ramps, Lifts and Escalator.

Unit - VI (07 Hours)

Roofs and Roof Coverings: Terms used. Roofs and their selection, Pitched roofs and their types, Steel trusses types and their suitability, Roof covering, Material, Details, Fixtures Mangalore tiles, A.C., G.I. and Precoated sheets, Concept of proflex (trussless) roof and their selection.

Concrete Flooring (Tremix Flooring)

Construction of upper floors: R.C.C. slabs, R.C.C. beams and slab. Flat slab floor.

Waterproofing: Materials, methods and systems.

CONTENTS

Section - I

Unit - I

1. Engineering Properties and Construction Materials .... 1.1 – 1.48

Unit - II

2. Basic Requirements of a Building .... 2.1 – 2.24

Unit - III

3. Stone and Brick Masonry .... 3.1 – 3.28

Section - II

Unit - IV

4. Arches and Lintels .... 4.1 – 4.22

5. Doors and Windows .... 5.1 – 5.34

Unit - V

6. Stairs .... 6.1 – 6.22

Unit - VI

7. Roofs and Roof Coverings .... 7.1 – 7.28

8. Concrete Flooring (Tremix Flooring) .... 8.1 – 8.20

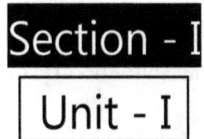

Chapter 1

ENGINEERING PROPERTIES AND CONSTRUCTION MATERIALS

INTRODUCTION

The materials required for construction of structures are known as building materials. It is very essential for an engineer, builder, architect and contractor, to be thoroughly conversant with these building materials. The knowledge of different types of materials, their properties and uses for different purposes is very essential for the builder in achieving overall economy.

Building material accounts for about 70% of the total cost of construction. Thus it is important that the building materials are easily and cheaply available. Civil engineering construction involves use of natural materials like stone, timber, sand, aggregates and manufactured materials like steel, plastic, cement etc. The correct use of materials leads to better structural strength, efficiency and economy in the long run. The commonly used materials required in civil engineering construction are discussed in this chapter in regards to their types, sizes, properties and uses etc.

1.1 STONE

1.1.1 Introduction

Stone has been used as a building material from very early times in the construction of buildings and other structures, both in India as well as in other parts of the world. Some of the ancient temples and forts are important examples of the extensive use of stone as a building material in our country over the ages. Today building stones are extensively used in various structures in different forms and can be used to fulfil a wide variety of requirements. Stone as a building material is the cheapest and most durable. It is quarried from rock.

1.1.2 Classification of Rocks

Stones are classified as per the classification of their parent rock.
1. **Geological Classification:** Igneous, sedimentary, metamorphic rocks.
2. **Physical Classification:** Stratified, unstratified, laminated rocks.
3. **Chemical Classification:** Siliceous, argillaceous, calcareous rocks.

(a) Igneous Rocks are formed by cooling the molten lava material which erupts from the interior of the earth. These are solid, massive and crystalline stones without stratification.
E.g.: Basalt, granite, and dolerite.

(b) Sedimentary Rocks are formed by denudation and deposition of existing rocks because of the weathering action of water, wind, frost, etc. Water is the most powerful medium of transportation of the disintegrated material from the primary rocks which ultimately gets deposited at the bottoms of lakes, streams and oceans. The consolidation of these deposited layers takes place under pressure by heat or by chemical agents acting as natural cements.
E.g.: Sand stone, lime stone, and gravel.

(c) Metamorphic Rocks are originally either igneous or sedimentary rocks that have undergone considerable changes in their constitution, i.e. in their shape, structure, and sometimes, even in their mineral composition, under the influence of agents of metamorphism. There are three principal agents of metamorphism, viz. heat, pressure, and chemically acting fluids.
E.g.: Marble, gneiss, slate, Schist etc.

(d) Stratified Rocks: These rocks show a layered structure in their natural environment. They possess planes of stratification or cleavage and can be easily split up along these planes. Stratified rocks are derived from sedimentary rocks.
E.g.: Sand stone, lime stone, slate.

(e) Unstratified Rocks: Rocks which do not have strata and cannot be easily split into thin slabs fall into this category. Their structure may be crystalline or granular.
E.g.: Marble, granite, trap etc.

(f) Siliceous Rocks: These rocks have silica as their main component. They are hard, durable and not easily affected by weathering agents.
E.g.: Sand stone, granite, trap etc.

(g) Argillaceous Rocks: These rocks have clay or alumina as their main component. Although these rocks are dense, compact and hard, they are brittle and cannot withstand shock.
E.g.: Slate, laterite etc.

(h) Calcareous Rocks: These rocks have calcium carbonate as their main constituent. The durability of these rocks depends upon the atmospheric constituents as they are acted upon by hydrochloric acid.

E.g.: Marble, lime stone etc.

1.1.3 Requirements of a Good Building Stone

Stone used in building construction should have following properties :

1. **Strength :** The stone should be strong enough to withstand all external loads coming over it. Crushing strength of various stones is sufficiently high, however, crushing strength of sedimentary and metamorphic rocks along the plane of stratification is very less. Hence, while laying such stones, it should be ensured that, the load is acting perpendicular to the plane of stratification as shown in Fig. 1.1 (a) and not as shown in Fig. 1.1 (b).

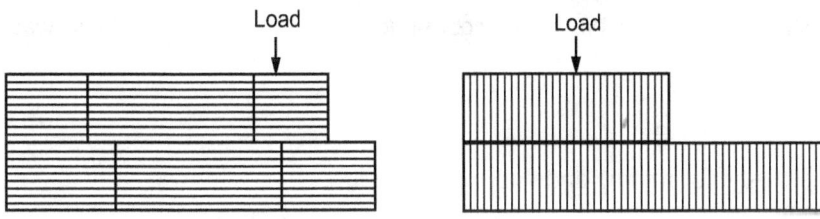

(a) Correct method of laying   (b) Incorrect method of laying of stone

Fig. 1.1 : Showing method of laying of stone

2. **Durability :** Durability of stone depends upon its chemical composition, homogeneity, and cementing material. A stone having high strength may not be durable, if various granular particles of stones are not held together by equally strong cementing material. (To check durability, stone chips of size 2 to 3 cm are placed in a beaker containing clean water, and stirred for about 30 minutes. If stone contains soluble minerals, then water will become dirty, indicating lesser durability).

3. **Resistance to weathering :** Through various industrial and chemical wastes, fumes of acid are emitted. These fumes are dissolved in rain water, which attack stone masonry gradually.

Sand stone, Gneiss have higher weather resistance, whereas Lime stone, Laterite rocks are less weather resistant.

4. **Colour/Appearance :** The exposed surface of stone masonry should have pleasing appearance/colour and should be in conformity with the desired effect of building.

5. It should be easy to work with and should be able to take polish.

Marble, sand stone are easy to work with for ornamental purposes. Granite is not easy to work with ornamental purposes, but can take very high polish.

6. Resistance to fire : The fire resistance of stone depends upon percentage of calcium carbonate and iron oxide present in stone. Lesser the percentage of the same, higher is the fire resistance. Relatively, sedimentary rocks have higher resistance fire than igneous or metamorphic rocks.

7. It should be free from crack, cavities, flaw, decay or patches of soft material.

8. The surface of a freshly broken stone should be sharp, clean and bright with uniformity of colour and texture.

9. The specific gravity of the stone should not in any case be less than 2.5.

10. It should be crystalline and homogeneous in structure.

11. It should not absorb more than 5 percent of its weight of water after immersion in water for one day.

12. It should be well seasoned.

13. It should be obtainable easily, economically and in large quantity in water for one day.

1.1.4 Uses of Stone

1. Slates are used for roofing and flooring material.
2. Stone blocks are mainly used in stone masonry in walls, foundations and ornamental facia work.
3. Granite is used for bridge abutments and pier, flooring, kitchen otta, steps, table top.
4. Marble is extremely suitable for ornamental and superior type of building work, monumental structures, floors, tiles.
5. Quartzite is used for rubble masonry, road metal, and aggregate for concrete.
6. Lime stone slabs are used for flooring, paving and roofing.

1.2 BRICKS

1.2.1 Introduction

Brick is a rectangular block of regular shape obtained by moulding a mixture of clay and sand, and generally burnt at high temperature. Bricks are easily moulded from plastic clays, also known as brick clay or brick earth.

Brick earth is derived by the disintegration of igneous rocks. Potash feldspars, orthoclase or microcline ($K_2O: Al_2O_3 \cdot 6SiO_2$) is mainly responsible for yielding clay mineral in the earth. This mineral decomposes to yield kaolinite, a silicate of alumina which on hydration gives a clay deposit $Al_2O_3 \cdot 2H_2O$ known as kaolin.

A good brick earth should be a mixture of pure clay and sand that when prepared with water can be easily moulded and dried without cracking or warping. It should contain a small quantity of lime which causes the grains of sand to melt and helps bind the particles of brick clay together.

1.2.2 Chemical Composition of Brick Earth

According to IS: 2117-1975, the clay selected should preferably confirm to the following mechanical composition:

        Clay   :   20 - 30 % by weight
        Silt   :   20 - 35 % by weight
        Sand   :   35 - 50 % by weight

The total content of clay and silt may preferably be not less than 50 % by weight.

1.2.3 Functions of the Constituents of Brick Earth

1. Silica or sand prevents shrinkage in brick earth, and cracking and warping of bricks.
2. Clay or alumina makes brick earth plastic and makes bricks hard.
3. Lime and oxides of iron both act as fluxes helping the grains of sand to melt and bind the particles of clay together.
4. Oxides of iron also impart a red colour to the brick but if in excess, it makes the bricks dark blue.
5. Magnesia present in clay, combined, with oxide of iron makes the brick yellow.

1.2.4 Manufacture of Clay Bricks

Bricks are made by treating suitable brick earth or clay, moulding it to shape and size, drying it, and then baking it at high temperatures in order to fuse the constituents to a hard, homogeneous mass. The process of manufacture is as follows:

1. Selection of site
2. Preparation of clay
3. Moulding of bricks
4. Drying of bricks
5. Burning of bricks

1.2.5 Properties of Bricks

As per IS: 1077-1976, the following are the standard properties of burnt clay bricks:

1. Size and Shape of Brick: Hand moulded or machine moulded bricks should be free from cracks, flaws and from nodules of free lime. Bricks of 9 cm height may be moulded with a frog 1 to 2 cm deep on one of its flat sides. Bricks should have smooth rectangular faces and sharp corners. The standard size of common building bricks is 19 cm (length) × 9 cm (width) × 9 cm (height).

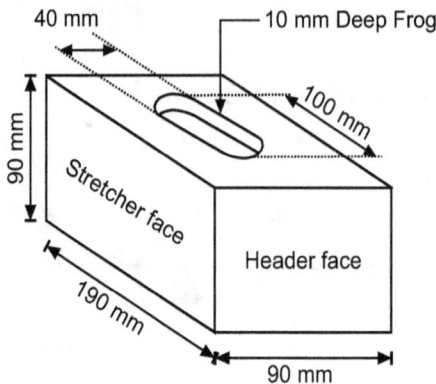

Fig. 1.2

2. **Water Absorption of Bricks:** After immersion in cold water for 24 hours, the average water absorption of common building bricks should not be more than 20 % by weight and 15 % by weight for higher classes.

3. **Efflorescence:** Salts such as sulphates of sodium and potassium, if present in bricks, are dissolved by the absorbed water. As and when drying conditions prevail, evaporation takes place at the outer face of the wall and the water previously absorbed is drawn to the face and along with it the salts also. As evaporation proceeds, the concentration of the salt in solution increases until a point is reached when the salt crystallizes out. According to IS : 3495-1976, the rating of efflorescence should not be more than moderate and slight for higher classes. The liability of efflorescence is reported as follows:

    Nil   :   When there is no perceptible deposit of efflorescence.
    Slight   :   When not more than 10 % of the area of the brick is covered with a thin deposit of salts.
    Moderate   :   When there is a deposit that is heavier than that mentioned under slight, and covering up to 50% of the exposed area of the brick surface, but unaccompanied by powdering or flaking of the surface.

4. **Strength of Bricks:** Bricks often have to withstand great compressive stresses. The durability of the masonry depends upon the strength of the bricks. The common building bricks should have a minimum strength of 35 kg/cm^2.

1.2.6 Types of Bricks

Bricks can be classified into two types:

(i) **Modular brick:** The bricks confirming to IS 1077-1976 are known as modular bricks. The size of brick is 19 cm × 9 cm × 9 cm. With mortar joint the size becomes 20 cm × 10 cm × 10 cm.

(ii) **Traditional brick:** These bricks are manufactured traditionally or right from ancient times. There is a slight variation in the size of the brick from place to place. The common size is 23 cm × 11.4 cm × 7 cm.

Classification of Bricks:

The bricks are also classified as per their quality. The comparison of properties of different classes of bricks is given in Table 1.1.

Table 1.1

Sr. No.	Description	First Class	Second Class	Third Class
1.	Moulding	Machine and Table	Hand and Table	Hand
2.	Colour and burning	Uniform red	Uniform red, may be slightly over burnt.	May be slightly over burnt or under burnt.
3.	Shape	Sharp straight edges, plain rectangular faces.	May have slightly blunt edges.	May have distorted round edges.
4.	Absorption of water by weight	Less than 20%	Less than 22%	Less than 25%
5.	Efflorescence	Nil	Slight	Moderate
6.	Compressive strength	Greater than 10.5 N/mm	Greater than 7 N/mm	Greater than 3.5 N/mm

1.2.7 Uses of Bricks

1. Bricks are used in brick masonry as a load bearing or a partition wall.
2. Bricks are used as flooring material.
3. Special refractory bricks are used as refractory lining.
4. Broken bricks are used as aggregates in lime concrete.
5. First class bricks are used in architectural compositions and face work of building.
6. Bricks are also used in the construction of roads.

1. Fly Ash Bricks :

Fly ash is the extremely fine ash flying along with flue gases is trapped in electrostatic precipitators and it is collected. This collected fly ash depending upon the sizes is used for the manufacturing of fly ash brick.

The fly ash brick can be used for an alternate of burnt brick.

The raw material required for fly ash brick is fly ash from thermal power plant station, sand, stone dust and ordinary Portland cement.

The raw materials required are mixed in a pan mixer and added water for the semi dry mix.

This dry mix is placed in a mould of hydraulic press.

The moulded bricks are dried for one or two days and the curing of the bricks is done for 14-21 days.

These bricks produced are sound, compact and of uniform shape.

Minimum fly ash content for fly ash bricks and blocks to quantify as fly ash based products shall be 50% of the total input material.

The fly ash bricks are used for the construction of residential building, commercial building, industrial building,

Fig. 1.3

2. Cellular Light Weight Concrete Bricks :

Cellular light weight concrete bricks are available in three grades :

Grade A : These bricks are used for load bearing structure and have a brick density in the range of 1200 kg/cum-1800 kg/cum.

Grade B : These bricks are used for non-load bearing structure and have a brick density in the range of 700 kg/cum-1000 kg/cum.

Grade C : These bricks are used for providing thermal insulation and have a brick density in the range of 400 kg/cum-600 kg/cum.

The raw material used for the brick is cement, fly ash (min fines 20%) water foaming compound.

The weight of the brick is lighter than the conventional burnt brick.

The dry density of the brick is 750-800 kg/m^2.

The compressive strength of the brick 25-30 kg/cm^2.

The sound insulation property of the cellular light weight brick is more superior than the burnt clay brick and hollow brick.

The brick can be easily cut with saw, nailed and it can be easily drilled.

It is an ecofriendly material as well as pollution free.

3. Autoclaved Aeraed Concrete Brick :

Autoclaved Aeraed concrete brick is highly thermally insulating concrete based material used both internal and external construction.

Autoclave brick is mostly suited for urban areas with high rise building and those with high temperature variations due to lower density high rise building structures require less steel and concrete for structural member of AACB.

When AAC is mixed and cast in forms, several chemical reactions take place that give AAC its light weight (20% of the weight of concrete) and thermal properties. Aluminium powder reacts with calcium hydroxide and water to form hydrogen. The hydrogen gas foams and doubles the volume of the raw mix creating gas bubbles up to 3mm (⅛ inch) in diameter. At the end of the foaming process, the hydrogen escapes into the atmosphere and is replaced by air.

When the forms are removed from the material, it is solid but still soft. It is then cut into either blocks or panels, and placed in an autoclave chamber for 12 hours. During this steam pressure hardening process, when the temperature reaches 190° Celsius (374° Fahrenheit) and the pressure reaches 8 to 12 bars, quartz sand reacts with calcium hydroxide to form calcium silica hydrate, which gives AAC its high strength and other unique properties. Because of the relatively low temperature used AAC blocks are not considered fired brick but a lightweight concrete masonry unit. After the autoclaving process, the material is ready for immediate use on the construction site. Depending on its density, up to 80% of the volume of an AAC block is air. AAC's low density also accounts for its low structural compression strength. It can carry loads of up to 8 MPa (1,160 PSI), approximately 50% of the compressive strength of regular concrete.

Advantages are as follows:
- Improved thermal efficiency reduces the heating and cooling load in buildings.
- Porous structure allows for superior fire resistance.
- Workability allows accurate cutting, which minimizes the generation of solid waste during use.
- Resource efficiency gives it lower environmental impact in all phases of its life cycle, from processing of raw materials to the disposal of waste.
- Light weight saves cost and energy in transportation, labour expenses, and increases chances of survival during seismic activity
- Larger size blocks leads to faster masonry work.

1.3 AGGREGATES

Water, cement and crushed rock or gravel and sand – are the chief ingredients of concrete. About 75% of volume of concrete is composed of aggregates and hence properties of aggregate greatly affect the properties of concrete such as workability, strength, durability and economy. Originally, aggregate was looked upon an inert material dispersed throughout the cement paste mainly for economic reasons. But, in fact, its physical, thermal and sometimes also chemical properties influence the performance of concrete. Aggregate being cheaper than cement, it is economical to put into the concrete as much of the aggregate as possible. But the aggregate is not used only from the economical viewpoint but the higher volume stability and better durability (than the cement paste alone), which is due to the aggregate, is more valuable.

1.3.1 Classification of Aggregates

The classification of the aggregates is generally based on their geological origin, size, shape, unit weight etc.

1.3.1.1 Classification According to Geological Origin

The aggregates are usually derived from natural sources and may have been naturally reduced to size (e.g. gravel or shingle) or may have to be reduced by crushing. The suitability of the locally available aggregate depends upon the geological history of the region. The aggregate may be divided into two categories; namely the natural aggregates and artificial aggregates.

Natural Aggregates: These are generally obtained from natural deposits of sand and gravel, or from quarries by cutting rocks. Cheapest among them are the natural sand and gravel which have been reduced to their present size by natural agents, such as water, wind and snow etc. The river deposits are the most common and have good quality. The second most commonly used source of aggregates is the quarried rock which is reduced to size by crushing. Crushed aggregates are made by breaking rocks into requisite graded particles by blasting, crushing and screening etc. from the petrological stand point. The natural aggregates, whether crushed or naturally reduced in size, can be divided into several groups of rocks having common characteristics. Natural rocks can be classified according to their geological mode of formation. i.e. igneous; sedimentary or metamorphic origin, and each group may be further divided into categories having certain petrological characteristics in common. Such a classification has been adopted in IS : 383: 1970.

Artificial Aggregate: The most widely used artificial aggregates are clean broken bricks and air-cooled fresh blast-furnace slag. The broken bricks of good quality provide a satisfactory aggregate for the mass concrete and are not suitable for reinforced concrete work if the crushing strength of brick is less than 30 to 35 N/mm². The bricks should be free from lime mortar and lime sulphate plaster. The brick aggregate is not suitable for waterproof construction. It has poor resistance to wear and hence it is not used in concrete for the road work.

The blast-furnace slag is the byproduct obtained simultaneously with pig iron in the blast furnace, which is cooled slowly in air. Carefully selected slag produces concrete having properties comparable to that produced by using gravel aggregate. However, the corrosion of steel is more due to sulphur content of slag, however, the concrete made with blast-furnace-slag aggregate has good fire resisting qualities. The other examples of the artificial slag are the expanded shale, expanded slag, cinder etc. Such aggregates should not contain more than one % of sulphates and should not absorb water more than 10% of their own mass.

1.3.1.2 Classification According to Size

The aggregates used in concrete range from few centimetres or more, down to a few microns. The maximum size of the aggregate may vary, but in each case it is to be so graded that the particles of different size fractions are incorporated in the mix in appropriate proportions. The particle size distribution is called the *grading of aggregate*. According to size, the aggregate is classified as: fine aggregate, coarse aggregate and all-in-aggregate.

Fine aggregate: It is the aggregate most of which passes through a 4.75 mm IS sieve and contains only so much coarser material as is permitted by the specifications. Sand is generally considered to have a lower size limit of about 0.07 mm. Material between 0.06 mm and 0.002 mm is classified as silts, and still smaller particles are called *clay*. The soft deposit consisting of sand, silt and clay in about equal proportions is termed as *loam*. The fine aggregate may be one of the following types:

(a) Natural sand, i.e. the fine aggregate resulting from natural disintegration of rock and/or that which has been deposited by stream and glacial agencies.
(b) Crushed stone sand, i.e. the fine aggregate produced by crushing hard stone, or
(c) Crushed gravel sand, i.e. the fine aggregate produced by crushing natural gravel.

According to size, the fine aggregate may be described as coarse, medium and fine sands. Depending upon the particle size distribution, IS : 383 - 1970, has divided the fine aggregate into four grading zones. The grading zones become progressively finer from grading zone I to grading zone IV.

Coarse aggregate: The aggregate most of which are retained on the 4.75 mm IS sieve and contain only so much of fine material as is permitted by the specifications are termed as coarse aggregates. The coarse aggregate may be one of the following types:
(a) Crushed gravel or stone obtained by the crushing of gravel or hard stone,
(b) Uncrushed gravel or stone resulting from the natural disintegration of rock, or
(c) Partially crushed gravel or stone obtained as a product of the blending of the above two types.

All-in-aggregate: Sometimes combined aggregates are available in nature comprising different fractions of fine and coarse aggregates, which are known as all-in-aggregate. The all-in-aggregates are not generally used for making high quality concrete.

Single size aggregate is the bulk of aggregate which passes one size on the normal concrete series and is retained on the next smaller size.

Graded aggregate is the aggregate comprising of a proportion of all sizes from a given normal maximum to 4.25 mm. When these sizes are so proportioned as to give a definite grading, it is a well graded aggregate.

1.3.1.3 Classification According to Shape

The aggregate shape is important as it affects the workability of concrete. The shape of aggregate is defined using certain geometrical characteristics of particles. Classification of aggregates based on the shape of aggregate as given by IS : 383 - 1963 is tabulated in Table 1.2.

Table 1.2: Particle Shape

Classification	Description	Example
Rounded	Fully water-worn or completely shaped by attrition.	River or sea shore gravels, desert, and wind blown sand.
Irregular or partly rounded	Naturally irregular or partly shaped by attrition and having rounded edges.	Pit sands and gravels, dug flints or rocks.
Angular	Processing well defined edges formed at the intersection of roughly plane faces.	Crushed rock of all types, talus, screens.
Flaky	Material usually regular of which the thickness is small relative to the width and/or length.	Laminated rocks.

To achieve the best possible strength, concrete should be as dense as possible i.e. it should contain minimum voids. The voids are greatly influenced by the shape of aggregates. The rounded particles can be packed to produce a concrete with 33% voids i.e. 67% of the volume of concrete is occupied by the aggregates. The rounded particles produce smoother mix for a given water-cement (W/C) ratio. On the other hand, the angular and flaky particles reduce the workability and demand more cement and water to give the specified strength of concrete mix. Not more than 10 to 15% of flaky particles should be used in concrete.

1.3.1.4 Classification According to Surface Texture

According to surface texture the aggregates are classified as glassy, smooth, granular, rough, crystalline and honeycombed. This classification is based on degree to which the particle surfaces are polished or dull and smooth or rough. The surface texture of aggregate depends on the properties of parent materials, such as hardness, grain size and pore characteristics. Examples of surface texture are as follows:

(a) Glassy   : Black flint
(b) Smooth   : Chert, slate, marble
(c) Granular   : Sandstone, oolite
(d) Rough   : Basalt, limestone
(e) Crystalline   : Granite, gabbro, gnesis
(f) Honeycombed   : Brick, pumice, trass, clinker.

1.3.1.5 Classification Based on Unit Weight

The aggregates can also be classified according to their unit weights as normal-weight, heavy-weight and light-weight aggregates.

Normal-weight aggregates: The commonly used aggregates i.e. sands and gravels; crushed rocks such as granite, basalt, quartz, sandstone and limestone; and brick ballast etc., which have specific gravities between 2.5 and 2.7 produce concrete with densities ranging from 2300 kg/m³ to 2600 kg/m³ and crushing strength at 28 days between 15 to 40 N/mm² are termed as normal-weight aggregates.

Heavy-weight aggregates: Some heavy-weight aggregates having specific gravities ranging from 2.8 to 2.9 but unit weights from 2800 kg/m³ to 2900 kg/m³ such as magnetite (Fe_3O_4), barytes ($BaSO_4$) and scrap iron are used in the manufacture of heavy weight concrete. Concrete having densities of about 3000 kg/m³, 3600 kg/m³ and 5700 kg/m³ can be produced by using magnetite, baryte and scrap iron, respectively.

Light-weight aggregates: The light-weight aggregates having bulk density upto 1200 kg/m^3 are used to manufacture the structural concrete and masonry blocks for reduction of the self weight of the structure. These aggregates can be either natural, such as diotomite, pumice, volcanic cinder etc. or manufactured, such as bloated clay, sintered fly ash or foamed blast-furnace-slag. In addition to reduction in the weight, the concrete produced by using light-weight aggregate provides better thermal insulation and improved fire resistance.

1.3.2 Mechanical Properties of Aggregates

The following important mechanical properties of aggregate when the aggregate is subjected to wearing surfaces, are:

1. Toughness
2. Hardness
3. Crushing value of aggregate (compressive strength).

The toughness of aggregate which is measured as the resistance of the aggregate to failure by impact is determined in accordance with IS : 2386 (part - IV) - 1963. The aggregate impact value shall not exceed 45% by weight for aggregate used for concrete other than those used for wearing surfaces and 30% for concrete for wearing surfaces.

The hardness of aggregate defined as 'its resistance to wear' and obtained in terms of aggregate abrasion value is determined by using Los Angeles machine as described in IS : 2386 (part-IV)-1963. The method combines the test for attrition and abrasion. A satisfactory aggregate should have an abrasion value of not more than 30% of aggregates used for wearing surfaces and 50% for aggregates used for non-wearing surface.

The aggregate crushing value is a relative measure of the resistance of an aggregate sample to crushing under gradually applied compressive load. The crushing value of aggregate is restricted to 30% for concrete used for road pavements and 45% for other structures.

1.3.3 Physical Properties of Aggregates

The physical properties of aggregates depend on:

(i) Size of aggregate
(ii) Shape of aggregate
(iii) Surface texture of aggregate
(iv) Bulk density

(v) Specific gravity
(vi) Moisture content of aggregate
(vii) Porosity and water absorption.

The shape of the aggregates, influence the workability of fresh concrete and bond between the aggregate and the mortar phase. The shape of aggregates are of four categories like rounded, irregular, angular and flaky. The angular aggregates having thickness smaller than the width and/or length are termed as flaky. The rounded aggregate requires lesser amount of water and cement paste for a given workability. On the other hand, the use of crushed aggregate may result in 10 to 20% higher compressive strength due to development of stronger aggregate-mortar bond. The flakiness index of a coarse aggregate is generally limited to 25%.

The surface texture is a measure of the smoothness or roughness of the aggregate. The surface texture may be classified as glassy, smooth, granular, rough, crystalline, porous and honeycombed.

Shape and surface texture of aggregate influence considerably the strength of concrete. The flexural strength is more affected than the compressive strength and the effects of shape and texture are more significant in the case of high strength concrete.

The bulk density of an aggregate can be used for judging the quality of aggregate by comparison with normal density for that type of aggregate. It is also required for converting proportions by weight into the proportions by volume.

The specific gravity is required for the calculations of the yield of concrete or of the quantity of aggregate required for a given volume of concrete. The specific gravity of an aggregate gives valuable information on its quality and properties. Higher the specific gravity of an aggregate, indicates the stronger and harder aggregate.

There is no theoretical relation between the strength of concrete and the water-absorption of the aggregate used. The pores of surface of the particle affect the bond between the aggregate and cement paste. Thus, affecting the strength. Also the porosity affect the bond between the aggregate and the cement paste, the resistance of concrete to freezing and throwing, resistance to abrasion and the specific gravity of aggregate.

1.3.4 Artificial Sand

In naturally available sand, often undesirable materials (like chlorides, harmful chemicals which adversely affect the concrete) are present in clayey material adhered to sand. On the contrary, the same are absent in manufactured sand. Thus, manufactured sand is clean and does not contain harmful or deleterious materials as it is produced from clean parent rock.

Due to advances in technology, now it is possible to manufacture sand which has following advantages :

1. Well graded.
2. Superior surface texture.
3. It can be compacted properly to produce low voids.
4. Lesser quantity of coating material (such as cement) is required.
5. Required quantity and quality of sand can be produced in a short time.
6. Wastage of sand is less.

If economy at large is considered, artificial sand, many times, proves the economical.

Uses of Sand :

1. Sand forms a major constituent in cement concrete. Roughly 45 to 50 volume of concrete is occupied by sand.
2. Sand is also required for making mortar used in brick work, stone masonry.
3. Sand is required in plastering to give a smooth surface to walls.
4. Sand serves as a draining material and is therefore used in filteration filling behind retaining wall, around foundation, filling well foundations, as a drain seepage water from earthen dams.

1.4 TIMBER

Timber is a natural, good old material suitable for building, carpentary or other engineering purposes. As per old English it means "to construct or build". At many locations it can be appropriately used such as beams, trusses, rafters, joists in floors, door-window shutters and frames, staircases, poles, piles, columns, partition, furniture etc.

The natural wood-timber as a living tree is known as **standing timber**. The timber obtained after falling a tree is known as **rough timber** and the one which is sawn and cut to suit the need is known as **converted timber**.

Day-by-day, its use is decreasing due to scarcity, high cost of labour and timber and availability of relatively cheaper and stronger material.

Classification of Timber : Timber is classified according to :

(a) Growth of Tree :
1. *Exogeneous* i.e. outward growing trees. Distinct consecutive rings are formed in the horizontal section of such trees known as annual rings. Further, it can be divided into two categories conifers and deciduous, Soft - Chir, Deodar, Fir, Pine, Spruce etc. Hard - Babul, Oak, Sal, Teak, Mahagony etc.
2. *Endogeneous* i.e. inward growing trees, such as palms, canes and bamboos.

(b) Durability : Indicative average life of group of trees.

(c) Strength :

(d) Refractiveness : Indicating resistance to defects during seasoning.

1.4.1 I.S. 399 - 1963 Classification

1. **Zonal :** Depending upon the zonal division of India i.e. North, South, East, West, Central.
2. **Uses :** Depending upon classification for timber, uses are as follows.
   (a) Construction,
   (b) Furniture and cabinet making,
   (c) Light packing cases,
   (d) Heavy packing cases,
   (e) Agricultural implements and tools,
   (f) Turnery articles and toys,
   (g) Veneers and plywoods.
3. **Availability :** Depending upon the quantum available per year, the classification is as under :
   (a) X – Most common with quantity ≥ 1000 tonnes/yr.
   (b) Y – Common with quantity 250 to 1000 tonnes/yr.
   (c) Z – Less common with quantity < 250 tonnes/yr.
4. **Durability and Strength :** If the trees are susceptible to various actions due to fungi, insects, chemicals, physical and mechanical agencies then the strength is less, thereby it will indicate a less durable tree.
   (a) Class I   – average life ≥ 120 months.
   (b) Class II – average life 60 to 119 months.
   (c) Class III – average life < 60 months.

Table 1.3 : Safe working stresses and other properties for Indian Timbers Commonly used : Standard grade

Trade Name	Ave. Wt. kg/m³	Modulus of Elasticity T/cm² All grades	Bending and tension along grain extreme fibre stress			Shear stress all locations		Compressive stress Parallel to grain			Compressive stress Perpendicular grain			Durability Grade or Class
			Inside Location	Outside Location	Wet Location	Horizontal	Along grain	Inside Location	Outside Location	Wet Location	Inside Location	Out-side Location	Wet Location	
1. Babul or Kikar	835	108	182	154	124	15.4	22.2	112	102	80	65.5	50.5	41.5	III
2. Benteak	675	110	138	112	92	9.2	13.0	88	78	64	41.5	32.5	26.0	I
3. Blue Pine	515	68	66	56	50	5.6	8.0	52	46	38	17.0	13.5	10.5	III
4. Chir	575	98	84	70	60	6.4	9.2	64	56	46	22.5	17.5	14.0	III
5. Deodar	560	95	102	88	70	7.0	10.2	78	70	56	26.5	23.0	17.0	I
6. Fir, Partal	465	94	78	66	56	6.0	8.4	60	52	42	16.0	12.5	10.5	III
7. Haldir	675	91	138	112	92	9.4	13.4	84	74	64	36.5	28.0	23.0	III
8. Kail	515	68	66	56	50	5.6	8.0	52	46	38	17.0	13.5	10.5	III
9. Sal	800	127	168	140	112	9.4	13.4	106	94	78	45.5	35.0	29.0	I
10. Spruce	480	92	78	66	52	6.0	8.4	56	50	42	17.0	13.7	10.5	III
11. Teak	625	96	140	116	94	9.8	14.0	88	78	64	40.0	31.0	25.5	I
12. Walnut	575	91	116	94	78	8.4	12.0	66	70	50	23.0	18.5	15.0	III

5. **Refractiveness :** It indicates resistance to defects during seasoning of timber.
   (a) Class A (Highly Refractive) : Timber which while air seasoning is not prone for development of any defect, fall under this category.

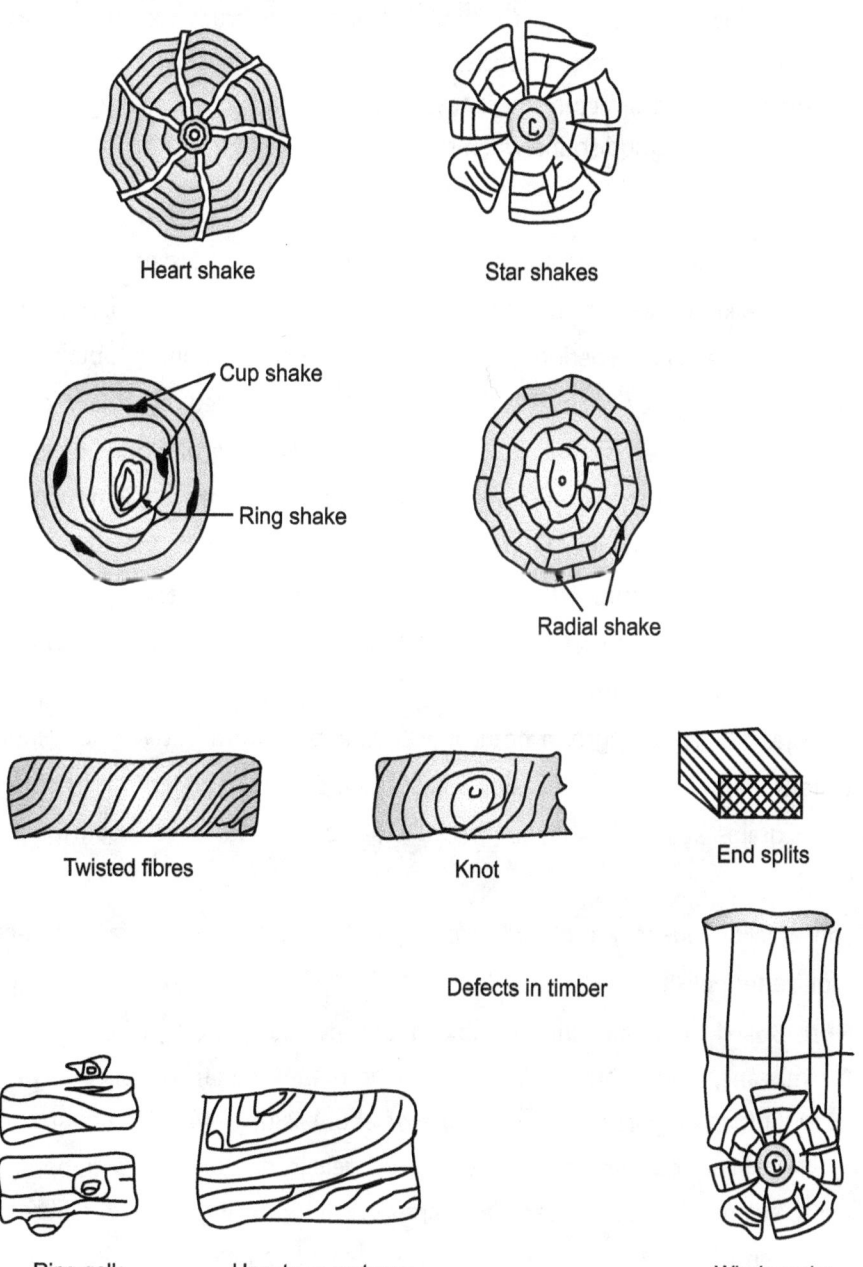

Fig. 1.4 : Defects - Diseases - Decay of timber

(b) Class B (Moderately Refractive) : Timbers under this class can be seasoned with appropriate precautions against rapid drying; e.g. Teak, Sheesam etc.

(c) Class C (Low Refractive) : These require special precautions during seasoning.

In general for a good timber, it must exhibit following properties viz. strength, durability, weather resistance, fire resistance, elasticity, workability, toughness and resistance to wear, sufficient weight, uniform structure, hardness, compact, dark colour, straight fibres, shiny appearance, sweet smell, good sound when struck etc.

Industrial Timber :

The timber which is manufactured scientifically in a factory to suit the need and to serve the desired purpose is known as industrial timber; such as veneers, plywood, particle board etc.

1. Veneers : These are superior quality thin sheets or slices of timber obtained by rotary cutting, peeling of logs or slicing. Large veneers are produced by rotary cut whereas attractive decorative veneer is obtained by slicing on radial face of woods of teak, walnut, rose wood, sheesam etc. The thickness of veneer varies from 0.4 mm to 0.6 mm or more.

2. Plywood : These are thin board formed by gluing together thin sheets of veneer. (Odd in number) under pressure ($70 - 150$ kg/cm^2). Placement of sheets is carried out in such a manner that grains of one layer are at right angles to the other. This offers greater resistance to cracking and splitting.

Advantages : Same strength in both directions and uniform but very less shrinkage in both directions. Inner veneers with grains parallel to face veneer are known as core whereas the one with grains at right angles are called cross bands. Adhesives used for gluing are synthetic resins.

Superior quality veneers are placed as outermost veneers on either faces to ensure the plywood for better polish.

3. Fibre Board : Manufacturing of fibre board involves pressing of pieces of wood of about 20 mm, cane, wood fibres, saw dust etc. The matter is initially boiled in water. Then passed to an autoclave where steam pressure of about 2300 kN/m^2 for about half minute and 7000 kN/m^2 for few seconds is applied and released. During this trapped water is vapourised to steam and wooden particles teared apart; producing fibres. The fibres are then spread on woven wire belt in the form of mat, subjected to heat and hydraulic pressure to form dry sheets. Thickness varies between 3 mm to 15 mm. (Normal sheet length $1.2 - 5.5$ m, width $- 1.2$ m).

They are good heat and sound insulators, sturdy, give smooth finish after suitable coat and used for form work and partitions as well.

Sr. No.	Category	Density	Use
1.	Low density or Semi-hard Board	480 – 800 kg/m^3	Ceiling, soft wall decor
2.	Hard board	800 – 1000 kg/m^3	Painted exterior cladding
3.	High density (for superior works)	> 1000 kg/m^3	Where more strength is required

4. Particle Board : Particles or chips are randomly mixed with strong adhesives and subjected to high pressures. Random orientation of particle indicates that the strength will depend upon quality of adhesive and shape of particles. This is weaker than plywood. Long thin chip during orientation will depict more overlap, hence give better strength. Cuboidal particles involving end grain joints in larger proportion results in weaker board.

Three layers with middle layer of longer chips and outer of small particles for better finish are pressed together to give final product.

5. Veneer Faced Boards : Thin veneers are used on either faces and are glued to the core. Veneer will give better look. Grains of veneer are at right angles to that of core. Depending upon core material further classification is :

Sr. No.	Name	Description	Uses
1.	Batten Boards	Core with about 8 cm wide strips i.e. battens.	Partitions, packing cases, furniture, ceiling decor etc., but liable to crack or split.
2.	Block Boards	Strip width is less than 2.5 cm.	Same as above.
3.	Laminated Board	Width is not more than 8 mm, hence the name. Cross band or Core may be continuous or cut and joint type. Stronger than block board. Thickness is 1 cm to 5 cm.	For interiors.

Category of Work	Used Indian Timber
Chaukhat - Frame	Sal, Teak, Deodar, Jamun, Chir, Kail etc.
Door - Window shutters	Teak, Jamun, Deodar, Kail, Chir etc.
Piles or posts	Sal, Sheesam, Jamun
Rail sleepers	Teak, Sal, Deodar, Chir
Handles and Cart wheel	Babul, Sheesam etc.

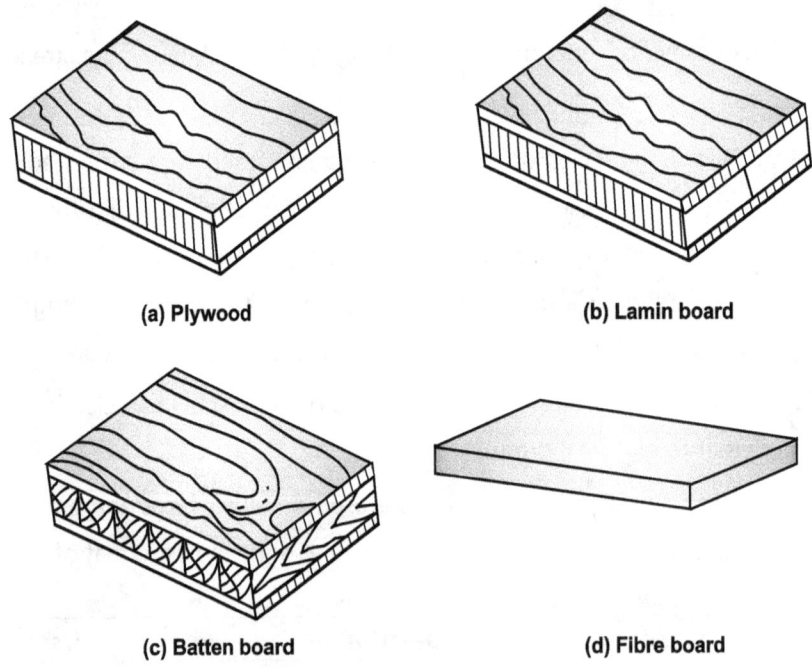

(a) Plywood   (b) Lamin board

(c) Batten board   (d) Fibre board

Fig. 1.5 : Plywood and allied products

1.5 REINFORCING STEEL

Reinforcing steel consists of bars, usually circular in cross section. These are available in three different grades viz. Fe 250, Fe 415 and Fe 500. Fe refers to ferrous metal and the number refers to the specified guaranteed yield stress in N/mm^2.

Steel is an intermediate form between cast iron and wrought iron. It is an alloy of iron and carbon containing carbon from 0.25 to 1.25%. Steels are highly elastic, ductile, malleable, forgeable, weld able.

1.5.1 Classification of Steels

Based on the physical and mechanical properties, the following three types of reinforcements are mainly used in reinforced concrete construction:

(a) Mild steel: Mild steel is used as a structural and non-structural steel in the form of various sections like I-section, channel, angle, flat and also in the form of round bars as reinforcement in concrete. It is designated as Fe 250 due to the yield strength of 250 N/mm^2.

(b) Tor steel: These bars are usually of steel which do not possess a well defined yield point. These bars have low ductility and low bend ability. Tor steel is extensively used as reinforcement in R.C.C work. It is available in two grades: Fe 415 and Fe 500 and a variety of diameters ranging from 8 mm to 40 mm.

(c) High tensile steel: Wires of high tensile strength (tendons) are used in pre-stress concrete. The diameter of wires is 1.5 mm to 8 mm with their ultimate stress ranging from 1500 N/mm^2 to 2350 N/mm^2. Tendons are grouped in the form of cables containing 7 to 8 wires.

1.5.2 Uses of Steel in Building Construction

1. Mild steel is used as distribution steel in R.C.C members.
2. Mild steel is used as rolled structural sections like I-section, T-section, channel section, angle iron, plates; round and square rods in construction work.
3. Plain and corrugated sheets of mild steel are used as roof coverings.
4. Mild steel is also used in the manufacture of various tools and equipments, machine parts, towers and industrial buildings etc.
5. Tor steel is used as main steel in R.C.C members.
6. High tensile steel wires are used in pre-stress concrete.
7. In the fabrication of steel tank, steel pipes.
8. In the fabrication of structural steel in trusses, stanchions, beams in the form of various sections.
9. In the fabrication of non-structural steel component for grills, door frame, windows and stairs.

1.6 CEMENT

The product obtained by burning and crushing to **powder form**, homogeneous and **well proportioned mixture of lime stone and clay** is known as cement. Commonly used greyish coloured cement is known as ordinary **Portland cement.**

1.6.1 Manufacture of Cement

"The raw materials required for manufacture of Portland cement are calcareous materials, such as limestone or chalk, and argillaceous material such as shale or clay. The process of manufacture of cement consists of grinding the raw materials, mixing them intimately in certain proportions depending upon their purity and composition and burning them in a kiln at a temperature of about 1300 to 1500°C, at which, the material sinters and partially fuses to form a nodular shaped clinker. The clinker is cooled and ground to a fine powder with the addition of about 2 to 3% gypsum. The product is known as cement. The oxide compounds in raw materials of cement are as follows.

Table 1.4

Oxide	Content (%)
CaO	60 – 67
SiO_2	17 – 25
Al_2O_3	3 – 8
Fe_2O_3	0.5 – 6.0
MgO	0.1 – 4.0
Alkalies	0.4 – 1.3
SO_3	1.0 – 2.75

The oxide compounds mentioned in Table 1.4 are in the form of:

- Tricalcium silicates (C_3S)   – $3 CaO \cdot SiO_2$
- Dicalcium silicates (C_2S)   – $2 CaO \cdot SiO_2$
- Tricalcium aluminates (C_3A)   – $3 CaO \cdot Al_2O_3$
- Tetracalcium alumino (C_4AF)   – $4 CaO \cdot Al_2O_3 Fe_2O_3$

1.6.2 Physical Properties of Cement

In order to judge suitability of cement, the following properties are important:

(i) Fineness: When cement is very fine, the number of cement particles present per gram of cement will be more and hence total surface area of all particles present in one gram of cement will be more. Therefore more surface area will be available for chemical reaction. Hence, with finer cement, more strength is developed.

Fineness of cement is measured either in terms of (i) surface area of cement in cm^2 per gm. or (ii) percentage of weight retained after sieving cement through 90 micron sieve.

As per I.S. surface area per gram of cement for ordinary Portland cement should not be less than 2250 cm^2/gm. I.S. specifies that the maximum residue after sieving through a 90 micron I.S. sieve should be limited to 10% by weight for ordinary Portland cement.

(ii) Setting Time: The phenomenon by which the plastic cement paste changes into hard mass is called setting of cement. When cement and water are mixed to form paste, water combines chemically with the particles of cement to form hydrates. This process is known as hydration.

(a) Initial Setting Time: Cement paste is initially in plastic state, it sets slowly. Initial setting is that stage at which a crack that may appear will not reunite. This is not a sudden change, but it takes place gradually. Initial setting time of cement should not be less than 30 minutes.

(b) Final Setting Time: This is the term which relates to the completion of the setting process. The setting time is influenced by the percentage of water, its temperature, the temperature and the humidity of air. The setting time is controlled by adding a small quantity of gypsum in cement. Final setting time of cement is about 3 to 6 hours, but it should be greater than 10 hours.

(iii) Compressive Strength: Cement mortar cubes of surface area 50 cm^2 are prepared and kept wet for 3 days or 7 days. Then they are tested in a compression testing machine. For ordinary Portland cement, 3 days strength should be more than 16 N/mm^2 and 7 days strength should be more than 22 N/mm^2.

(iv) Soundness: Due to presence of lime and magnesium oxide, expansion of cement takes place as it comes in contact with water. Such expansion of cement is harmful and cement with less or no expansion is called sound cement. Expansion by Le Chatelier's apparatus should not be more than 10 mm.

1.6.3 Types of Cement

The various types of cements available in the market can be classified as follows:
1. Portland Cements
    (a) Ordinary Portland cement
    (b) Rapid hardening Portland cement
    (c) Low heat Portland cement
    (d) Sulphate resisting cement
    (e) Blast furnace slag cement
    (f) White and coloured cement

2. Super Sulphated cement
3. Natural cement
4. High Alumina cement
5. Special cements:
   (a) Portland Pozzolana cement
   (b) Masonry cement
   (c) Oil-well cement

1. Portland Cement:

(a) Ordinary Portland cement: Nearly 60% of the cement used is ordinary Portland cement. It is admirably suited to all construction work. It is not affected by sulphates. It has medium rate of strength development and heat generation. It has adequate resistance to dry, shrinkage and cracking, but has less resistance to chemical attack.

(b) Rapid hardening Portland cement: This cement is called rapid hardening Portland cement because the strength developed in a standard mortar cube after 3 days is the same as 7 days strength of ordinary Portland cement. This is because of higher percentage of C_3S present in this cement.

(c) Low heat cement: Percentages of C_3S and C_3A are lower in this cement while that of C_2S is higher. This results in a slower rate of reaction, lower evolution of heat of hydration and lower early strength, but the ultimate strength remains more or less unaffected.

(d) Sulphate resisting cement: In hardened cement, there exist two compounds which are sensitive to sulphate attack, viz. calcium aluminate hydrate which reacts with sodium sulphate and magnesium sulphate to form sodium-magnesium sulphoaluminate. This reaction results in an increase in volume of solid paste to the extent of 200 to 400% of the original calcium or magnesium aluminate hydrate. The surrounding concrete, therefore, slowly disintegrates.

(e) Portland Blast Furnace Slag cement: Slag is a waste product in the manufacture of pig-iron. Slag is a mixture of lime, silica, and alumina. It is similar to ordinary Portland cement and can be used in all places where ordinary Portland cement is used. But in view of its low heat evolution it can also be used in mass concrete structures, such as dams, retaining walls, foundations, bridges and abutments. Blast furnace slag cement is more resistant to sulphate attack and is specified for marine works or pipe carrying water containing chemicals or sewage.

(f) White and Coloured cement: White Portland cement is made from raw materials containing very little iron oxide and manganese oxide. China clay is used together with chalk or limestone free from impurities. Oil is used as a fuel instead of coal to avoid contamination. White cement is costly and is used only for interior decoration and architectural finish.

Coloured cement is obtained by mixing the pigments (oxide of lead etc.).

2. Super Sulphated Cement:

Super sulphated cement is made by inter grinding a mixture of 80 to 85% of granulated slag with 10 to 15% of calcium sulphate and about 5% Portland cement clinker and ground to a fineness of 4000 to 5000 cm^2/g.

It is highly resistant to sea water and can withstand the highest concentration of sulphates normally found in soil or ground water and is also resistant to peaty acids and oils.

3. Natural Cement:

It is obtained by calcining and grinding the so-called cement rock, which is a clayey limestone containing about 25% argillaceous material. The resulting cement is similar to Portland cement and it is really an intermediate product between Portland cement and hydraulic lime. Being calcined at very low temperatures, it contains practically no C_3S and is, therefore, it slowly hardens. It is very rarely used, since manufacture of natural cement cannot be controlled.

4. High Alumina Cement:

It is manufactured by the fusion of bauxite and limestone. Bauxite consists of hydrated alumina, oxide of iron and titanium with a small quantity of silica. It is not attacked by carbon dioxide dissolved in pure water and is, therefore, suitable for manufacture of RCC pipes.

5. Special Cement:

(a) Portland Pozzolana Cement: This is a cement of inter-ground or blended mixture of Portland cement and pozzolana. Pozzolana is a natural or artificial material containing silica and alumina in a reactive form. Pozzolanic material is most found in: volcanic ash, pumice, opal shale and cherts, burnt clay, fly ash etc.

The proportion of pozzolana used varies between 10 to 25% according to the weight of cement. Because of free lime is removed, pozzolana concretes have a high resistance to chemical attack. Portland pozzolana cement also has a lower rate of strength development. It is widely used for hydraulic structures such as dams, weirs etc.

(b) Masonry Cement: It is the product obtained by inter-grinding the Portland cement clinker with inert materials (non-pozzolana) such as limestone, dolomite and dolomite gypsum and an air-entraining plasticizer in suitable proportions so that the resulting product confirms to the requirements laid down by the Indian standards.

Masonry cement has been recently used in India because of its property of producing a smooth, plastic, cohesive, strong yet workable mortar when mixed with tint aggregate. Masonry cement is a good substitute for the normally used mortars.

(c) Oil-well Cement: A special type of cement is required for sealing oil-wells. Sealing is necessary to prevent the side of the freshly drilled well from collapsing and to keep ground water out of well shaft.

1.6.4 Field Testing of Cement

It is not always possible to check the quality of cement in a laboratory. In order to check the quality of cement on field, following methods are adopted:

1. When cement is thrown into a bucket of water it should float for sometime before sinking.
2. If one's hand is plunged into a bag of cement he should feel cool and not warm.
3. A thin paste of Portland cement with water should feel sticky between the fingers.
4. If the cement is found in the form of impalpable powder (felt between fingers by rubbing) the cement may be trusted. The quality of cement is suspected, if it is felt gritty.
5. Colour of the cement should be greenish grey and should not show any visible lumps.

1.6.5 Uses

1. Ordinary Portland cement is used in the preparation of cement mortar and cement concrete in the construction of buildings.
2. It is used in the manufacturing of tiles.
3. It is used as a base in paints.
4. It is used for soil stabilization.
5. Rapid hardening cement is used in the construction of highway slabs.
6. Low heat cement is used in mass concreting of gravity dams, retaining walls.
7. White and coloured cement is used for ornamental works, face plastering to give a decorative finish.
8. Sulphate resisting cement is used in the construction of surfaces exposed to sulphate action.

1.7 TILES

1.7.1 Ceramics

Materials whose melting points are very high relative to room temperature are called refractories, may be metallic or non-metallic (i.e. ceramics). Their absolute maximum service temperatures may be as high as 90% of their absolute melting temperatures.

Various types of ceramic products are used in construction industry.

1.7.1.1 Ceramic Tiles

For areas not subjected to heavy traffic, concentrated loads or excessive amount of water, organic adhesive is used for fixation or cement mortar usually. Appearance and resistance to wear make ceramic tiles suitable for use in kitchens and bathrooms, roof etc., available in various colours and cheap.

Types : Glazed, unglazed mosaic, marble, granite, laminated, vitrified etc.
Kitchen sinks or laboratory sinks. Ceramic.

Rectangular Hollow Receptacles : One piece with or without rim, drainer board; sloping towards the waste outlet. Height of top is around 90 cm.

Kitchen sinks	– 600 × 450 × 150 mm
	– 600 × 450 × 250 mm
	– 750 × 450 × 250 mm
Laboratory sinks	– 400 × 250 × 150 mm
	450 × 300 × 150 mm
	500 × 350 × 150 mm
	600 × 400 × 200 mm

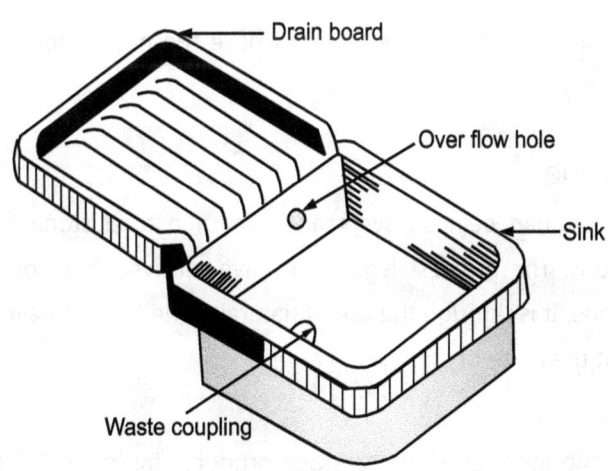

Fig. 1.6 : Kitchen sink

1.7.2 Vitrified Tile

Vitrified tile is a tile produced using vitrification. By this process the tiles created have very low porosity making it stain-resistant and strong. It is an alternative to marble and granite flooring.

Process

Vitrified Tile is made by baking fine minerals like clay and silica, at extreme high temperatures where the individual grains or particles melt and fuse make a vitreous surface. Thus creating a single mass making them extremely hard with low porosity.

Types

- Soluble salt vitrified tiles are screen printed and polished.
- Double charge vitrified tiles are fed through a press that prints the pattern with a double layer of pigment, 3 to 4 mm thicker than other types of tile. This process does not permit complex patterns but results in a long-wearing tile surface, suitable for heavy traffic commercial projects.
- Full body vitrified tiles have pigment in entire body (thickness) of the tile. This makes chips and scratches less noticeable and make this an ideal choice for high traffic zones, but the process significantly increases the cost.
- Glazed vitrified tiles (GVT) have a glazed surface. They offer a wide variety of design, art work and surface textures like wood grain, bamboo, slate or stone. This is also an expensive process, but the cost is dropping as digital printing techniques are introduced.
- Digital Digital

Disadvantages

As a manufactured product, vitrified tiles do not have the natural textures and patterns of marble or granite.

1.7.3 Natural Stone

Throughout history, human beings have made use of natural stone for their social and cultural manifestations. The greatest legacy we have received from our ancestors derives from their use of stone. It is through the use of natural stone that we have found out most of what we know about their way of life.

Definition

The term natural stone includes all those stony products traditionally used by men in the construction industry, including those used in decoration and indoor flooring and walls. The applications of this material are manifold and, as is the case with other materials, new products and applications are continuously found. However, natural rock is more than just a mere construction element to be used for a given work. It is a product that is full of symbolism, has excellent durability and great plastic beauty. This has been proven by stone work carried out by human beings throughout History.

Features and Properties

The most relevant characteristics of natural rock are hardness, resistance to different stress types, composition, porosity, colour, and durability. The latter is perhaps the most important technological feature. There are numerous architectural remains where stone has been the only remaining material, which demonstrates it stability at real scale. The best uses of natural stone require good knowledge of its properties, which are determined through testing. The European standards of these products establish the specific parameters to be determined in the laboratory, namely,

- Petrographic analysis to determine composition and structure.
- Resistance to bending stress.
- Resistance to compressive stress.

1.7.4 Paving Blocks

A paver is a paving-stone, -tile -brick or brick-like piece of concrete commonly used as exterior flooring. In a factory, concrete pavers are made by pouring a mixture of concrete and some type of coloring agent into a mold of some shape and allowing to set. They are applied by pouring a standard concrete foundation, spreading sand on top, and then laying the pavers in the desired pattern. No actual adhesive or retaining method is used other than the weight of the paver itself except edging. Pavers can be used to make roads, driveways, patios, walkways and other outdoor platforms.

Amongst the concrete blocks there is an enormous variety of shapes, sizes, colours, and textures now available, with all the major concrete paving manufacturers producing their own versions of the standard rectangular block, and also special shapes, "olde-worlde" looking tumbled or antiqued units, and an ever increasing array of textured blocks.

Fig. 1.7

1.8 MISCELLANEOUS
1.8.1 Aluminium and Alloys
The most popular non-ferrous metal is Aluminium. Other non-ferrous metals are lead, copper magnesium, nickel, tin, zinc etc.

Main ore for aluminium is bauxite. Bluish-silver white lustrous metal i.e. aluminium is obtained from it. The necessary provision for extracting aluminium from its ore is continuous abundant electric supply. This is the main drawback in commercial exploitation of rich bauxite deposits in India.

Aluminium Plants	States in India (With Hydroelectric Power Supply)
Belgaum	Karnataka
Mettur	Tamil Nadu
Koyana	Maharashtra
Renukoot	U.P.

Procedure : Crushed ore is treated with caustic soda forming sodium aluminate. This is separated by filteration and converted into Aluminate hydrate by precipitation. Finally, after calcination what is obtained is aluminium oxide called alumina. Alumina thus obtained is deoxidised by electrolysis of molten solution. Further, subjected to purification which give 99.5% pure aluminium.

Properties of Aluminium :
1. It is soft, ductile, light in weight (specific gravity 2.7), malleable metal with high luster, corrosion resistant (due to formation of tough adherent oxide film when exposed to air).
2. It melts at 658°C and is a good conductor of heat and electricity.
3. The tensile strength of aluminium is about 100 N/mm^2 for pure metal but for alloys it can reach to 500 N/mm^2.
4. During cold work strength goes to 150 N/mm^2 but there is considerable loss of ductility.

Uses :
1. Production of utensils, electric wires, machine parts etc.
2. Structural load bearing members.
3. Construction of aeroplanes.
4. Roofing sheets.
5. Post-panels-balustrade formation.
6. Door-window frames etc.

7. Aluminium paints, glazing bars, rods etc.
8. Bathroom fittings, surgical instruments, explosive manufacturing, precession survey etc.
9. Flash bulbs for photography.
10. Self-lubricated sintered aluminium bearing (improved corrosion resistance, high thermal conductivity, greater oil retention and stability, less frictional coefficient).

Alloys of Aluminium :
Pure metal does not satisfy all requirements of an engineering structure. The properties exhibiting in case of pure metal can be improved by adding one or more element to it; thereby forming an alloy.

Alloy Preparation : First, metal with highest melting point is heated upto that point in fire clay crucible. Subsequently to this molten metal, other metal/metals with decreasing melting points are added in molten state. Homogeneous mixture is obtained by continuous stirring, agitation, which is poured into suitable moulds and cooled to solidify.

Aluminium alloys find uses in structural applications because strength to weight ratio is often more favourable than that of other materials. This also requires minimum maintenance since aluminium stabilizes in most varied atmospheric conditions.

Aluminium forms alloys after adding one or more elements such as : (1) Copper, (2) Silicon, (3) Iron, (4) Magnesium, (5) Nickel, (6) Manganese etc. Out of different alloys widely used alloys are : Duralium, Aldural, Y-alloy etc.

Sr. No.	Composition Elements	Duralium	Aldural	Y-alloy
1.	Aluminium	94%	10%	92.5%
2.	Copper	4% average, 2 to 6%	90%	4%
3.	Magnesium	Max. 0.5%	–	1.5%
4.	Manganese	Max. 0.4%	–	–
5.	Silicon	Max. 0.5%	–	–
6.	Iron	Max. 0.5%	–	–
7.	Nickel	Max. 0.5%	–	2%

(a) Duralium :
(i) Slightly heavier than Al, with specific gravity 2.85 and as strong as steel.
(ii) It can be forged and machined, hence applications are wide such as reciprocating pistons, air crafts, I.C. engines, with less weight for moving parts.
(iii) It can take high polish, hence can substitute german, silver, brass, copper.
(vi) After heat treatment (heating and quenching), it acquires strength in 2 - 3 days because of its ageing property and it offers more resistance to corrosion.

(b) Aldural : It can be produced in rolled form and consists of duralium with coating of purest Al. More corrosion resistance than duralium.

(c) Y-alloy : Similar to duralium, possesses high strength at high temperature. It can be forged and machined. Being a good conductor of heat suitable for gear boxes, propellers, engine pistons etc.

1.8.2 Glass

It is an important engineering material and it has many applications in construction industry.

Manufacturing Process : It is an amorphous, transparent or translucent, coloured or colourless material which is obtained by fusing a mixture of pure sand (SiO_2), soda (NaOH or KOH) and chalk ($CaCO_3$) with some quantity of broken glass. These ingredients are grounded to fine powder and are melted and fused in a furnace known as Tank Furnace at about 800 to 950°C. The molten mass is poured into moulds of required shape.

Many varieties of glass have been developed so far and it is possible to make glass lighter than cork, softer than cotton or stronger than steel.

1.8.2.1 Types of Glasses

1. **Crown Glass (Soda Ash Glass) :** Major constituents are 75 parts silica, 12.5 parts soda, alumina and cullet (pieces of glass). It represents cheapest quality and used for window panes, bottles, bulbs etc.

2. **Sheet Glass (Window Glass) :** Transparent, thin (2 to 6 mm), glossy, apparently smooth surface (with some wavy texture visible at an acute angle or in reflected rays). Transmits light rays of visible portion (85 to 90%) and blocks ultraviolet rays. Properties like density, strength, thermal conductivity are similar to that of soda - lime - silica glass. Used for glazing, interior doors, skylights and if thickness > 3 mm then employed for multiple glass units, exterior doors, shop windows, showcases etc.

3. **Flint Glass :** Major constituents are 100 parts (by weight) of sand or silica, 70 parts of lead, 33 parts of potash, 100 parts of cullet. It is a very fine variety of glass and is used for making glassware, art glass, radio valves. Very fine polished surface can be obtained for this variety.

4. **Ground Glass :** It is semi-transparent or translucent variety, hence to be used in situations where light transmission without transparency is essential. One of the surface is made rough either by grinding or by melting powdered glass over it.

5. **Pyrex Glass :** Very much heat resistant variety. Sand 90 parts, lime 36, borax 0.5, feldspar 0.5 and cullet 90 parts by weight. Used for laboratory apparatus, cooking utensils, electric insulators etc.

6. Plate Glass : Thickness ranges within 5 mm to 25 mm and is available in larger sheets (upto 4.5 m × 3.5 m). There is no distortion of vision at any angle of observation. It is obtained by mechanical grinding and polishing or by floating molten glass on the surface of molten tin contained in tank. Manufactured glass is usually flat. It has very high compressive strength (about 1200 MPa). Bending and impact strength can be improved by tempering, ion exchange or alike methods.

As light transmission is good (around 87%), it is used for shopping glass window, showcases, mirrors, furniture etc. Also in case of public building fenestration it is employed.

7. Tempered Glass : Tempering dates back to 17th century but commercial production began in 1930s. It has high mechanical strength and heat resistance. Manufactured by heating thick sheets (thickness > 5 mm) to a temperature of 700 to 900°C and then subjected to rapid but uniform cooling with a stream of air or a liquid (By immersion, spraying or hosing).

Glass products to be tempered are fully shaped in advance as tempered glass cannot be cut, ground, drilled etc. Bending strength is 5 to 6 times and resistance to heat is twice as that of ordinary annealed glass.

Used for shop windows, public building fenestrations, flush doors etc. and where impact load is predominantly to be resisted.

8. Wired Glass : It is an ordinary plate glass 5 to 6 mm thick with wire mesh reinforcement. Like tempered glass, it constitutes no hazard when shattered. It is more heat resistant as steel wires are good conductor of heat.

9. Glass Blocks : These are hollow or solid, translucent masonry units made from structural glass annealed to withstand the stresses. Available in various sizes 140 × 140 × 100, 190 × 190 × 100 or 194 × 194 × 98, 244 × 244 × 98 mm (depending upon the partition wall thickness appropriate use is expected). Block units are formed by fusing two sections at a high temperature which are casted separately. They may have one or two air cells. Partial vacuum in the interior improves heat insulation capacity. The joining edges are painted internally and sanded externally to form a key to mortar and front and back faces are decorative or plain. Blocks are laid in cement lime mortar 1 : 1 : 4. If the height is upto 150 mm then expanded metal strip reinforcement is placed in every third or fourth course, however if the height is more than 250, it is to be provided in every course. Provision for thermal expansion is made along jambs and heads of each panel. Glass bricks are also casted with joggles and end grooves to form glass wall; glass claddings.

Capsule Lift

Roof Truss with Tie Beam Purlins Rafter Post Etc.

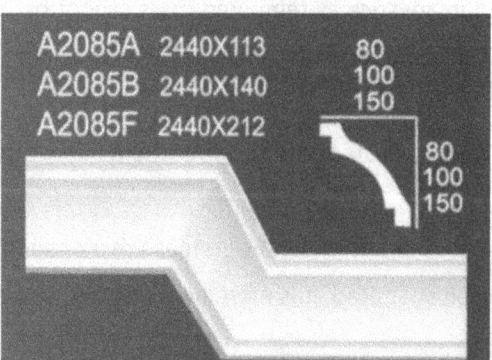
Fire proof Gypsum Plaster

Slab Underpining

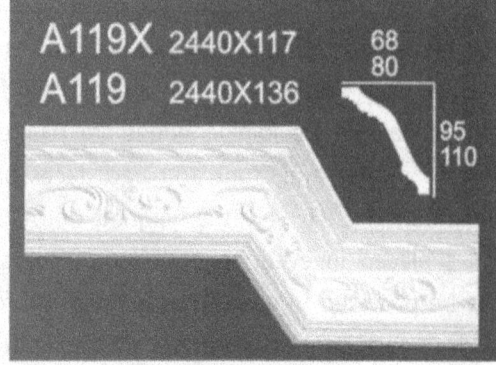
Gypsum Plaster Cornice
Moulding Crown Moldings

Underpinning

Thatch Roof

Exterior Wall Cladding

Aluminium Composite Panel

Cork Tiles

Glazed Door and Roof

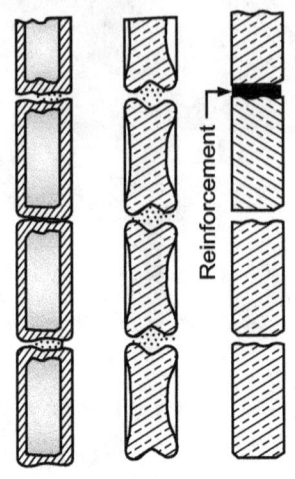

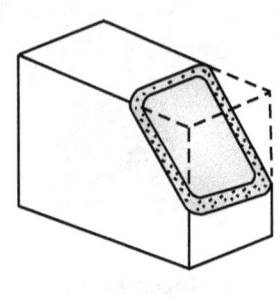

(a) Glass block walls　　　　　　(b) Hollow glass block

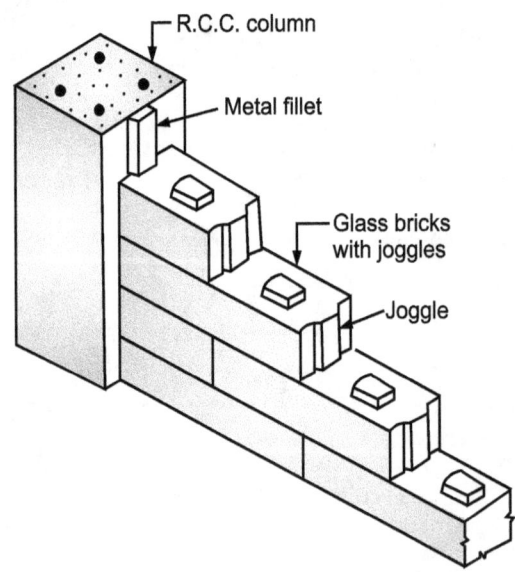

(c) Glass brick wall

Fig. 1.8 : Glass block and glass brick

Properties :

   Compressive strength — 1.5 MPa (min)
   Toughness — 0.8 joule
   Light transmission — 30 to 50%
   Thermal conductivity — 0.5 W/machine
   Fire resistance — upto 2.4 hrs.

Uses : Exterior claddings, external walls, partitions, windows or in combination with concrete, masonry work, roofing where concrete members serve as a skeleton.

Advantages :
1. Non-porous, impervious, non-absorbent of moisture.
2. Diffused light admittance, at desired tinge of colour, pleasing to eye.
3. As the surface is smooth, less catch to dirt/dust.
4. Does not allow condensation on the internal surface.
5. Provides good architectural effect.
6. Sound proof, fire proof, heat proof to some extent.
7. If used as external cladding, no necessity to provide windows, at the same time admittance is less and diffused, hence partial privacy is maintained.

1.8.2.2 Glass and Aluminium Cladding

All the mega cities in the world are adopting a modern international look, for their residential and commercial projects. For improving the exterior facades of any building whether old or new; techniques like cladding are adopted. The material used for cladding is glass, aluminium, tiles etc.

1.8.2.3 Aluminium Composite Panel Cladding

It is basically a typical metal curtain wall system. Its applications include Exterior claddings, Column covers, In-fill panels, Fascias-Canopies, Clean rooms, Interior walls and partition panels, Sunshades, Cornices etc.

Characteristics : Light in weight, modern finish, available in many colours, ease in installation, weather proof coats, colour consistency, flatness, can take various forms of bends and curves, recyclable, non-toxic etc.

It consists of 3 mm thick flame resistant polyethylene compound sandwiched between 0.5 mm thick aluminium foil facings with coating of polyvinyledene fluoride for one of them with thickness 0.25 microns.

1.8.2.4 Glass Cladding

Realizing the fact that glass can be transparent or translucents, wider applications of glass are observed. Glass cladding fulfills functional requirements of building such as lighting, heat retention etc. with visual impact creation.

Characteristics : Total safe, aesthetical, recyclable, energy saver, time saver (constructional aspect), no flaws of plaster and paint, attractive colours, can take any shape etc.

Tempered Safety Glass : (Plain or coloured) It is easy in cleaning and maintenance can be used for cladding. Tempered glass also provides resistance to pressure, temperature variations and impact loads.

Ceramic or Vitrified Glass : Stable, available in wide colour - range/varieties, abrasion resistance, virtually any pattern can be screen printed, enhanced solar control performance, covers spandrel panels.

Spandrel panels are the areas between the floors which has concrete, pipings, floor slabs, ceilings etc.

1.8.3 Plastic/Polymers

It is an organic material of high molecular weight which is plastic at some particular stage of their manufacture, hence can be moulded into required shape.

Natural substances like coal, petroleum, cellulose are the major constituents and binders are resins or cellulose derivatives. The chemical process of manufacturing is condensation or polymerization whereas physical processes worked out are - moulding (compression, injection, transfer and cold moulding), extruding, laminating, blowing, machining and cementing. Compounds used are binders, fillers, plasticizer, solvents/catalysts, pigments, lubricants etc.

Broad Classification :

1. **Thermoplastics :** These are softened under application of heat and regain the original properties during solidification, without any chemical change. Hence, moulding and remoulding by applying pressure is possible.
2. **Thermosetting Plastics :** When heated, chemical changes occur and solidify even when hot. Not possible to reshape them as no appreciable softening is seen on heating.

Following **thermoplastic resins** have different applications in building construction industry:

Sr. No.	Name	Properties	Applications
1.	Acrylics	Clarity, transparency, softer than glass, optimum combination of flexibility and rigidity, can have any colour combination, readily formed into any shape.	Transparent windows, parts of lighting equipments, decorative panels.

... (Contd.)

Sr. No.	Name	Properties	Applications
2.	Acrylonitrile Butadiene Styrene (ABS)	Tough, hard, chemically resistant resins.	Pipes and fittings.
3.	Polycarbonate	Excellent transparency, high resistance to impact, good resistance to weathering.	Safety glazing, (with interlayer of polyvinyl butyral) general illumination.
4.	Polyethylene	Flexible, waxy, translucent, partly crystalline.	Insulating material for wires, corrosion proof lining for tanks.
5.	Polypropylene	Harder, stronger, more temperature resistant.	Water cisterns for water closets.
6.	Polyvinyl Fluoride	Inertness to chemical attack, weathering.	Thin film overlays for exposed building boards.
7.	Polyvinyl Formal Resins	Tough, water resistant.	Insulating enamel for electric wires.
8.	Vinyl Chloride Polymers and Copolymers	Hard, rigid but can be plasticized, abrasion resistance.	Insulation, floor coverings (i.e. tiles), tubing, pipes.
9.	Vinylidene Chloride	Highly resistant to inorganic chemicals, organic solvents, impervious to water on prolonged immersion.	Where less impact, shock resistance is required.
10.	Polystyrene	Light weight, ease in moulding, less expensive, good dimensional stability, negligible water absorption, resistance to chemicals.	Light weight concrete.
11.	Thermoplastic Resins	With marble chips and similar aggregate for decorating elements.	Finish, protective coat.
12.	Polyimide	Impact, abrasion resistance, chemical resistant.	Coating to wires.

Cellulose Derivatives : It is naturally occurring polymer in woody plant tissues, cotton etc. Oldest plastic is cellulose nitrate.

Sr. No.	Name	Properties	Applications
1.	Cellulose Acetate (C.A.)	Provides basis of safety films, may be hard - rigid and soft - flexible.	For temporary enclosures of buildings during construction (when reinforced with wire mesh).
2.	Cellulose Acetate Butyrate	Softer and flexible than cellular acetate but has good impact resistant.	Tubing is used as irrigation and gas lines.
3.	Ethyl Cellulose	High impact, toughness.	Same as in case of C.A.
4.	Cellulose Nitrate	Tough, high impact strength.	Commercial photographic film, commercial leaquer for furniture.

Thermosetting Plastics : Following thermosetting plastics have different applications in construction industry.

Sr. No.	Name	Properties	Applications
1.	Polyester Resins	Water resistant.	Thermosetting concrete with other fillers like gravel, quartz, stone dust, fly ash etc.
2.	Phenol Formaldehyde	Hard rigid, glossy surface, does not burn readily and does not support combustion, light weight.	Electrical field, decoration, thermal applications.
3.	Epoxy and Polyester Resins	Resistance to thermal and mechanical shocks. Adhesion to various materials.	Combinations with copper, brass, steel, aluminium, are used at appropriate places and for concrete is in (1).
4.	Polyester Moulding Materials	Compounded with fibres (like glass).	Putties and premixes.

... (Contd.)

Sr. No.	Name	Properties	Applications
5.	Melamine Formaldehyde Materials	Unaffected by organic solvents, oils, weak acids and alkalies, less water absorption, flame resistant.	Electrical accessories.
6.	Polyurethane	Thermal insulation, occupancy in irregular shapes.	Clear or colour coatings and finishes for floors, walls, furniture, its rubber form is employed for sprayed or troweled on roofing.
7.	Alkyds - (Alongwith Fillers)	High impact strength.	Electrical appliances.
8.	Urea Formaldehyde	Opaque colour, light fastness, resistant to organic solvents, mild acid and alkalies.	Not recommended for continuous water exposures.
9.	Silicons	Inert, durable, difficult to mould, low water absorption.	Moisture resistance to walls, base for paints.

Typical Applications of Composites :
1. **Fibre Reinforced Polymer Plastics :** Made from fibre glass reinforced plastics.
   Characteristics : High strength, light weight, weather resistant, fire resistant, opaque, hence they compete with wood products.
2. **Aluminium Plastic - Paper Composite Boards :**
   Characteristics : High strength, ease in installation and maintenance, excellent heat insulation, impact resistance etc.
   Applications : In case of exterior applications and to have light weight for structures.
3. **Coir Polymer Composite :**
   Characteristics : Made from coir fibre, strong, rigid, flame retardant, eco-friendly, economic, flexible, ease in working, easy nailing etc.
   Applications : Substitute for wooden furniture decor, masonry etc.
4. **Jute Fibre Polyster Composite :**
   Characteristics : Adequate tensile strength, impact strength, weather resistance etc.
   Applications : Tiles, shutter, sanitary units.
5. **Unplasticized PVC Pipes :**
   Characteristics : Ecofriendly i.e. recycling is possible, adequate acid/alkali resistance.
   Applications : Bath/W.C. pipe, pipe fittings etc.

6. **Fibre Reinforced Polymer (Plastics) :**
   Characteristics : Energy efficient, mouldable, highly aesthetics, strong, weather resistant.
   Applications : External cladding, roofing, ceiling, flooring etc.
7. **Non-conventional Concretes :**
   Polymer cement concrete : Polymer fills up gaps/voids in concrete and makes it dense. Imparts more compressive strength, fatigue resistance, impact resistance, acid alkali resistant.
   Polymer impregnated concrete : Obtained by impregnating precast cured hydrated concrete with low viscosity monomer (methyl methecrylate) and polymerized in situ. Creep reduces almost to zero value and elastic modulus is twice that of ordinary concrete. Used for beams, prestressed members, slabs, sewers, pipes etc.

1.8.4 Admixtures

1.8.4.1 Introduction

A material other than cement, water and aggregate that is used as an ingredient of concrete and added to batch before or during mixing is called as *admixture*. Admixtures are used in concrete to improve a certain property of concrete. The properties which are commonly modified by adding admixture are rate of hydration, setting time, workability, dispersion and air entrainment. Generally the quantity of admixture added is small.

1.8.4.2 Functions of Admixtures

1. Admixtures are used to accelerate the rate of hydration.
2. Used to reduce the initial setting time.
3. Used to increase the strength of concrete.
4. Used to improve the workability.
5. Reduces the heat of hydration.
6. Helps in improving the durability of concrete.
7. Helps in controlling shrinkage, creep and swelling of concrete.
8. Increases the impermeability of concrete.
9. Improves the pumpability of concrete.
10. Used to increase the bond between old and new concrete layers.
11. Prevents the corrosion of concrete.
12. Increases the resistance to chemical attack.
13. Used to produce cellular concrete.
14. Used to produce coloured concrete or mortar.
15. Used to produce concrete of fungicidal, germicidal and insecticidal properties.

1.8.4.3 Classification of Admixtures

Admixtures are classified as follows :

1. Plasticizers (water reducer) : Reduce water requirement and to increase workability (high range water reducer).
2. Superplasticizers : Improved version of plasticizer.
3. Accelerators : Accelerate the harding process, so used for urgent repair work.
4. Retarders : Slows down the chemical process of hydration, so used in hot weather.
5. Grouting admixtures.
6. Air entraining admixtures : Produce air bubble, hence increase the fluidity of concrete.
7. Air detraining admixtures : Remove excess air bubble.
8. Gas forming admixtures : Reduce gas bubble for light-weight concrete.
9. Expansion producing admixtures.
10. Waterproofing admixtures : Improve workability, reduce water, make dense and impervious concrete.
11. Corrosion inhabiting admixtures : Prevent corrosion of reinforcement.
12. Fungicidal, germicidal and insecticidal admixture.
13. Bonding admixture : Increase bond strength between old and new concrete.
14. Pozzolanic or mineral admixture : More resistant to action of salt.
15. Colouring admixture : Add pigment to obtained coloured concrete.
16. Workability admixtures : Improve workability of concrete.

1.8.5 Plasticizers

As we have discussed earlier concrete requires different workabilities in different situations. The workability of concrete can be increased either by making changes in the quantities of ingredient or by adding excess water. But by adding excess water only fluidity of concrete is increased not the workability and another disadvantage of excess water is loss of homogeneity, effect on the strength and durability of concrete, increase in tendency of segregation and bleeding etc.

Now-a-days we are having plasticizers and superplasticizers which can be used to improve the workability without using the extra water. These are also called as *water reducers*. In practice, now-a-days use of plasticizers and superplasticizers is increased all over the world for reinforced concrete works and even for mass concreting work to reduce the water requirement and to increase the workability of concrete. Due to the use of superplasticizers the water-cement ratio is reduced for given workability, which naturally increases the strength of concrete and durability of concrete. The quantity of plasticizers used in concrete is about 0.1% to 0.4% by weight of cement. For these doses for constant workability the reduction in water requirement is about 5% to 15%. At the same time the increase in workability at same water-cement ratio may be about 30 mm to 150 mm slump. This naturally increases the strength.

As discussed above, the plasticizers are mainly used to fluidise the mix and improve the workability. The mechanism due to which this happens is dispersion. The portland cement has tendency to flocculate in wet concrete. Some amount of water get entrapped in the flocs. When the plasticizers are used, they get absorbed on the cement particles and creates particle to particle repulsive force. Due to which, particles are deflocculated or dispersed, which releases water entrapped into flocs and make it available to fluidify the mix.

The basic products used as plasticizers are :
1. Anionic surfactants – Lingosulphonates, salts of sulphonates, hydrocarbons.
2. Non-ionic surfactants – Polyglycol esters, acid of hydroxylated carboxylic acids.
3. Carbohydrates etc.

1.8.6 Superplasticizers

These are improved version of plasticizers also called as high range water reducers. By using superplasticizers the reduction of water requirement for same workability is about 30% whereas it was 15% in case of plasticizers. The practical application of superplasticizers is for production of flowing, self levelling, self compacting and high strength and high performance concrete. The mechanism of action of superplasticizer is more or less same as plasticizers. By using superplasticizers it is possible to use water-cement ratio as low as 0.25 or even lower than this, to obtain the high strength concrete. Along with the increased strength with lower water-cement ratio, it also permits a reduction of cement content.

The products used as superplasticizers are :
1. Modified lingosulphonates.
2. Sulphonated melamine – Formaldehyde.
3. Sulphonated naphthalene – Formaldehyde.
4. Acrylic polymer based.
5. Cross-linked acrylic polymer.
6. Multicarboxylatethers etc.

1.8.7 Mineral Admixtures and Other Admixtures

Pozzolanic materials are siliceous materials, which themselves does not possess cementitious value, but meet with calcium hydroxide in presence of water to form compound of low solubility having cementitious properties. The action is termed as pozzolanic action.

Pozzolanic materials are of two types, first natural pozzolans such as clay or shale, opaline cherts, diatomaceous earths, volcanic stuff and pumicites and second, artificial pozzolans such as fly ash, blast furnace slag, silica fume, rice husk ash, metakaoline, surkhi etc.

The pozzolanic materials can be used as partial replacement of portland cement. The quantity of material replaced may be between 10 to 35%. By using pozzolanic materials in the concrete, concrete may be more permeable but more resistant to the action of salt, sulphate or acids. The gain of strength is somewhat slower than the normal concrete. Pozzolana when used in concrete improves the workability, and resistance of chemical attack. It also lowers the heat of hydration and thermal shrinkage. Some pozzolans reduce the expansion caused by the alkali-aggregate reaction. Pozzolanic materials may be used as some replacement of cement resulting reduced cost.

IS 456-2000 permits the use of pozzolanas (clause 5.2) like fly ash, silica fume, rice husk ash, metakaoline, ground granulated blast furnace slag (GGBS) (i.e. fly ash confirming to grade I of IS : 3812 and GGBS confirming to IS : 12089).

1.8.8 Fly Ash

Fly ash conforming to grade I of IS : 3812 may be used as part replacement of OPC provided uniform blending with cement is ensured. Fly ash is the residue from the combustion of powdered coal collected by the mechanical or electrostatic separators from the fuel gases of thermal power plants. Fly ash mainly consist of spherical glassy particles ranging from 1 to 150 microns in diameter. Now-a-days the use of fly ash is increased to produce high strength and high performance concrete. The use of fly ash as concrete admixture has not only technical advantages but it contributes also to the environmental pollution control. In our country, we are producing about 75 million tons of fly ash per year, the disposal of which is serious problem.

Fly ash can be used in two ways in the concrete, one, grind the certain per cent of fly ash with cement clinker in factory to produce portland pozzolana cement and second, use the fly ash as admixture on site at the time of making concrete.

The fly ash produced at different factories has different chemical properties, therefore it is not available in ready to use condition. The chemical requirements of fly ash as per IS 3812 is given in Table 1.5.

Table 1.5 : Chemical Requirements (IS : 3812-1981)

Sr. No.	Characteristics	Requirement
(1)	(2)	(3)
(i)	Silicon dioxide (SiO_2) plus Aluminium oxide (Al_2O_3) plus Iron oxide (Fe_2O_3) per cent by mass, (Min.)	70.0
(ii)	Silicon dioxide (SiO_2), per cent by mass, (Min.)	35.0
(iii)	Magnesium oxide (MgO), per cent by mass, (Max.)	5.0
(iv)	Total sulphur as sulphur trioxide (SO_3), per cent by mass (Max.)	2.75
(v)	Available alkalis, as sodium oxide (Na_2O), per cent by mass, (Max.) (See Note 1)	1.5
(vi)	Loss on ignition, per cent by mass, (Max.)	12.0

Note 1 : Applicable only when reactive aggregates are used in concrete and are specially requested by the purchaser.

Note 2 : For determination of available alkalis, IS : 4032-1968 'Method of chemical analysis of hydraulic cement' shall be referred to.

Silica Fume : Silica fume (very fine non-crystalline silicon dioxide) is a by-product of the manufacture of silicon, ferrosilicon or the like, iron quartz and carbon in electric arc furnace. It is usually used in proportion of 5 to 10% of the cement content of mix. Silica fume is essentially silicon dioxide in non-crystalline form. The silica fume is very much finer than the cement particles. The average diameter of the particle is about 0.1 micron i.e. about 100 times smaller than average cement particles.

Silica fume does not contribute to the strength, but use of it being a very fine pozzolanic material creates dense packing and pore filling of cement paste. By using silica fume it is possible to produce a concrete of about 60 to 90 MPa compressive strength.

Rice Husk Ash (RHA) : Rice husk ash is produced by burning rice husk and contain large proportion of silica. To achieve amorphous state, rice husk may be burnt at controlled temperature. RHA exhibit high pozzolanic characteristics and contribute to high strength and high impermeability of concrete. Each ton of paddy produces about 40 kg of RHA.

1.8.9 Metakaoline

Metakaoline is obtained by calcination of pure or refined kaolintic clay at a temperature between 650°C and 850°C, followed by grinding to achieve a fineness of 700 to 900 m^2/kg. The resulting material has high pozzolanic characteristics. IS : 456-2000 suggest that metakaoline having fineness 700-920 m^2/kg specific surface area may be used as pozzolanic material in concrete.

Ground Granulated Blast Furnace Slag (GGBS) : GGBS is a non-metallic product consist of silicates, and aluminates of calcium and other bases. The molten slag is rapidly chilled by quenching in water to form a glassy sand like grains, further these grains are ground to fineness less than 45 microns. IS : 456-2000 suggests, GGBS obtained by grinding granulated blast furnace slag confirming to IS 12089 may be used as part replacement of OPC provided uniform blending with cement is ensured.

The chemical composition of GGBS is similar to that of cement clinkers. When the GGBS is used as a replacement of cement the water requirement reduces to obtain the same slump. It also reduces the heat of hydration. Refinement of pore structure is obtained by using GGBS in concrete. The main advantage of use of GGBS is reduction in permeability and increased resistance to chemical attack. Therefore GGBS is best applicable in the marine structure or concreting in saline environment.

REVIEW QUESTIONS

1. What are the various requirements of a good building stone ?
2. Explain the various uses of stones.
3. Write a short note on manufacturing of bricks.
4. Explain the aggregate with origin, type, particle, size and shape.
5. Write a short note on artificial sand.
6. What are the mechanical properties of aggregates ?
7. Explain the physical properties of aggregates.
8. Differentiate between coarse aggregate and fine aggregate.

9. Differentiate between natural and artificial wood.
10. Explain the various applications of timber in civil engineering.
11. Explain the various types of steel.
12. Explain the use of steel in building construction.
13. Write a short note on tiles.
14. Write short notes on :
    (a) Aluminium
    (b) Glass
    (c) Plastic
    (d) Admixtures
    (e) Plasticiser
    (f) Superplasticity

Unit - II

Chapter 2

BASIC REQUIREMENTS OF A BUILDING

2.1 INTRODUCTION

Man requires different types of buildings for his activities, stations, houses, bunglows and flats for his living; hospitals and health centres for his health; schools, colleges and universities for his education; banks, shops, offices, buildings and factories for doing work; railway, bus stations and air terminals for transportation; clubs, theatres and cinema houses for recreation; and temples, mosques, churches etc. for worship. The above building activities are an important indicator of the country's social progress. Fundamental requirements of these buildings are that they should fulfill the physical, emotional, social and biological needs of the person or persons who are going to occupy them.

All the requirements can be grouped under two main headings - Form and Function. "Form" covers the emotional and aesthetic portion of the human requirements while "Function" covers the biological, social and physical needs. Both form and function are important and if possible should be achieved to the maximum extent. But in case of comparison, of the importance of the two "Function" out weighs "Form". Functionally, a building should be well satisfied before one can skip on to the importance of "Form". If a piece of architecture does not fulfill the basic requirements of function and all importance is stressed on "Form", then it reduces to mere piece of sculpture and ceases to be architecture.

The building design has traditionally been the responsibility of the architect, though the building construction has been the responsibility of the civil engineer. Also, the structural designs of the building are the responsibility of a civil engineer. The main considerations in architectural design of buildings for all purposes are as follows :

1. Climate and its effect.
2. People and their requirements.
3. Materials for construction and method of construction.
4. Regulations and bye laws of sanctioning authority.

2.2 DEFINITION

National Building Code of India (SP : 7 - 1970) defines the building "as any structure for whatsoever purpose and of whatsoever materials constructed and every part thereof whether used as human habitation or not and includes foundation, plinth, walls, floors, roofs, chimneys, plumbing and building services, fixed platforms, verandah, balcony, cornice or projection, part of a building or anything affixed there to or any wall enclosing or intended to enclose any land or space and signs and outdoor display structures". Tents, shamianas and tarpaulin shelters are not considered as building.

A building can also be defined as enclosed space covered by roof. The building has to perform many functions such as utility of the buildings, structural safety, fire safety and it should also satisfy the requirement of sanitation, ventilation, day light. These requirements will vary from building to building and the design of building is dependent on the minimum requirements prescribed for each of the functions mentioned above.

2.3 BASIC REQUIREMENTS OF BUILDING

The planning and construction of a building should be aimed at fulfilling the following requirements :

1. **Strength and Stability :** Building should be capable of transferring the expected loads in its life period safely to the ground. Design of various structural components like slabs, beams, walls, columns and footing should ensure safety. None of the structural components should buckle, overturn and collapse.

2. **Dimensional Stability :** Excessive deformation of structural components give a sense of instability and result into crack in walls, flooring etc. All structural components, should be so designed that deflections do not exceed the permissible values specified in the codes.

3. **Resistance to Dampness :** Dampness in a building is a great nuisance and it may reduce the life of the building. Great care should be taken in planning and in the construction of the building to avoid dampness.

4. **Resistance to Fire :** Regarding achieving resistance to fire, the basic requirements laid down in the codes are :
   (a) The structure should not ignite easily.
   (b) Building orientation should be such that spread of fire is slow.
   (c) In case of fire, there should be means of easy access to vacate building quickly.

5. **Heat Insulation :** A building should be so oriented and designed that it insulates interior from heat.

When there is difference in temperature of inside of a building and outside temperature, heat transfer takes place from areas of higher temperature to those of lower temperature. This transfer of heat may take place by any or more of the three methods namely, conduction, convection and radiation. In colder regions, when the buildings are internally heated and where outside temperature is cool, it is necessary to check this heat loss of the building. Similarly in very hot regions, when buildings are internally cooled and the outside temperature is unbearably warm, it is essential to check the entry of heat from outside into the building. The term thermal insulation is used to indicate the construction or provisions by way of which transmission of heat from or in the room is retarded. The main objective of thermal insulation is to conserve a constant heat or temperature inside the building, irrespective of temperature changes outside.

6. **Sound Insulation :** Buildings should be planned against outdoor and indoor noises. Sound insulation or sound proofing is a measure used to reduce the level of sound when it passes through the insulating building component. The materials and methods used for sound insulation should be such that desirable insulation is obtained. Table ???? gives the desirable levels of sound insulation between individual rooms (air borne).

7. **Protection from Termite :** Buildings should be protected from termites.

8. **Durability :** Each and every component of the building should be durable.

9. **Security against Burglary :** This is the basic need the owner of the building expects.

10. **Ventilation :** For healthy and happy living, natural light and ventilations are required. Diffused light and good cross ventilation should be available inside the building.

Where no products of combustion or other contaminants are to be removed from air, the amount of fresh air required for dilution of inside air to prevent vitiation of air by body odours depends on the air space available per person and the degree of physical activity. The amount of air requirement increases with decrease in air space per person and it may vary from 20 to 30 m^3 per person per hour.

Requirement of air for different occupancies may be expressed in terms of air changes per hour which indicate the replacement of air in an occupancy by fresh air, expressed as the number of times such replacement is effected in an hour.

The following values of air changes are recommended by the National Building Code of India, based on maintenance of required levels of oxygen, carbon dioxide and other air quality parameters and for the control of body odours when no products of combustion or other contaminants are present in the air.

11. Comforts and Conveniences : For healthy and happy living, natural light and ventilations are required. Diffused light and good cross ventilation should be available inside the building.

12. Daylighting : The ultimate source of daylight is of course the sun, but the light reaching the earth from the sun may be partly diffused by the atmosphere and the local climatic conditions which in turn determine how this light will reach a building.

If we consider a point inside a building, light may reach it from the sun in the following ways :

(i) direct sunlight along a straight path from the sun, through the window, to the given point,

(ii) light reflected externally by the ground or other buildings, through an opening,

(iii) light reflected internally from walls, ceiling or other internal surfaces and

(iv) diffused or skylight through an opening.

Day light is an integral part of the design of a majority of modern buildings. The requirements for good lighting design can be achieved by skillful application of daylighting techniques. These differ from the design methods for electric lighting because of variations in the amount of daylight, the changing position of the sun, the desire for a view of the outdoor etc.

13. Water Proofing Techniques : All the flat roofs in the modern age are generally constructed of reinforced cement concrete. This material removes all the defects of flat roofs except that the roof should be made water-proof by employing any one of the following four methods.

1. Finishing
2. Bedding concrete and flooring
3. Mastic asphalt and jute cloth
4. Use of water proofing compounds.

(1) Finishing : For ordinary buildings of cheap construction, the finishing of roof surface is done at the time of laying cement concrete. The finishing of flat roof is carried out in cement mortar of proportion 1 : 4 i.e. one part of cement to four parts of sand by volume.

(2) Bedding concrete and flooring : In this method, the surface of R.C.C. slab is kept rough and on this surface, a layer of concrete is laid. The concrete may be brickbats lime concrete 1 : 2 : 4 or brickbats cement concrete 1 : 6 : 12 or 1 : 5 : 10. The thickness of the concrete layer is about 100 mm. The surface of the bedding concrete is provided by a suitable flooring such as tiles, terrazzo, Indian patent stone, etc. A convex corner joint is provided at the junction of parapet wall and roof as shown in Fig. 2.1.

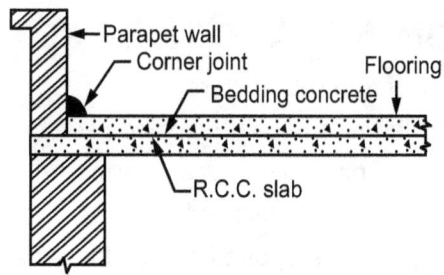

Fig. 2.1 : Water proofing of flat roofs

(3) Mastic asphalt and jute cloth : In this method, a layer of hot mastic asphalt is laid on the roof surface. The jute cloth is spread over this layer. Then one more layer of mastic asphalt is applied so that the jute cloth is sandwitched between the two layers of mastic asphalt. The sand is then sprinkled over the entire surface of roof. For better grip, the lead sheets are inserted at the junction of parapet wall and roof as shown in Fig. 2.2.

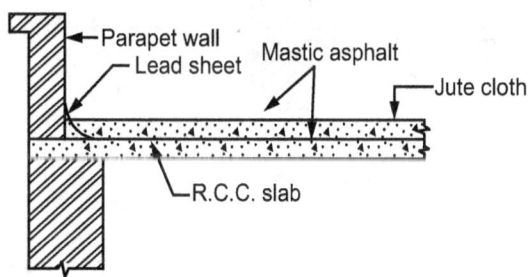

Fig. 2.2 : Water proofing of flat roofs

(4) Use of water-proofing compounds : Some of the water-proofing compounds like Pudlo, Impermo etc., are available in the market and when such a compound is added to cement during construction, it prevents seepage, leakage and damp caused by the capillary absorption of the moisture in cement, mortar and concrete. The quantity of water-proofing compound to be added is also very small, say 2% and thus a bag of cement will require only about 10 N of such a compound.

The water-proof compounds are available in the powder form and they are to be mixed thoroughly with cement by hand before the cement is mixed with the aggregate. The advantages claimed by using a water-proofing compound of good quality are as follows :

(i) It corrects a badly proportioned concrete mixture.

(ii) It cures immature green concrete.

(iii) It makes good concrete from the poor materials.

(iv) It permits less rigid supervision of the workmanship.

2.4 BASIC COMPONENTS AND THEIR REQUIREMENTS

The following are the components of substructure.

   1. Foundation : It is the lowest artificially prepared part of a structure below the ground level which provides base for superstructure and transmits all loads from the component parts of the building to the soil on which the building rests.

   2. Plinth : It is the portion of a structure between the surface of the enclosing ground and the surface of the floor first above the ground.

   3. Damp Proof Course (DPC) : It is the layer between superstructure and the substructure. It does not allow the moisture to move from the foundation level to the superstructure.

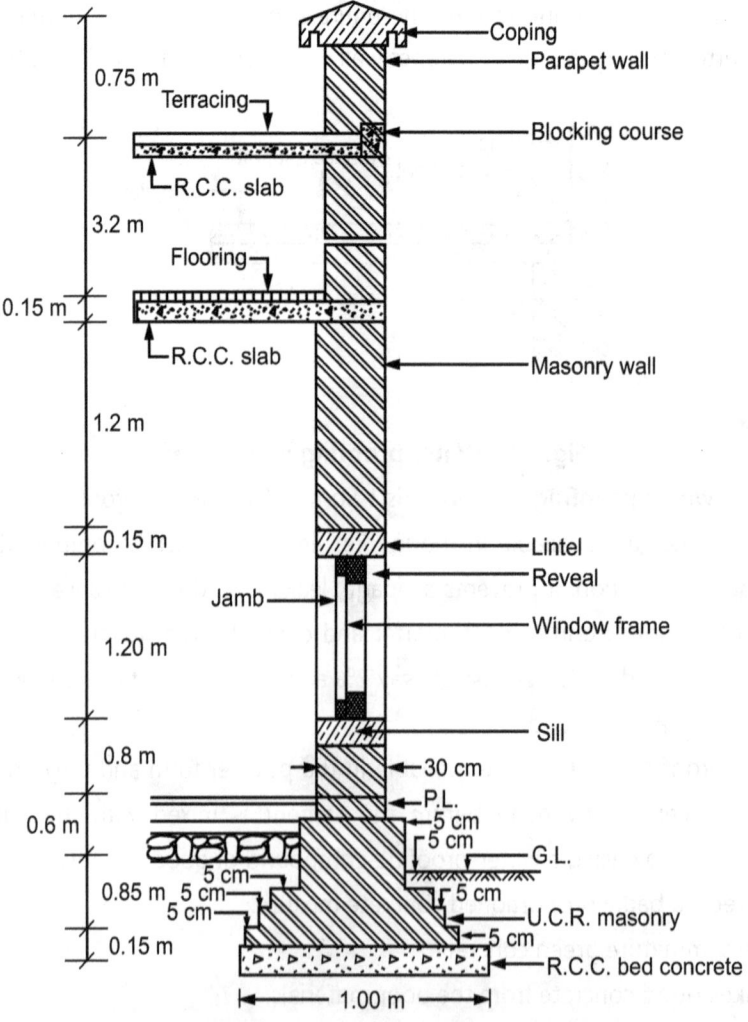

Fig. 2.3 : Cross-section through a load bearing wall

Introduction :

It is that part of the structure which is constructed above the plinth level or ground floor level. The various components of superstructure are walls, floors, doors and windows, roofs, stairs, sill, lintel, weather sheds, finishes for wall, utility fixtures etc. The functions of various components of superstructure are as follows :

1. **Walls :** The vertical components of the building, which are constructed to enclose the space are called walls. They are also constructed to divide the space into various rooms and small compartments as per the requirements of the building.

2. **Floors :** Floors are the horizontal elements of a building structure which divide the building into different levels for the purpose of creating more accommodation within the restricted space one above the other and to provide support for the occupants, their furniture and requirements in the building.

3. **Doors :** The openings provided in the walls of the building to connect the internal rooms, to be used as a means of free movement inside and outside the building.

4. **Windows :** The openings provided in the outer walls of the building for the purpose of light and air.

5. **Roofs :** The uppermost horizontal or inclined part of a building provided to cover the space enclosed by the walls is called the roof. Roofs protect living spaces from direct sun, rain or snow and wind.

6. **Stairs :** The component of the building which is provided for climbing from one floor to another floor is called stairs.

7. **Lintel :** Lintel is the component of the building provided over the openings i.e. doors and windows. It supports the load of the brick or stone masonry above the opening and transfers the same on either side of the supporting walls.

8. **Sill :** Sill is the component of the building provided between the bottom of a window frame and the wall below it. It protects the top of the wall from wear and tear. Window sills are usually weathered and throated to throw the rain water off the face of the wall.

9. **Weather sheds :** The horizontal slabs projecting from the external wall just above the doors, windows, verandas, etc. are called weather sheds or sun shades or chhajjas. They are monolithically constructed with the lintels. They protect the doors, windows etc. from the direct effects of the sun and rain.

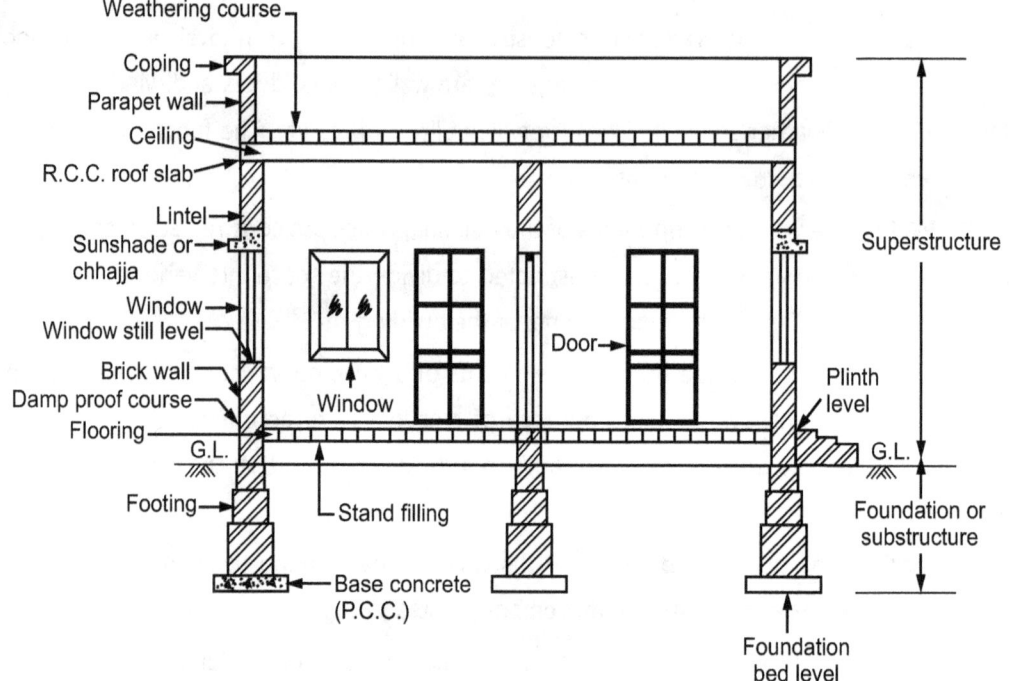

Fig. 2.4 : Components of a building

10. Finishes of wall : Finishes are of several types such as pointing, plastering, distempering, decorative colour washing etc. that are applied on the walls. The main functions of these finishes are as follows :

(i) They provide an even and smooth finished surface and also improve the aesthetic appearance of the structure as a whole.

(ii) They rectify, rather cover to some extent, the poor or defective workmanship.

(iii) They protect the structure from the effects of weather, such as rain, sun.

11. Utility fixtures : These are built-in items of immovable nature, which add to the utility of a building and hence, are termed as utility fixtures. The most common of such built-in fixtures are cupboards, shelves, smokeless chulas, etc.

2.5 FORM WORK

Forms are the moulds and dies for concrete construction. They mould the concrete to the desired size and shape and control its alignment and position. Form work also carries the weight of freshly placed concrete besides live load due to materials, equipment and workmen.

The objectives of Form work are three fold – quality, safety and economy. Economy is a major concern since form work cost may range anywhere from 25 to 60% of the cost of the concrete structure. Judgment in selection of materials and equipment, in planning fabrication and erection procedures, in scheduling reuse of forms and in deployment of trained and experienced man power helps to save form work cost and at the same time expedite the job. The Structural Engineer or the Architect can also contribute to help save form work cost by keeping the requirement of form work economy in mind when he is designing the structure.

However, to achieve economy, quality and safety should not be sacrificed. Cutting corners in design and practice could be responsible false economy as rectification of defective concrete may require expensive chipping and grinding.

The economy measures which may lead to form work failure; also defeat the very purpose as the costs due to loss of human lives and materials will totally outweigh the savings due to economic measures.

It is necessary to understand the requirements of form work before going into the details of materials, erection, inspection and other essential steps for successful and proper job.

2.6 REQUIREMENTS OF FORM WORK

The following are essential requirements :
1. To obtain the required shape, size, finish, position and alignment of concrete members.
2. Form work has enough load carrying or transferring capacity to take pressure or weight of fresh concrete and any other loads, without distortion, deflection, leakage, failure or danger to workmen.
3. To have design for quick erection and removal (stripping).
4. To handle easily using available equipment or man power.
5. Joints between form work must be tight enough to prevent leakage of grout.
6. Form work provides easy and safe access for concrete handling and placing.
7. Form work avoids damage to concrete or form work itself while stripping.

2.7 MATERIALS USED FOR FORM WORK

1. **Wooden Materials :**

Timber and plywood are the most commonly used materials for form work because these can be cut or assembled easily on site. Use of wooden props (ballies) and bamboo props is still persisting in many construction works. Even large floor heights are constructed using these props without proper interconnection for the extended length or without proper bracing. These often result in serious failures. It is not recommended to use wooden props specially when floor heights are large requiring connecting one prop over the other using inadequate method of connections. In any case, the load carrying capacity of any wooden or bamboo prop is often not known and difficult to ascertain, depending on the type and quality of wood, its moisture content, size and shape.

Plywoods of different types and quality are used. It is usual to frame up the materials into largest size panels that can be handled by the available equipment on the site or is convenient for manual handling. The size will also depend on the shape of the structural member being cast.

The plywood panels are suitable for large smooth areas like walls and floors. For complicated shapes, timber frames with plywood face are usually more economical than timber boards or other materials specially when high number of reuses are required.

Ply surfaces get easily damaged, hence adequate care has to be taken during assembly, erection, casting, (removal) and storage. The soft surfaces and edges are more prone to damage than other surfaces and therefore, they need to be protected. The cut edges of ply and tie holes should be sealed and protected to prolong the life of the plywood panels so that more number of usages are obtained.

2. **Steel :**

There are two ways in which steel is used in form work and false work :

   (a) In proprietary form work.

   (b) Purpose made form work.

(a) **Proprietary Form work :** These systems are available in different forms, some of which are listed as follows :

(i) Steel framed panels with either steel plate or plywood facing.

(ii) Telescopic supporting trusses.

(iii) Adjustable props (tubular).

(iv) Yokes and fastening devices.

(v) Tie rods and spacers.

(vi) Clamps and bracings (tubular).

(b) Purpose Made Form work : These form works are specially designed for a particular type of job work as in case of linings inside tunnels, culverts, slip form work for tall structures, curved surfaces of water tanks, shells, domes, parabolieds and other jobs which have unusual shape.

3. **Other Materials :**

There are several other types of materials used in form work such as glass reinforced plastics, vacuum formed plastic facings etc. Although these types of form work offer many uses, additional care has to be taken while placing and vibrating concrete to avoid damage to the form face. Scrapers cannot be used when concrete is being poured into these form works.

Cleaning also needs to be done immediately after deshuttering. Wet cloth cleaning is necessary to remove dust and cement concrete paste sticking to the surface.

2.8 FOUNDATIONS

The part of structure, which is above ground level is called as super-structure and the part of structure which is below ground level is called as sub-structure.

Foundation is the part of sub-structure, which receives load of super-structure and transmits it to lower and firmer strata safely without causing excessive settlement or stresses or any damage to super-structure.

It is very difficult and costly to carry out any repairs to foundation after it is constructed. Hence, it is essential to understand basic principles of foundations.

2.8.1 Definition and Purpose of Foundation

Definition: *It is the part of structure below ground level, which is directly in contact with subsoil to receive load of superstructure and to transmit it to firm strata below safely.*

Purpose: Foundation of a building is designed to achieve the following objectives :

1. **It should carry loads safely :** The soil strata, on which foundation is to rest, should be strong enough to safely bear the loads imposed on it.
2. **Settlement of structure should be uniform and within permissible limits :** Due to loads imposed on foundation, structure is likely to settle. Foundation is so designed that, the settlement is as uniform as possible throughout and is within permissible limits.
3. **Differential settlement should be less :** If a part of foundation settles more than the other part then the difference between the two settlements is called as 'Differential

settlement'. This differential settlement induces heavy stresses and cracks appear in super-structure thereby endangering safety of structure.
4. It should offer required stability to structure against uplift forces sliding, overturning.
5. It should be strong enough to resist attack by harmful substances and strong undercurrents (if any) present in subsoil.
6. Construction of foundation should not cause adverse effects on adjoining structures and on environment. e.g. Vibrations during pile driving or pumping out of ground water may cause large settlement of adjoining structures.

2.9 TYPES OF FOUNDATIONS

Depending upon ratio of depth D and width W, foundation is classified as under :

1. Shallow Foundation = $\left(\dfrac{D}{W} < 1\right)$ = D < 5 m

2. Deep Foundation = $\left(\dfrac{D}{W} > 1\right)$

2.9.1 Shallow Foundation

Shallow Foundation is further classified according to distribution of load on soil as shown in following chart and in Fig. 2.5.

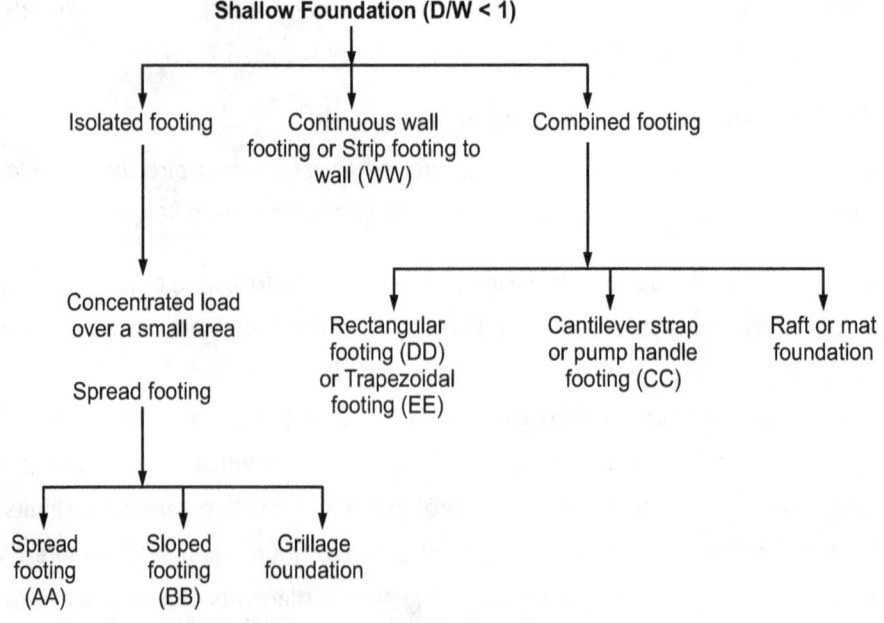

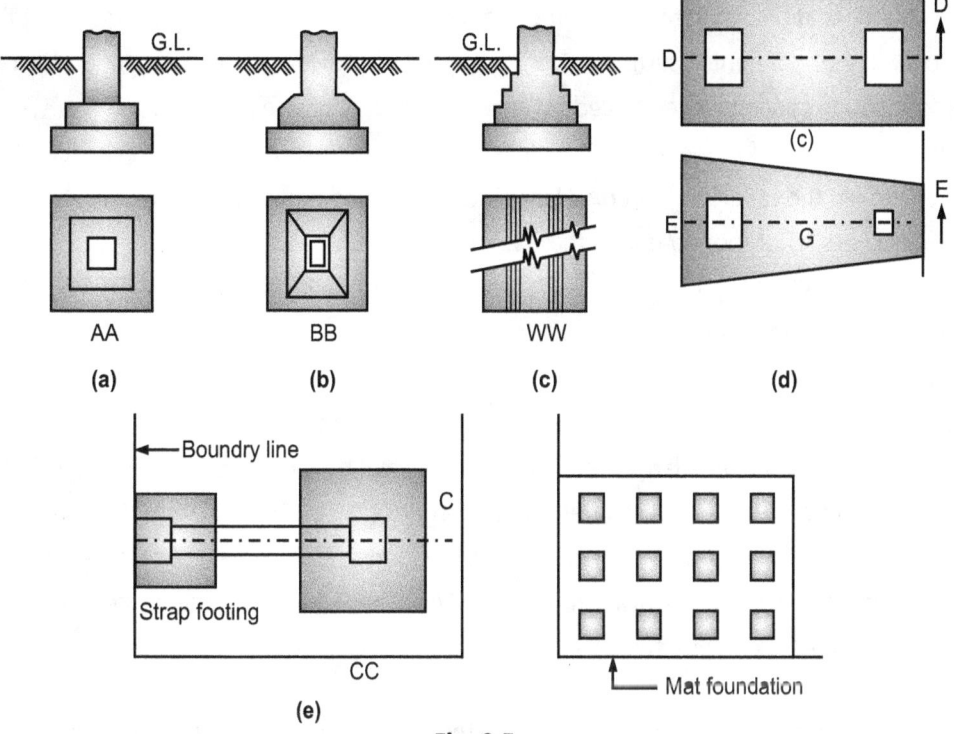

Fig. 2.5

(A) Spread Footing :

It is the most common type of shallow foundation used to transmit load of wall or isolated column. The base of wall of column is enlarged or spread to distribute load over a large area (to reduce intensity of load). Spread footing does not directly rest on soil. Usually, about 15 to 30 cm thick lean concrete of mix (1 : 4 : 8) called as foundation concrete is first laid, as a base course to cover small pockets in foundation and to provide level surface for laying spread footing.

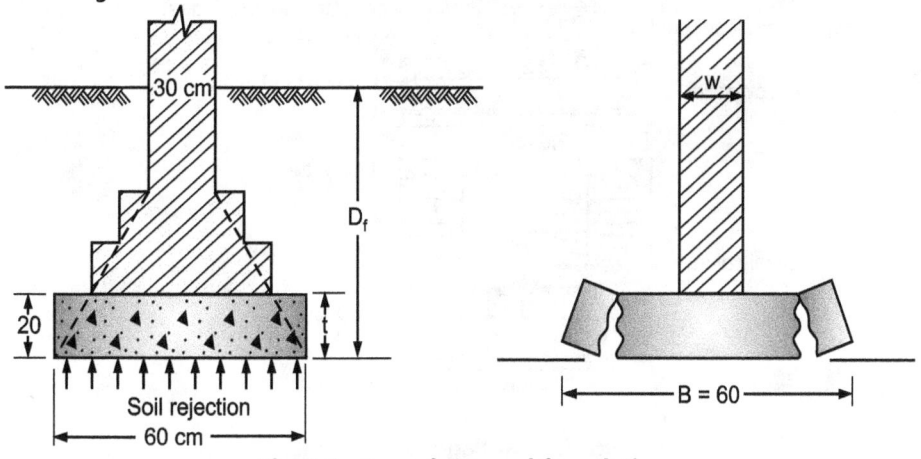

Fig. 2.6 : Spread stepped foundation

Over this foundation concrete, spread footing rests. If load of wall footing is high and if there is probability of differential settlement, then instead of providing plain foundation concrete, the foundation concrete is reinforced by providing steel reinforcement.

1. If projection of footing beyond wall is excessive, the footing may crack due to soil reaction in the cantilever portion. Hence, stepped foundation is provided.
2. If thickness "t" of footing is less, the wall may punch in the footing.
3. Depth of foundation (D_f) should be adequate to give necessary safe bearing capacity. Minimum depth of foundation of 90 cm is provided.

(B) Grillage Foundation :

This type of foundation is used to transmit heavy loads from steel columns to soils having low bearing capacity over a large area. It consists of steel beams (called as Rolled Steel Joists) in one or two tiers. Beams in each tier are held in position by 20 to 25 mm diameter spacer bars. This type of foundation avoids deep excavation and provides large area to reduce intensity of load. Depth of excavation is limited to 1.2 to 1.5 m only. The space between the beams is filled with concrete to protect steel beams from corrosion.

In water logged area, sometimes, instead of steel beams, wooden logs are provided in 2 or 3 tiers. This eliminates possibility of corrosion of steel and foundation is economical. Since, total quantity of steel required is large, this type of foundation becomes costly and hence has become outdated.

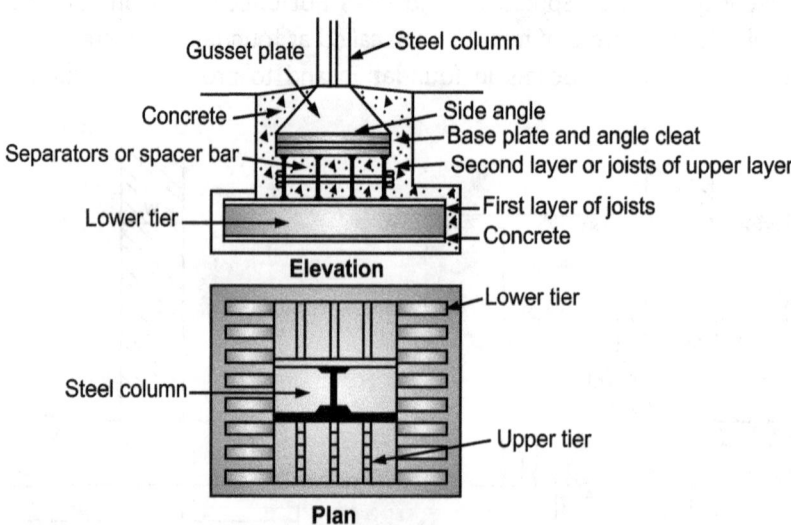

Fig. 2.7 : Grillage foundation

For continuous wall foundations (plain or reinforced), adequate reinforcement should be provided, particularly at places where there is abrupt change in load or variation in ground support.

On sloping sites, the foundation should have a horizontal bearing and stepped and lapped at charges of levels for a distance at least equal to thickness of foundation or twice the height of step, which ever is greater. The steps should not be of greater height than thickness of the foundation.

The foundation of walls on sloping ground may be at one level or stepped as shown in Fig. 2.8.

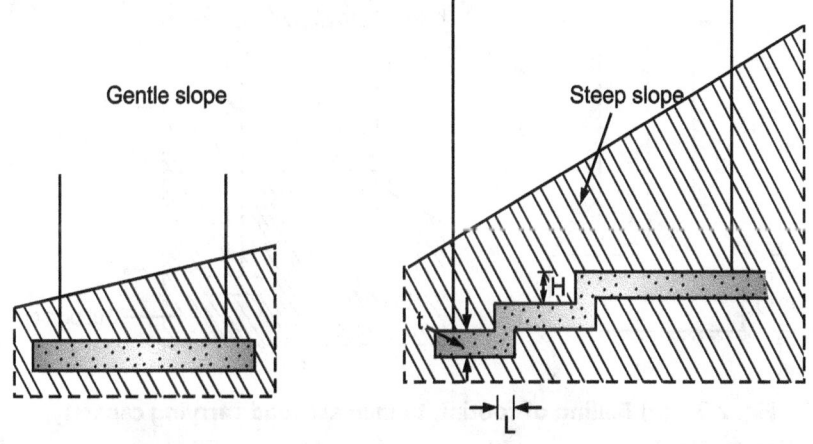

(a) Footing on gentle sloping ground   (b) Footing on steep sloping ground

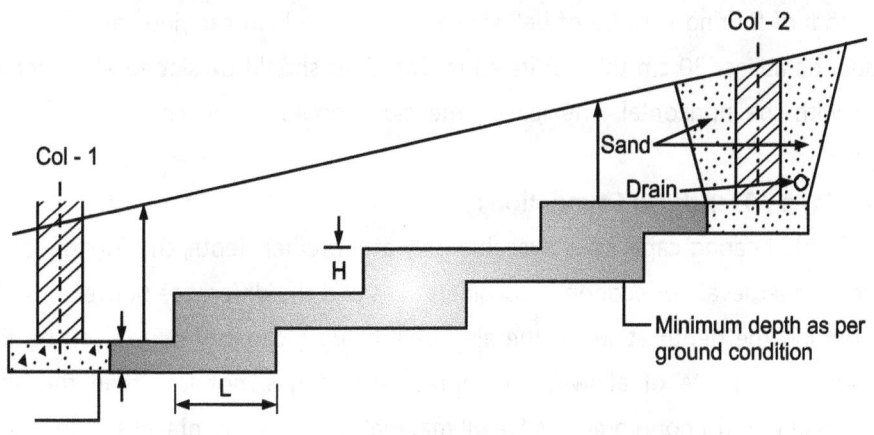

(c) Details of footing on sloping ground

Fig. 2.8

Where the slope is gentle, the foundation may be at one level, but if the slope is steep, a portion of floor rests on filled up portion as a portion rests on excavated and levelled ground. Cutting is extended beyond the wall at the highest point and arrangements are made to drain out water, so that the stability of ground at highest level is not in danger.

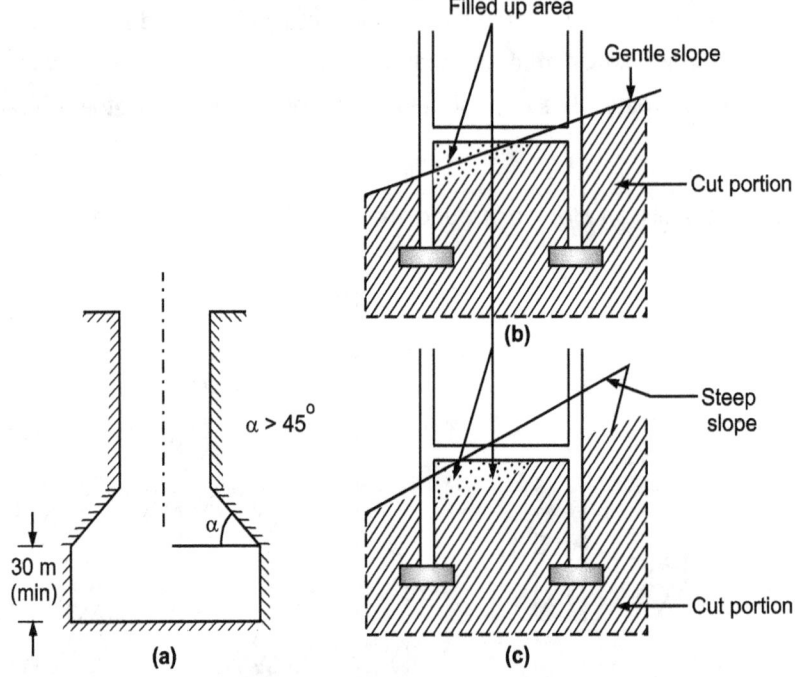

Fig. 2.9 : (a) Belling of footing to increase load carrying capacity,
(b) Footing on sloping ground with gentle slope. Floor on filled up compacted soil,
(c) Footing partly in cut section and partly in filled up section

If the bottom of footing is to be of bell shape, to increase load carrying capacity, then such bell should be atleast 30 cm thick at its edge. The sides should be sloped at an angle more than 45° with the horizontal. The least dimension should be 60 cm (circular, square or rectangular).

(C) Deep-Strip / Trench Fill Foundation :

If the allowable bearing capacity is available only at a greater depth, the foundation can be rested at a higher level, for economic considerations and the difference between the base of foundation and the depth at which the allowable bearing capacity occurs can be filled up either with (a) concrete of allowable compressive strength, not less than the allowable bearing pressure or (b) non-compressible fill material such as sand, gravel etc., in which case, the width of fill should be more than the width of foundation by an extent of dispersion of load from the base of foundation on either side at the rate of 2 vertical to 1 horizontal.

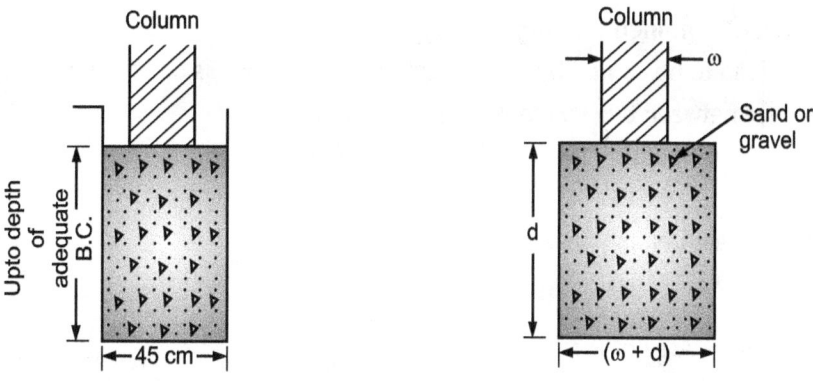

(a) Deep trench with PCC filling (b) Deep trench with sand filling

Fig. 2.10 : Deep strip foundation

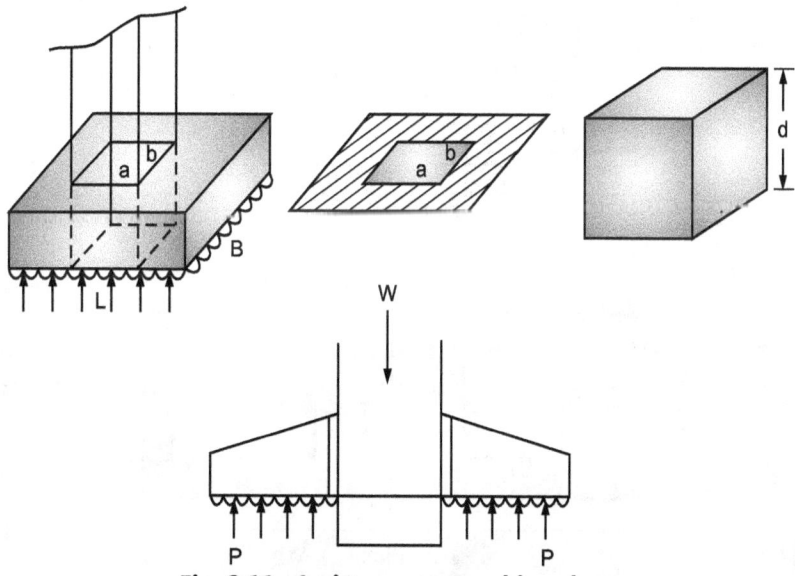

Fig. 2.11 : Assistance to punching shear

(D) Combined Footing :

Combined footings are provided under the following situations :
1. When loads on adjacent columns are very high.
2. Bearing capacity of soil is relatively less and
3. There is possibility of heavy differential settlement.

In combined footing, a common footing is provided for two or more columns. Combined footing is very rigid, hence the columns settle together and thereby eliminate possibility of differential settlement. Depending upon different loading conditions, following varieties of combined footing are provided :

(a) Rectangular Combined Footing : This type of footing is provided,
- (i) When load to be carried by the two columns is high and is nearly same.
- (ii) Distance between two columns is less.
- (iii) Projection of footing beyond columns is permitted.

Considering the safe bearing capacity of soil, and total load to be carried, area of footing is worked as under : -

$$A = \text{Area of footing} = \frac{\text{Total load } (\Sigma W)}{\text{Safe bearing capacity}} \quad \bar{x} = \frac{W_1 \cdot l}{W_1 + W_2}$$

Knowing individual column loads W_1, W_2 and spacing of columns, C.G. of load is found out. Footing is arranged in such a way that, C.G. of load coincides with C.G. of area of footing.

$$L = 2[a + \bar{x}] \text{ and } B = A \div L$$

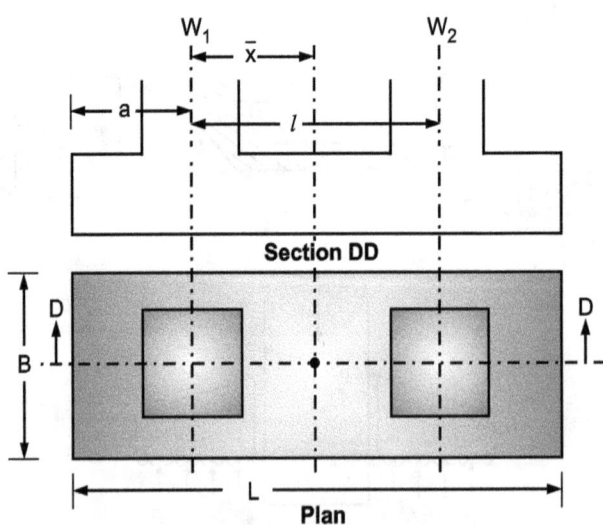

Fig. 2.12 (a) : Combined rectangular footing

(b) Trapezoidal Footing : This type of combined footing is provided when,
- (i) Loads to be carried by two adjacent columns are high.
- (ii) Difference between the two column loads is large and
- (iii) Bearing capacity of soil is less.

Trapezoidal footing consists of proportionately more width near heavier column and less width near lighter column as shown in Fig. 2.12 (b).

If two column loads W_1 and W_2 spaced at a distance l, then total load $(W_1 + W_2)$ will act at a distance $\bar{x}$ from heavier column W_1.

$$\bar{x} = \frac{W_1 \cdot l}{W_1 + W_2} \quad W_1 > W_2$$

Footing width "a" near heavier column is more than footing width "b" near lighter column such that,

$$A = \text{Area of footing} = \frac{(a + b)}{2} \cdot L = \frac{W_1 + W_2}{\text{Safe bearing capacity}}$$

where, L = Length of footing

C.G. of the trapezoidal footing from side "b" will be at a distance,

$$x' = \left(\frac{a + 2b}{a + b}\right) \cdot \frac{L}{3}$$

Projection of footing beyond column face is adjusted in such a way that $\bar{x}$, the C.G. of loads W_1 and W_2 coincides with x', the C.G. of footing.

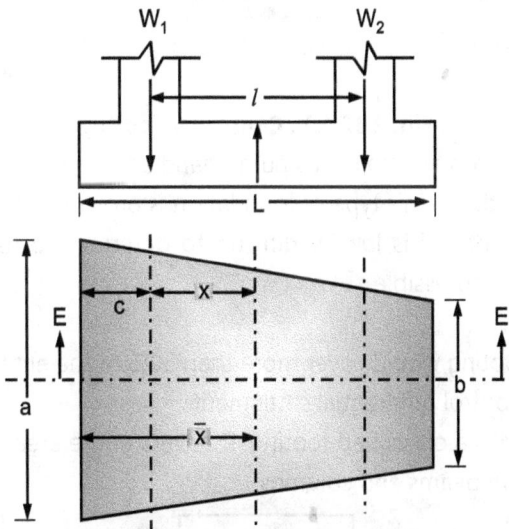

Fig. 2.12 (b) : Trapezoidal footing

(c) Cantilever Footing or Strap footing : This type of footing is provided when,
  (i) Column footing is not permitted to project beyond column face as in case of a column near compound wall.
  (ii) When the distance between the two columns for which a combined footing is to be provided is more. In such a case, rectangular footing is not economical.

Individual Column Footing is provided in proportion to reactions R_1 and R_2 below columns C_1 and C_2 (Refer Fig. 2.12 (c)). Two footings are connected together rigidly by a beam. Hence, the footings settle together and avoid differential settlement. Due to cantilever action, the reaction R_1 is more than cantilever load W_1.

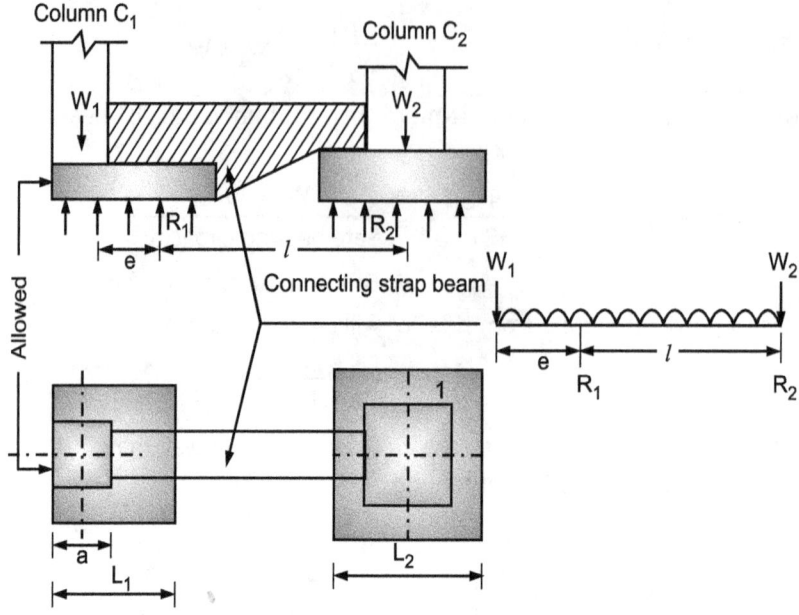

Fig. 2.12 (c) : Cantilever footing

Sometimes this footing is also called as pump handle footing.

(d) Mat or Raft Foundation : This type of foundation is provided when :
 (i) Bearing capacity of soil is low or difficult to determine or is of doubtful nature or strata is highly compressible.
 (ii) Loads are heavy.
 (iii) Use of spread footing would cover more than 50% of the entire area.
 (iv) It is difficult to control differential settlement.

A mat or raft foundation is a combined footing. It covers entire area beneath a structure and supports all walls through beams and columns.

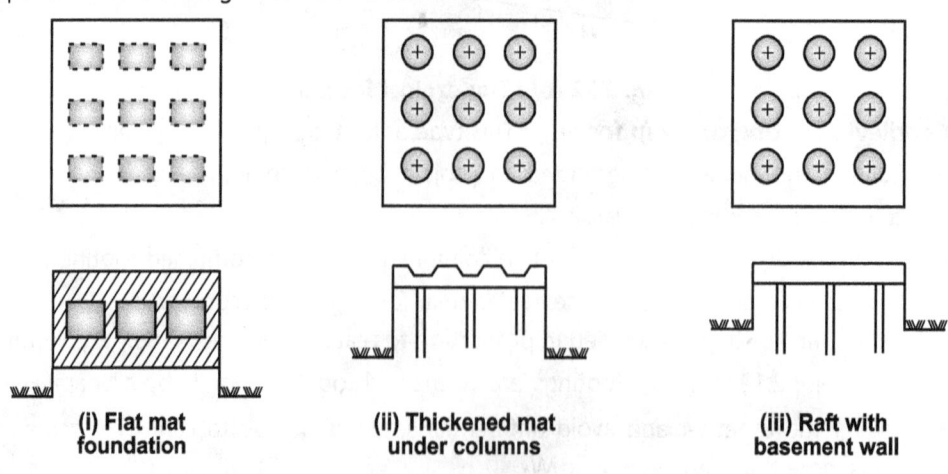

Fig. 2.12 (d) : Mat/Raft foundation

Raft consists of thick, heavily reinforced inverted slab using heavy beams from column to columns. Raft tends to bridge over erratic deposits and hence eliminate differential settlement. For this reason, total settlement of 75 to 100 mm is permitted for raft foundation. In case of highly compressible strata, raft foundation is taken to such a depth that,

Weight of excavated soil = Weight of structure and loads on structure.

Such type of foundation is called as **floating foundation**.

Sometimes, to reduce the self weight of thick raft, cellular foundation or reinforced basement walls serves as raft. A few types of rafts are shown in Fig. 2.12 (d).

2.9.2 Deep Foundation

These foundations carry heavy loads from structure through weak, compressible soils or fills on stronger and less compressible soils or rock at depth.

Some of the types of deep foundations are mentioned below :
  (1) Pile foundations,
  (2) Well foundations,
  (3) Caissons,
  (4) Pier foundations.

Pile Foundation :

Pile foundation is preferred under the following situations :

(a) When open foundation is not possible or for structure such as in deep-sea, or river, or where there is heavy seepage.
(b) When open excavation upto firm strata is difficult and uneconomical or when water table is high or strata consists of expansive soils.
(c) When loads are heavy, non-uniform and there is possibility of differential settlement at shallow depth.

Classification of Piles :

Piles are classified based on :

(a) Mode of transmission of load such as end bearing or friction piles.
(b) Method of construction such as bored or driven piles.
(c) Material of construction such as timber, steel, concrete.

  (a) **End Bearing Piles :** *When pile passes through poor, weak strata and its tip penetrates for a small depth into hard strata, and transfers load to hard strata, it is called as end bearing pile.* The hard strata should be available at a reasonable depth. Size of pile depends upon strength of hard strata.

(b) Friction Pile : When a pile passes through deep strata of limited bearing capacity, the strata offers sufficiently higher frictional resistance along the surface of piles, then it is called as friction pile. These piles derive support mainly from surrounding soil although a very small load is carried at the lower tip of pile.

This type of pile is provided when hard rock/hard strata is available to a great depth. Length and size of pile depends upon type of soil, load etc.

(c) Under Reamed Piles : These piles are provided in expansive soils such as black cotton soil, to resist tensile stresses due to changes in moisture content. By special equipment called under reamer, diameter of pile can be enlarged. The surface of enlarged bulb of pile helps in resisting tensile stresses.

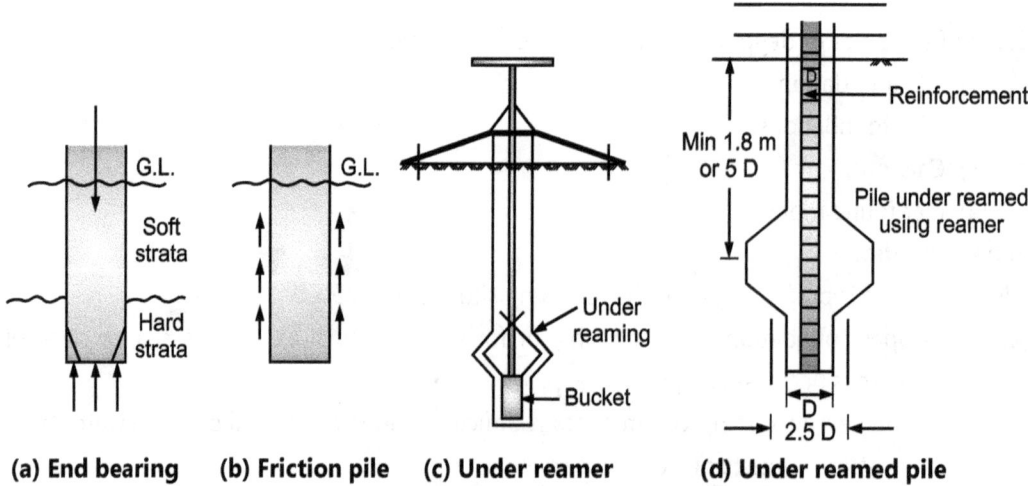

(a) End bearing   (b) Friction pile   (c) Under reamer   (d) Under reamed pile

Fig. 2.13

Foundation for Radar Antenna, Microwave and T.V. Towers :

(a) Uplift load becomes an important governing criteria for selection and design of foundation of these structures. Uplift loads are assumed to be counteracted in case of shallow foundations by the weight of the footing *plus* the weight of an inverted frustum of pyramid of earth on the footing pad, with sides inclined at angle of upto 30° with the vertical (Refer Fig. 2.14). A footing on rock, for uplift may be considered to develop strength by the dead load of the concrete and the strength of all bars anchored under the footing or embedded in concrete in drilled holes.

(b) Allowable settlement and maximum allowable differential settlement shall be as under :

	Type of Tower	Allowable settlement	Allowable differential settlement
1.	Radar antenna tower	12 m	6 mm
2.	Microwave towers with dish antenna	16 mm	12 mm
3.	T.V. towers.	50 mm	20 mm

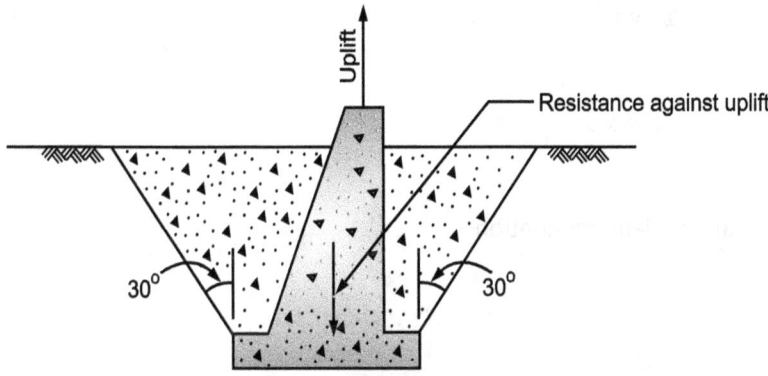

Fig. 2.14 : Conventional Assumption – Resistance against uplift by weight of frustum of earth plus weight of concrete

(c) Raft foundations become good choice if
   (i) Basements are provided.
   (ii) Soils are weak with low settlement value.
(d) Isolated footings are provided in case of lattice towers resting on good soils with medium to high bearing capacity and when tower legs are spaced far apart.
(e) Bored piles with enlarged bases, usually provide economical type of footing where under-reaming is possible.

REVIEW QUESTIONS

1. What are the various requirements of a building as a whole ?
2. Explain the various water proofing techniques.
3. What are the various building components and their requirements ?
4. Write short notes on :
   (a) Form work

(b) Strip footing

(c) Water proofing techniques

(d) Foundation

(e) Walls and columns.

5. Explain the various types of foundation.
6. Explain the suitability of foundation.
7. Differentiate between :

   (a) Stepped and isolated.

   (b) Combined and strip.

   (c) Spread and grillage foundation

Unit - III

Chapter 3

STONE AND BRICK MASONRY

3.1 INTRODUCTION TO STONE MASONRY

Stone is the oldest building construction material known to man. It is known to man since "Stone age". Beautiful structures have been constructed, with the help of this age old material. Out of seven wonders of the world, three wonders have been constructed using stone viz.

(1) The great wall of China, (2) "Pyramids" in Egypt, (3) The famous "Taj Mahal" in Agra.

Apart from these historical buildings, forts, docks, harbours, dams, bridges, arches, rail tracks, plain and reinforced concrete works, beautiful statues, temples, thousands of kilometres of roads etc. have been constructed using stones. Stones are strong, durable, can take polish and are available not only in large quantity, but have variety of pleasing colours.

In this section, characteristics of good building stones, natural bed, defects in stones, different types of tests carried on stone, etc. UCR and CR masonry, etc. are discussed.

Table 3.1 : Physical Properties and Engineering Uses of Familiar Stones

Sr. No.	Type of rock and classification	Properties and Engineering Uses	Locality where available	Physical Properties		
				Compressive strength kg/m²	Sp. gravity G	Density γ, kg/m³
1.	Sand stone (sedimentary)	Hard, strong, non-absorbent, easy to work. Can resist heat (if mica is absent). **Uses :** Ornamental work, floor, wall, columns, steps, road metal.	A.P., M.P., H.P., U.P., Gujarat, Karnataka, T.N., Maharashtra	650	2.6 to 2.9	2200
2.	Deccan trap (Igneous)	Hard, tough durable difficult to work. Not suitable for ornamental work. **Uses :** Suitable for rubble masonry work, road metal, paving stone, flay stone.	Maharashtra, Gujarat, Bihar, M.P.	1500 – 1900	2.9	2800 – 2900

3.	Granite (Igneous)	Very strong available in pleasing colours, difficult to work with highly durable (in absence of feldspar and mica). **Uses** : Bridge piers, walls, columns, steps, sills, road metal, ballast.	Karnataka, M.P., U.P., Gujarat, Punjab, Rajasthan, Bihar, Orissa, Kashmir	700 – 1300	2.6 – 2.7	2600
4.	Lime stone (sedimentary)	Soft, liable to be affected by acid, easy to work. **Uses** : Walls, floors, steps, road work, manufacture of cement, as a flux	A.P., M.P., U.P., Gujarat, Maharashtra, Rajasthan	550	2 to 2.7	1700
5.	Marble (metamorphic)	Easy to work, taken polish, available in pleasing colours. Can be easily swan and carved. **Uses** : Ornamental work, columns, floors, steps.	Rajasthan, Gujarat, Maharashtra, A.P., M.P., U.P.	720	2.65	2700
6.	Laterite (metamorphic)	Porous, cellular structure, can be quarried in blocks, available in different colours. **Uses** : Building stone, road metal.	Bihar, Orissa, A.P., M.P., Maharashtra, T.N.	20 to 30	2.2 to 2.5	1200 – 1600
7.	State (metamorphic)	Non-absorbent, splits along natural bedding plane.	Flooring, roofing, sills, damp-proofing.	750 – 2100	2.9	2600

3.2 MASONRY

Masonry is defined as assemblage of masonry unit properly bonded together with mortar. Masonry units are individual units which are bonded together with the help of mortar to form a masonry element such as wall, column, pier, buttress etc.

3.2.1 Types of Masonry

Masonry units may be of the following types :

1. Stones
2. Common burnt clay bricks, sand-lime bricks
3. Concrete/lime based blocks
4. Burnt clay hollow blocks
5. Autoclaved cellular concrete blocks
6. Gypsum partition blocks; which are used only for construction of non-load bearing walls.

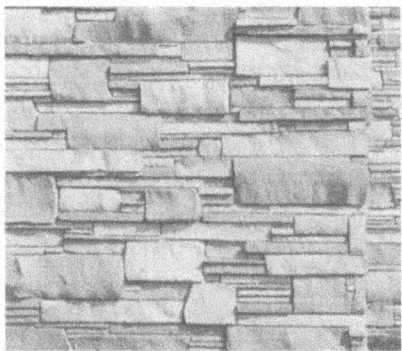
Stone Masonry Riser Leveller

Stone Masory

Brick Cavity Wall Insulation

Randon Rubble Stone Masonry

Plumb Check for Masonry Work

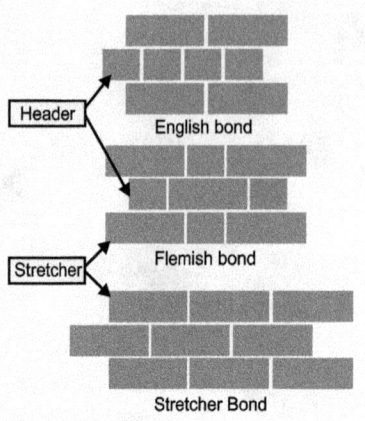
Bonds

Flemish-bond

FlemishBond

Jack Arch

Artificial-Stone

Jack Arch

Cavity Wall Insulation

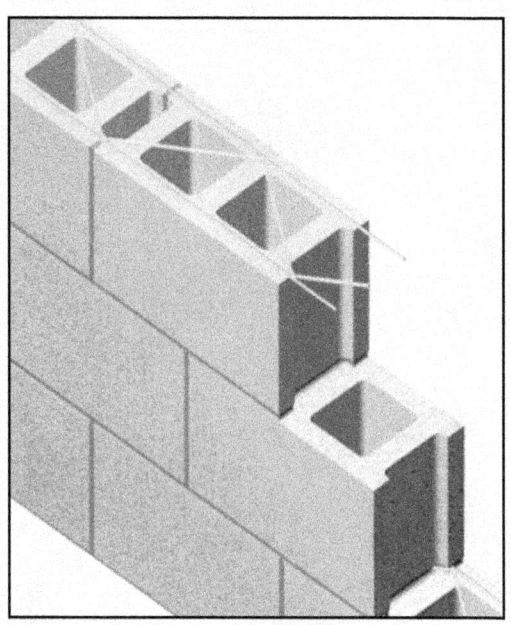

Hollow Block Masonry

Hollow Blocks

Cavity Wall Construction

Ridge Tile

Manglor Tiles

Flooring

Roofing Tiles

Epoxy-Floor-Paint-Coating

Rubber Flooring

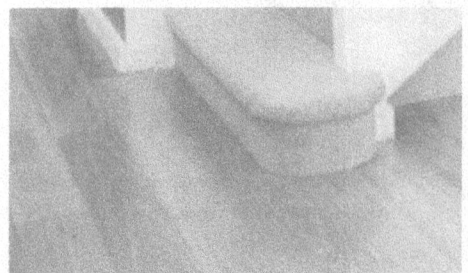
Wooden Floor

Wooden Floor

A wall is a continuous vertical structure of stone, brick, concrete etc. thin in proportion to its length and height, which encloses a building,
  (i) to carry designed vertical and horizontal load, on it,
  (ii) to protect it from rain, dampness, heat and
  (iii) to divide building in suitable rooms.

3.3 TERMS USED IN STONE MASONRY

Some of the terms used in stone masonry are explained as follows :
1. **Bed / Bed surface / Bedding plane :** It is the surface of a stone perpendicular to the line of pressure.
2. **Quoins :** These are the stones used at the corners of wall. In order to give better appearance, these are properly dressed and selected from larger stones having better appearance. Where good stones are not available, precast concrete blocks of suitable size are provided.
3. **Cornice and Corbel :**
    (a) **Cornice :** It is a moulded stone, with ornamental treatment, having large projection and is placed at the junction of wall and ceiling and is finished so as to throw rain water.
    (b) **Corbel :** It is also a stone projecting outside to support a structural member to serve as support to wall plate. Thus,
      (i) Although both cornice and corbel are stones projecting, cornice has ornamental appearance whereas corbel may not have ornamental treatment;
      (ii) Cornice is exposed to atmosphere and is having slope to drain off rain water, whereas corbel is not exposed to weather and is intended to support structural member.

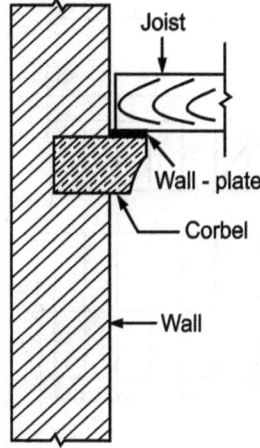

Fig. 3.1 : Corbel

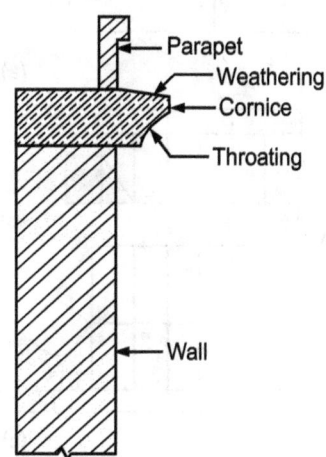

Fig. 3.2 : Cornice

4. **String Course, Drip stone and Throating :**
   (a) **String course :** It is a continuous horizontal course, projecting from the face of wall and is intended to throw off rain water. It is provided at floor level. It may or may not have groove at the underside to drain off water.
   (b) **Drip stone :** It is a projected stone moulding having throating under surface to drain out rain water off wall.
   (c) **Throating :** These are the grooves cut on the under surface of sills, copings, string courses to drain off rain water trickling from walls.
5. **Through Stone :** These are non-porous strong, and thick stones (or precast concrete block) extending throughout the thickness of wall, (i) to reduce ingress of moisture and (ii) to increase stability of wall. Even if a wall settles, these stones being strong will not crack.
6. **Heads and Header :**
   (a) **Heads :** These are the stones provided at the top of openings of doors, windows, etc. with sufficient bearing on either side of the opening. This is another name to stone lintel.
   (b) **Header :** It is a brick or stone which lies in its greatest length at right angles to the face of the work. In stone masonry, it is sometimes called as through stone. In case of brick masonry, the course, in which all the bricks are laid as headers is known as header course.
7. **Jambs and Reveals :**

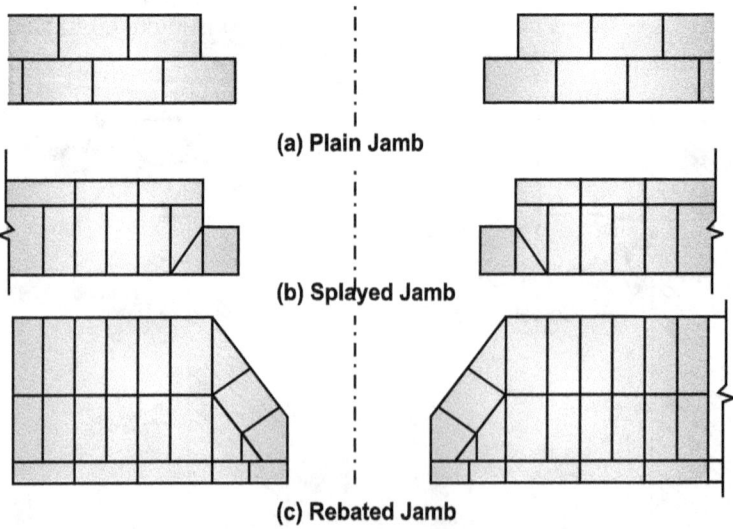

(a) Plain Jamb

(b) Splayed Jamb

(c) Rebated Jamb

Fig. 3.3 : Jambs

(a) **Jambs :** These are the vertical surfaces of an opening for doors and windows. These may be (i) plain or (ii) splayed or (iii) rebated to receive the frames of doors and windows.

(b) **Reveals :** These are the exposed vertical surfaces left on the sides of opening, after the door or window frame has been fitted in the position.

8. **Buttress, Pier, Pilaster :**

    (a) **Buttress :** It is sloping or stepped masonry projection from a tall wall intended to strengthen the wall against the thrust of a roof or arch or pressure of wind or soil.

    (b) **Pier :** It is an isolated vertical mass of stone or brick masonry to support beams or lintels. If it is made monolithic with the wall and project from wall (to support concentrated load) it is called as pilaster.

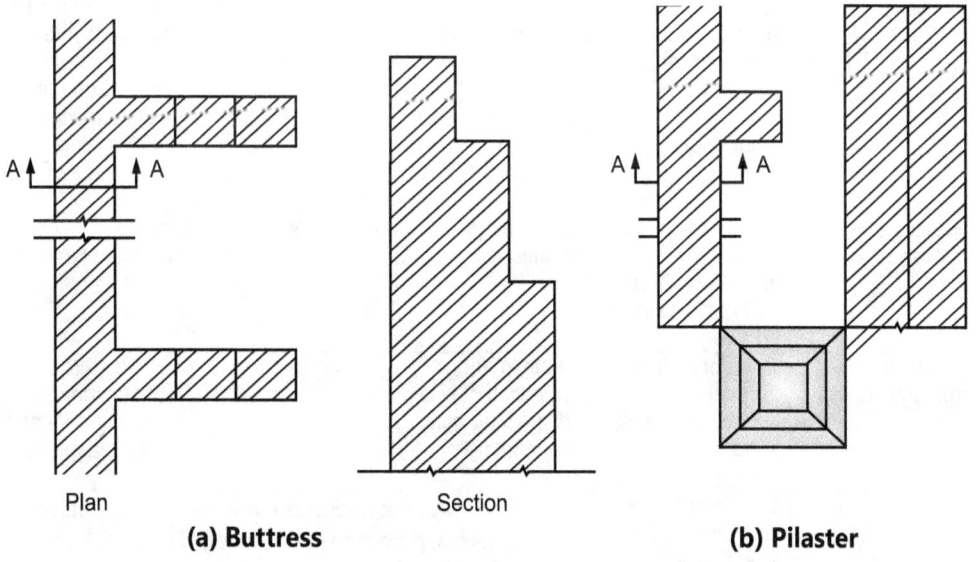

Fig. 3.4

9. **Dowel :** It is a pin or peg let into two pieces of stone or wood for joining.
10. **Spalls :** These are small pieces of stones, placed vertically and embedded in the mortar in the central portion of wall, to fill the voids.

3.4 DIFFERENCE IN DIFFERENT TYPES OF RANDOM RUBBLE AND SQUARE RUBBLE MASONRY

Difference in different types of random rubble and square rubble on important aspects is as follows.

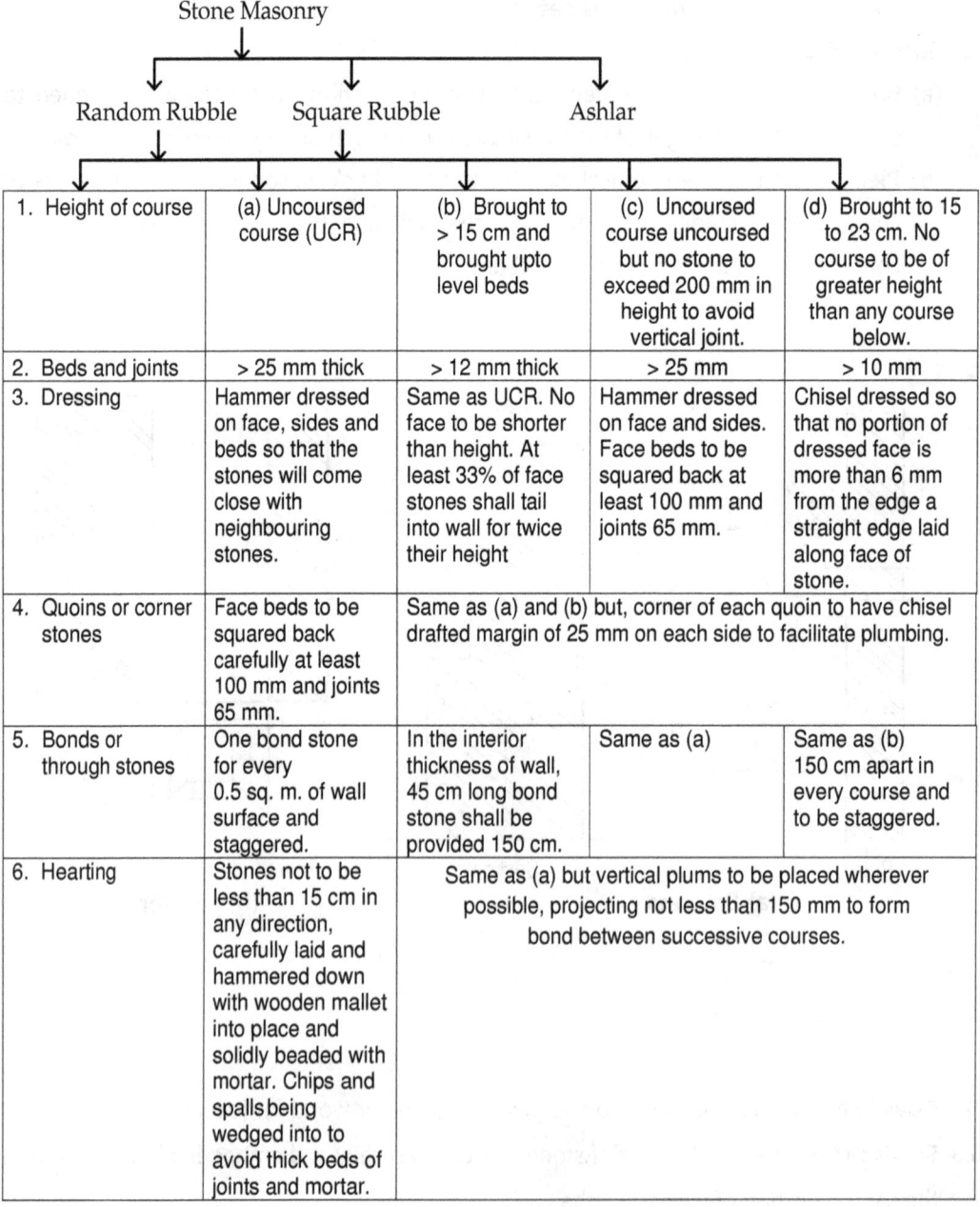

	Random Rubble	Square Rubble		Ashlar
	(a) Uncoursed course (UCR)	(b) Brought to > 15 cm and brought upto level beds	(c) Uncoursed course uncoursed but no stone to exceed 200 mm in height to avoid vertical joint.	(d) Brought to 15 to 23 cm. No course to be of greater height than any course below.
1. Height of course				
2. Beds and joints	> 25 mm thick	> 12 mm thick	> 25 mm	> 10 mm
3. Dressing	Hammer dressed on face, sides and beds so that the stones will come close with neighbouring stones.	Same as UCR. No face to be shorter than height. At least 33% of face stones shall tail into wall for twice their height	Hammer dressed on face and sides. Face beds to be squared back at least 100 mm and joints 65 mm.	Chisel dressed so that no portion of dressed face is more than 6 mm from the edge a straight edge laid along face of stone.
4. Quoins or corner stones	Face beds to be squared back carefully at least 100 mm and joints 65 mm.	Same as (a) and (b) but, corner of each quoin to have chisel drafted margin of 25 mm on each side to facilitate plumbing.		
5. Bonds or through stones	One bond stone for every 0.5 sq. m. of wall surface and staggered.	In the interior thickness of wall, 45 cm long bond stone shall be provided 150 cm.	Same as (a)	Same as (b) 150 cm apart in every course and to be staggered.
6. Hearting	Stones not to be less than 15 cm in any direction, carefully laid and hammered down with wooden mallet into place and solidly beaded with mortar. Chips and spalls being wedged into to avoid thick beds of joints and mortar.	Same as (a) but vertical plums to be placed wherever possible, projecting not less than 150 mm to form bond between successive courses.		

3.5 SPECIFICATIONS FOR UNCOURSED RUBBLE MASONRY

1. **Stone :** Stone should be tough, hard, dense, durable and of uniform colour; should be free from flaws, veins, etc. When immersed in water for 24 hours, should not absorb more than 5% of its dry weight.
2. **Size of Stone :** Width and height shall not be less than 15 cm and length shall not be less than 1.5 times its height.
3. **Dressing :** Stones shall be hammer dressed, weak corners and edges shall be removed.
4. **Face Stones :** Stones with larger sides, having good beds shall be used for face work. At least 50% of them shall be more than 10 litres in volume. The beds and joints shall have a minimum bearing of not less than 2 cm. Face stones shall be dressed in straight lines and these sides shall be in one plane.
5. **Through Stones :**
   (i) Through stones shall be about 0.03 m^2 in face area and shall occupy full width of wall, if thickness of wall is upto 60 cm.
   (ii) If thickness of wall is more than 60 cm, a line of headers over lapping each other by at least 15 cm shall be provided.
   (iii) Through stones shall be marked on their faces by paint.
   (iv) Through stones / headers shall be laid @ 2 stones / m^2. Each stone shall break joint with the stone in course below or above by at least 8 cm.
6. **Hearting and Backing Stones :** 30% of stones used in hearting and backing shall exceed 10 litres in volume.
7. **Quoins :** Quoins shall be of size 30 cm × 15 cm × 15 cm. The faces of quoins shall be hammer dressed. Each side of exposed corner shall be chisel drafted to a width of 40 mm. The quoins shall tail into wall to a length not less than 20 cm and 10 cm measured at right angles to the shorter and longer face respectively.
8. **Thickness of Joint :** No face joint shall exceed 16 mm in thickness; and all joints shall be raked to a depth of 16 mm.
9. **Raising of Masonry :** Face work and hearting shall be brought up evenly, but top of each course shall not be levelled. The rate of raising masonry shall not exceed 60 cm per day.
10. **Laying Stones :** All stones shall be laid full in the mortar, both in bed joints and side joints. Clean chips and spalls shall be wedged into the mortar joints in hearting.
11. **Quantity of Mortar :** The volume of mortar used per cubic metre of masonry shall be between 0.30 to 0.35 cubic metre.

3.6 SPECIFICATIONS FOR COURSED RUBBLE MASONRY [FIRST SORT]

1. **Stones :** Same as that for uncoursed rubble masonry.
2. **Size of Stones :** Height of stone shall be 15 cm. Breadth shall be more than height and shall tail back into the masonry 1.5 times the height.
3. **Scaffolding :** It shall be double scaffolding and shall be sufficiently strong.
4. **Face Stones :** Bushing on the face of stone shall not be more than 4 cm. The beds and tops shall be rough tooled to atleast 8 cm from face and the vertical faces shall be rough tooled to at least 4 cm from face.
5. **Through Stones :** The height of the through stones shall be the full height of the course and the width shall not be less than height. Rest same as that for UCR.
6. **Hearting and Backing Stones :** Same as that for UCR.
7. **Quoins :**
   (i) The faces of quoins shall be rough tooled and the sides of exposed corner shall be provided with a chisel draft of about 4 cm from the face.
   (ii) These shall be of the same height as that of the course.
   (iii) The length (L) of quoins on the longer face shall not be less than twice their height (H) and on shorter face not less than height.
   The quoin shall tail into the wall to length of not less than 20 cm and 10 cm measured perpendicularly to the shorter and larger sides respectively.
8. **Joints :** The thickness of joint shall not exceed 10 mm. Horizontal joints shall be truely horizontal and vertical joints shall be truely vertical.
9. **Raising of Masonry :** Same as that for UCR masonry.
10. **Laying :** The stones shall be laid in horizontal course of 15 cm height. All courses shall be of equal height.
11. **Quantity of Mortar :** The volume of mortar used per cubic metre of masonry shall be between 0.25 to 0.30 cubic metre.

Notes :
   (1) In Course Rubble Masonry of second sort, each course need not be of the same height but not more than two stones are used in the height of the course.
   (2) In Course Rubble Masonry of third sort not more than three stones are used in the height of the course.

Thus, in Course Rubble of first sort, second sort and third sort, one stone, two stones and three stones are used respectively in the height of course.

3.7 GENERAL POINTS TO BE OBSERVED DURING THE SUPERVISION OF STONE MASONRY WORK

Various points as regards thickness of joints, quoins, through stones, dressing, height of course, hearting have been summarized and given in the chart for Random Rubble and Square Rubble Masonry and in the specifications for DCR and CR masonry. In addition to this, the following points should be observed :

1. The stones should be properly wetted so that stones do not absorb moisture in mortar.
2. The stones should be dressed as per requirement, before placing in position.
3. Positioning, spacing of centre line of walls must conform as per drawings; during the entire construction of the wall. The same must be checked with the help of reference points located outside.
4. Verticality of the wall should be checked from time to time, with the help of plumb bob. This is to ensure that, the loads acting on the wall is concentric.
5. The various courses should be brought to level with the help of thin string stretched between the ends of walls.
6. Construction of stone masonry should commence at prominent corners of walls. Masonry between corners should be raised gradually, uniformly and in plumb.
7. Good and bad examples of (i) Stretcher stone, (ii) Quoins, (iii) Through stones and (iv) Faulty construction are shown in the following sketches. Faulty materials and methods should be avoided.
8. All surfaces should be kept wet while the work is in progress. After completion of work, the masonry should be cured in 2 to 3 weeks.

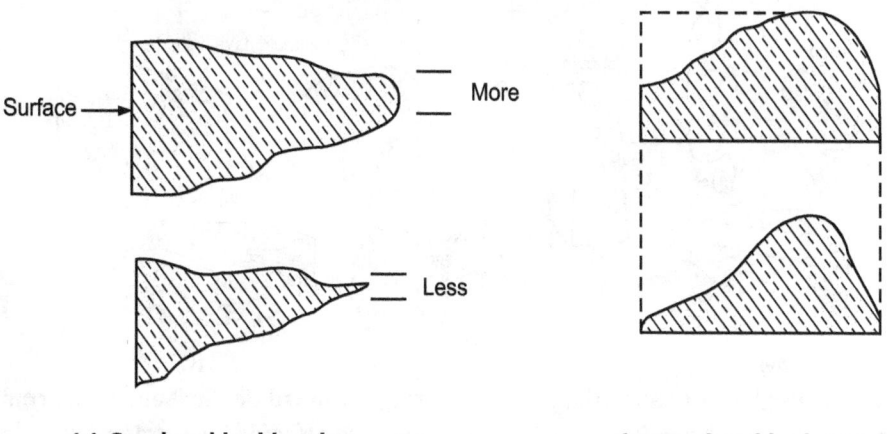

(a) Good and bad header **(b) Good and bad stretcher**

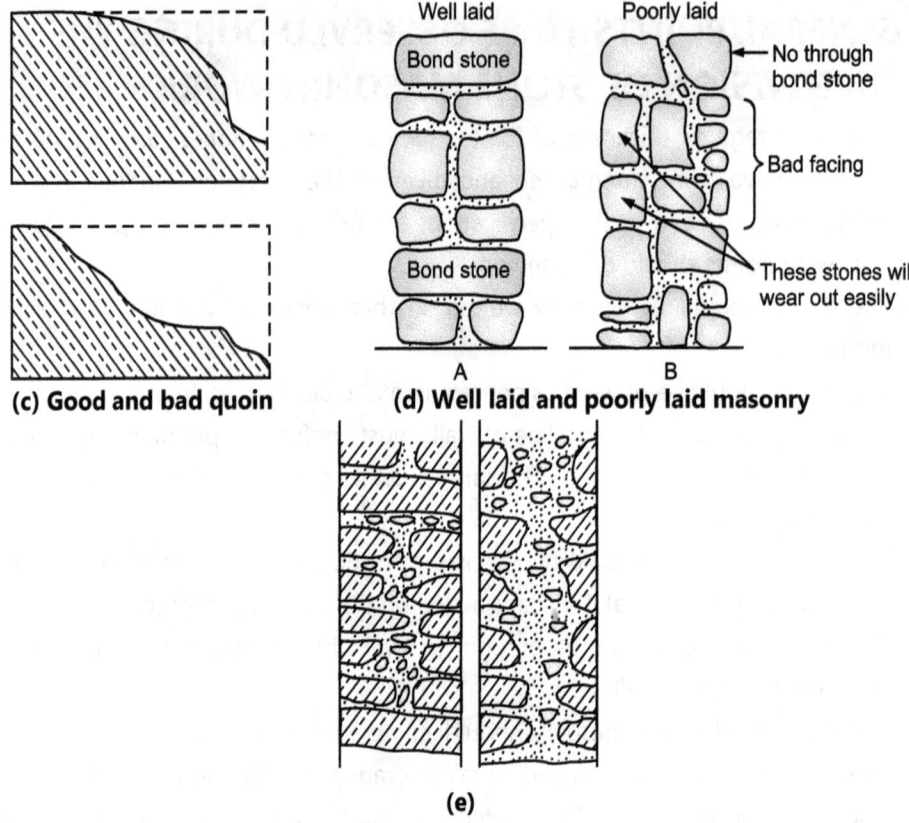

(c) Good and bad quoin
(d) Well laid and poorly laid masonry
(e)
Fig. 3.5 : Section through a good and bad masonry wall

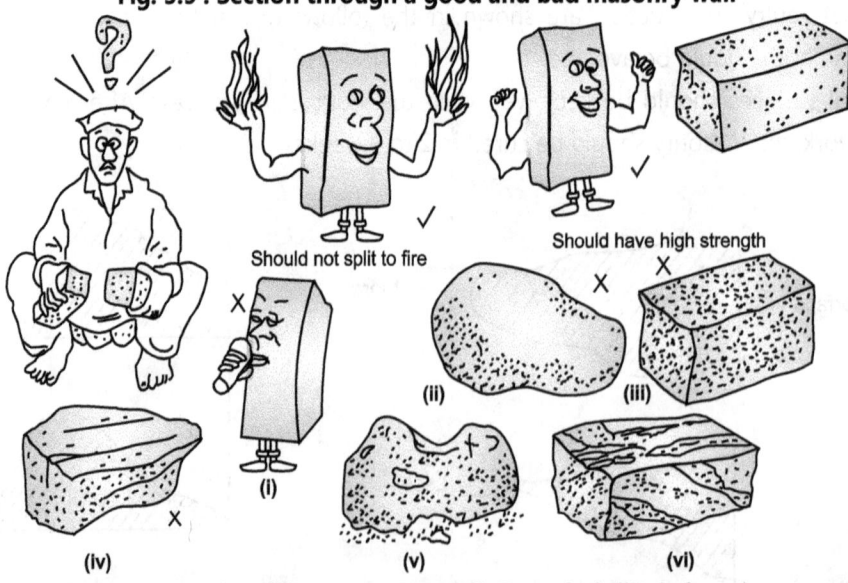

Fig. 3.6 : Avoid (i) Stones absorbing more water (ii) Rounded (iii) Soft and stone composed of sand and soil (iv) Irregular flat pointed (v) Likely to affected by weather (vi) With dark spots and bonds of different colours

(1) Soak stones in water before use

(2) Masonry with thin joints and PCC (1 : 4 : 8)

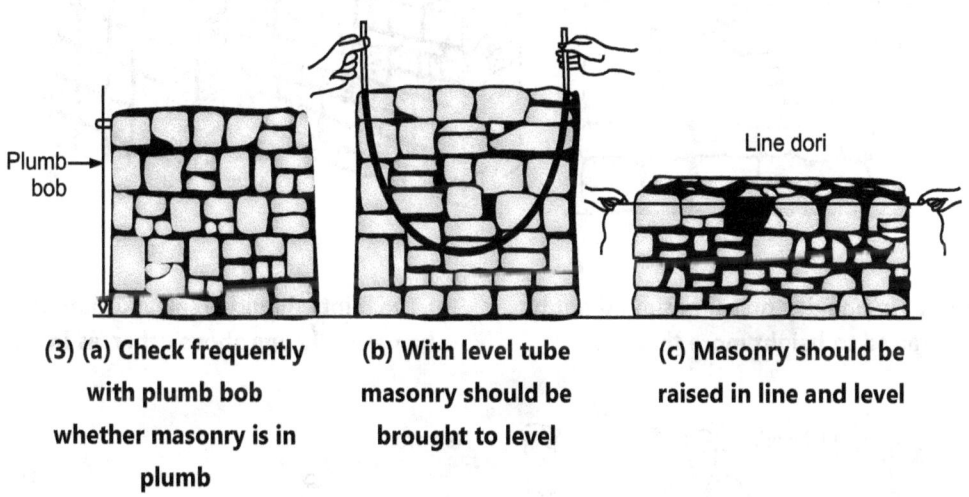

(3) (a) Check frequently with plumb bob whether masonry is in plumb

(b) With level tube masonry should be brought to level

(c) Masonry should be raised in line and level

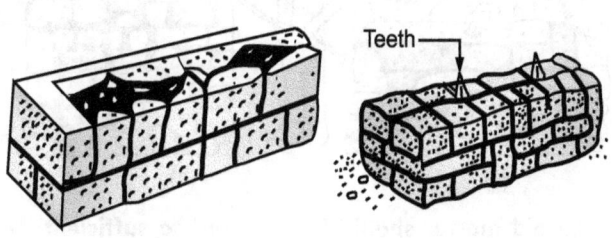
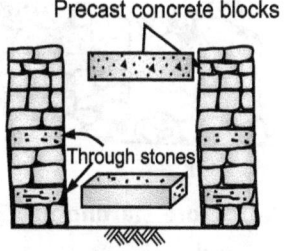

(4) (a) Fill voids between stones using spalls in hearing

(b) At the end of day's work, provide pointed stones as shown. This will help in providing grip in further work

(c) Provide through stones for full width of wall. Sometimes precast concrete blocks are provided, in place of through stones

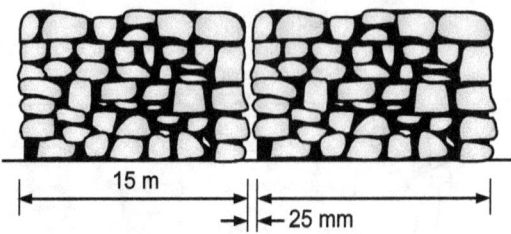

(5) If the length of compound wall exceeds 15 m, then provide a gap of 25 mm throughout width and height to serve as expansion joint

Fig. 3.7 : Seven commandments for good stone masonry (continued)

(6) (a) In one day masonry should not be raised to height more than 0.6 m

(b) The joints should break and should not be vertically one above other, as in (c)

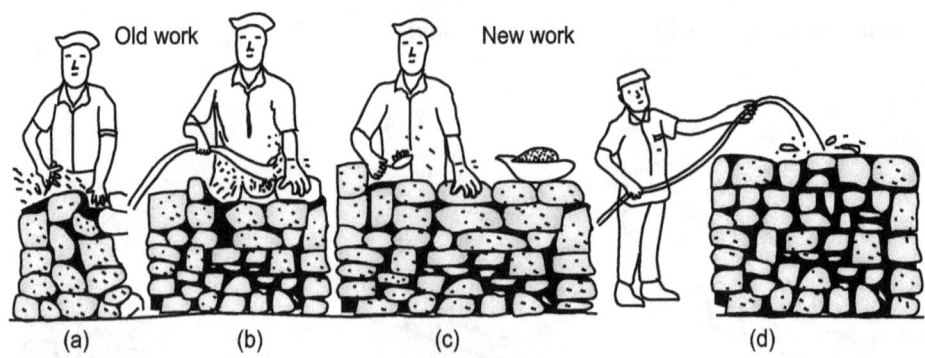

(7) (a) Before starting new work, the old mortar should breaked out to sufficient depth and

(b) Then masonry work is soaked with water

(c) Provide fresh mortar "into the masonry" and not on the previous levelled surface to obtain good grip. Keep mortar just near the work (and not at far away and too low level) to speed up construction.

(d) After completion of work, it should be cured atleast for 15 days.

Fig. 3.8 : Seven commandments for good stone masonry

3.8 INTRODUCTION TO BRICK MASONRY

Although beautiful structures can be constructed using naturally available stones, it has its limitations; such as :
1. Availability of stones of desired quality and quantity at economically viable cost.
2. Stones are required to be dressed to attain desired finish.
3. Stones are required to be quarried and transported.
4. Usually stones are heavy and wall thickness is more whereas bricks are light, wall thickness is less hence, dead weight of wall is less.
5. Speed of construction of stone masonry is less and more quantity of morter is required.

In view of above, many times it is advantageous to use light bricks of regular shape and size. Usually mouldable earth, suitable for manufacture of bricks is easily available.

The advantages and disadvantages of bricks as compared with stone as a building material are given below :

(i) Bricks are lighter in weight and can be more easily handled. The size and shape of bricks are such that the brick layer can continuously lay them for hours together without fatigue.

(ii) Bricks may be easily moulded from clay into required size and shape at a moderate cost. But stones are usually more costly than bricks, difficult and expensive to quarry and dress down the required size and shape and plaster does not stick well to stone as it does to bricks.

(iii) Bricks do not absorb as much heat as stones and are also more fire-resisting than stones.

(iv) Good bricks stand the effects of weather and of chemicals in the atmosphere better than stones. Under certain atmospheric conditions, stones are not suited.

(v) Walls with bricks can be easily constructed to the required thickness viz. 100 mm, 200 mm, 300 mm, and above, whereas walls with stones are to be constructed to a thickness of 400 mm or above for ease of construction and strength.

(vi) Bricks are not so strong or durable as stones. For public buildings and works of monumental nature bricks are not so suitable as stones; as a better architectural effect can be obtained in stones than in bricks.

(vii) Bricks absorb more water than stones and are not heavy as stones. Hence, bricks are not suitable for heavy engineering works.

(viii) In walls, the faces of bricks are generally to be covered by means of lime or cement plaster in order to prevent the absorption of moisture. But stones do not require plastering.

3.9 CHARACTERISTICS OF A GOOD BRICK

Good bricks which are to be used for the construction of important structures should possess the following qualities :
1. Bricks should be well-burnt in kilns, copper coloured, free from cracks, with sharp and square edges.
2. Bricks should be uniform in shape and should be of standard size.
3. Bricks should give clear ringing sound when struck with each other.
4. Bricks when broken should show homogeneous and compact structure.
5. Bricks should not absorb water more than $1/8^{th}$ to $1/6^{th}$ of its weight, when soaked in water for a period of 24 hours.
6. Bricks should be sufficiently hard. No impression should be left on brick surface, when it is scratched with finger nail.
7. Bricks should not break *when droped on hard* ground from a height of about one metre.
8. Bricks should have low thermal conductivity and they should be sound proof.
9. Crushing strength of brick varies from 4 N/mm^2 to 7 N/mm^2 depending upon type or class of bricks.

3.10 BRICK MASONRY

Using different varieties of stones, such as marble, granite, basalt, beautiful, polished, massive, strong structures have been built. However, use of stone masonry has certain limitations and drawbacks such as availability of suitable stones at a economically viable cost, weight, necessity of dressing the stones and resistance to fire. Some of these limitations and disadvantages of stone masonry can be overcome by using small sized, light bricks having regular shape and size. Strong and beautiful structures have been built using bricks. Brick masonry has certain over-riding advantages over stone masonry, especially where stones of desired quality and quantity can not be made economically available and where bricks can be manufactured easily by making use of locally available clayey soils (with certain modifications).

3.10.1 Comparison of Brick Masonry with Stone Masonry

Following are the advantages of Brick Masonry over Stone Masonry :
1. **Labour :** Comparatively more number of highly skilled labourers are required to quarry stones, dress them to required size and shape. Further special tools and tackles are required to lift heavy stones; whereas bricks being small, of regular size and shape and light in weight, no dressing is required and no special tools are required for lifting.

2. **Time :** Bricks being of regular size and shape, construction of brick masonry is fast.
3. **Quantity of Mortar :** Thickness of joint in Ashlar masonry is less; but voids in respect rubble masonry in hearting are more. Hence, more quantity of mortar is required for stone masonry than for brick masonry. For one cubic metre of random rubble masonry about 0.35 to 0.45 cu. m of mortar is required whereas for one cu. m of brick masonry only 0.23 to 0.27 cu. m of mortar is required.
4. **Thickness of Wall :** Comparatively thickness of stone masonry wall is more than that of brick masonry. As a result, dead weight of stone masonry is more and lesser carpet area is available.
5. **Resistance to Fire :** Brick masonry is comparatively more fire resistant than stone masonry.

However, the brick masonry has the following disadvantages.
1. **Strength :** Strength of stone masonry is more than that of brick masonry.
2. **Water Tightness :** Stone masonry absorbs less moisture than brick masonry. Therefore, to protect brick masonry from weathering action, external surfaces are required to plastered / pointed.
3. **Aesthetical Effects :** Aesthetical effects which can be obtained due to availability of variety of pleasing colours, due to dressing and polishing of stones can not be attained by use of brick masonry.
4. **Resistance to Weathering and Maintenance :** Stone masonry is more weather resistant and requires very less maintenance when compared to brick masonry.

Size of Brick :

Bricks of different sizes are available in market. I.S. advocates use of modular sized bricks, i.e. bricks of size 19 × 9 × 9 cm with a thickness of joint of 1 cm, the nominal dimension would be 20 × 10 × 10 cm. However, despite of advantages of modular size, still in many places use of old sized bricks is continuing.

Standard sizes for 9" bricks as prescribed in various PWDs in India are :

$9" \times 4\frac{1}{2}" \times 2\frac{1}{2}"$, $9" \times 4\frac{1}{4}" \times 2\frac{3}{4}"$, $9" \times 4\frac{3}{8}" \times 2\frac{3}{4}"$, $8\frac{7}{8}" \times 4\frac{1}{4}" \times 2\frac{3}{4}"$, $8\frac{7}{8}" \times 4\frac{1}{4}" \times 3"$, $8\frac{3}{4}" \times 4\frac{1}{4}" \times 2\frac{3}{4}"$

Now-a-days, wider bricks popularly known as "Thokala Bricks" of size $8\frac{1}{2}" \times 6" \times 3\frac{1}{2}"$ are also available in market.

3.11 CLASSIFICATION OF BRICKS

I.S. does not classify bricks into first class brick, second class brick and third class brick. However, in many organizations such as PWD, MES etc. bricks are classified as first class, second class and third class bricks. The difference between these three bricks and three classes of brick masonry is summarized as under.

No.		1st Class Bricks	2nd Class Brick	3rd Class Brick
1.	Burning	Well burnt	Slightly over burnt but not vitrified	Under burnt
2.	Colour	Uniformly reddish	Non - uniform	Yellowish
3.	Shape and size	Regular, sharp, straight and right angled edges	Somewhat irregular with rough surface	May be distorted with round edges.
4.	Sound when struck	Clear ringing	Clear ringing	Dull sound
5.	Water absorption %	< 20%	< 22% When soaked in water for 24 hours	< 25%
6.	Efflorescence	Not appreciable when dried in shed	Not appreciable either in wet or dry state	Moderate signs of efflorescence
7.	Curshing strength	$\geq 105 \text{ kg/cm}^2$	$\geq 70 \text{ kg/cm}^2$	–
8.	Flaws	Free from flaws, cracks, chips, nodules of lime or kankar	Slight chips or flaws or surface cracks but free from lime.	–
9.	Uses	All masonry works, Floaring, Face work, reinforced brick work	In unimportant works interior walls	Inferior and temporary buildings if not subjected to heavy rains, scaffolding and centering.
10.	Thickness of joint	For 1st class brick masonry thickness of joint should not be more than 10 mm	< 12 mm	–

3.12 TERMS USED IN BRICK MASONRY

Various terms used in brick masonry are explained as follows :

1. **Arrises :** The edges formed by the intersection of plane surfaces of a brick are called the arrises and they should be sharp, square and free from damage.
2. **Quoin :** A corner or external angle on the face side of a wall is called as Quoin.
3. **Course :** It is a complete layer of brick or stone, laid on the same bed. A header course consists of only headers whereas stretcher course consists of stretchers only as seen in elevation. In general, the courses are of the same height.

4. **Bond**: It is the method of arranging bricks in courses so that the individual units are tied together. Bonds are distinguished by their face appearance or elevation.
5. **Bed Joint**: The horizontal layer of mortar upon which bricks are laid is known as a bed joint.
6. **Lap**: The horizontal distance between the vertical joints in successive courses is termed as a lap and for a good bond, it should be one-fourth of the length of a brick.
7. **Stretcher**: This is a brick laid with its length parallel to the face or front or direction of a wall. The course containing stretchers is called a stretcher course.
8. **Header**: This is a brick laid with its breadth or width parallel to the face or front or direction of a wall. The course containing headers is called a header course.
9. **Perpends**: The vertical joints separating the bricks in either length or cross directions are known as perpends and for a good bond, the perpends in alternate courses should be vertically one above the other.

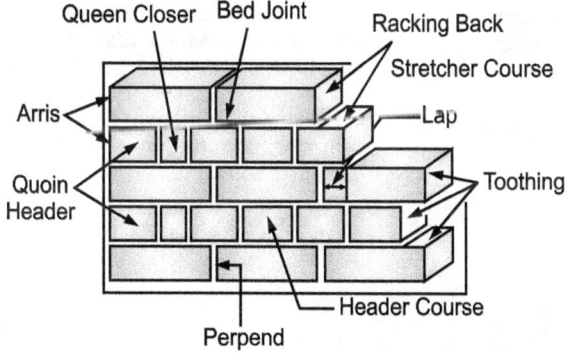

Fig. 3.9 : Brick terms

3.13 TYPES OF BOND

Following are some of the types of bonds used in brick masonry :
1. English bond
2. Single and double Flemish bond
3. Header bond
4. Stretcher bond
5. Herring bone bond
6. Diagonal bond
7. Garden wall bond.

3.13.1 English Bond

This bond is considered as the strongest in brick work and is used extensively. Following are the features of English bond. (Refer Fig. 3.10 and 3.11).

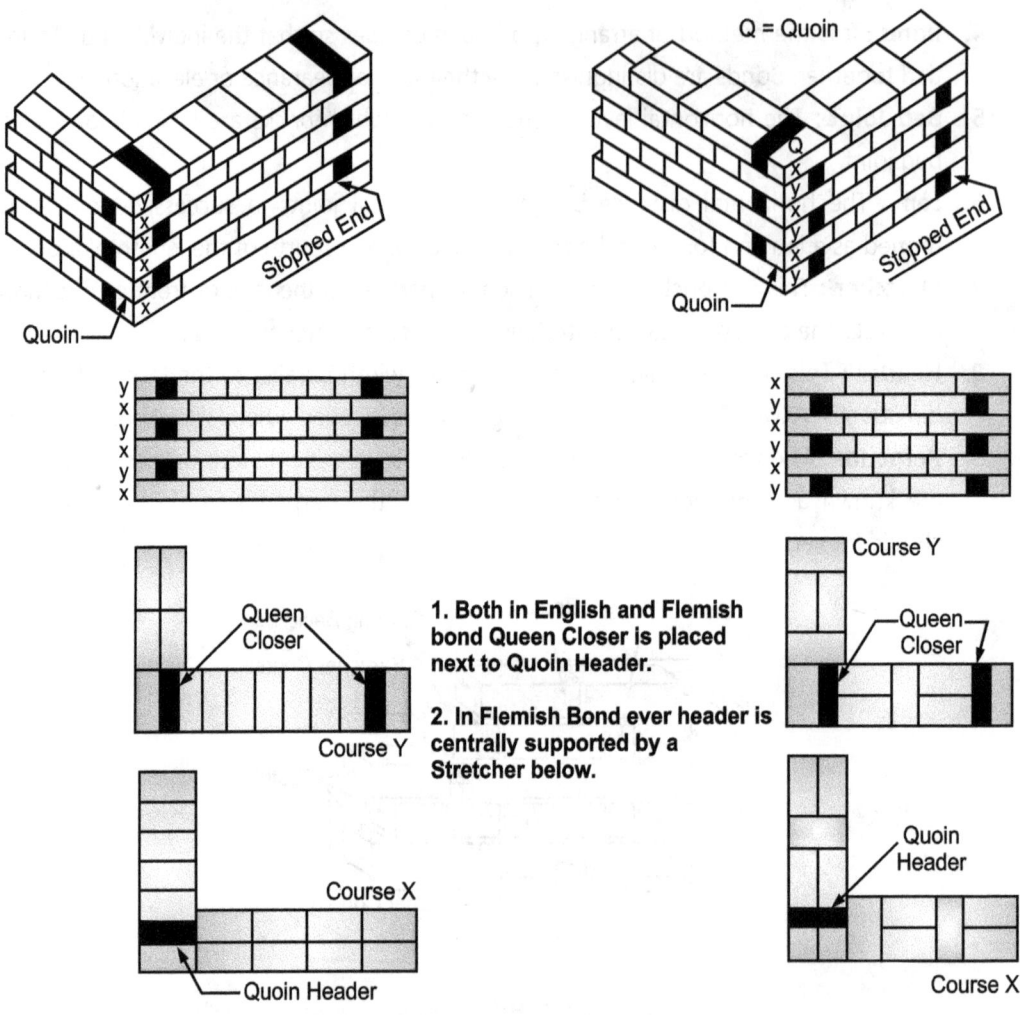

Fig. 3.10 : Brick wall with corner and stopped end

1. Queen closer is placed next to Quoin header and Queen closer is not required in stretcher course.
2. In alternate courses, headers and stretchers are provided.
3. No continuous vertical joint is formed.
4. Lap between header and stretcher course in successive courses is not less than $1/4^{th}$ of length of brick.
5. For 1, 2 and 3 brick thick wall in both front and rear elevation, the same course shows headers or stretchers.

However, for $1\frac{1}{2}$, and $2\frac{1}{2}$ thick brick wall, if header is infront elevation, stretcher will be seen in rear elevation for the same course.

6. Since, the number of joints in header courses are double than that in stretcher course, these joints should be thin, so that desired lap is maintained.

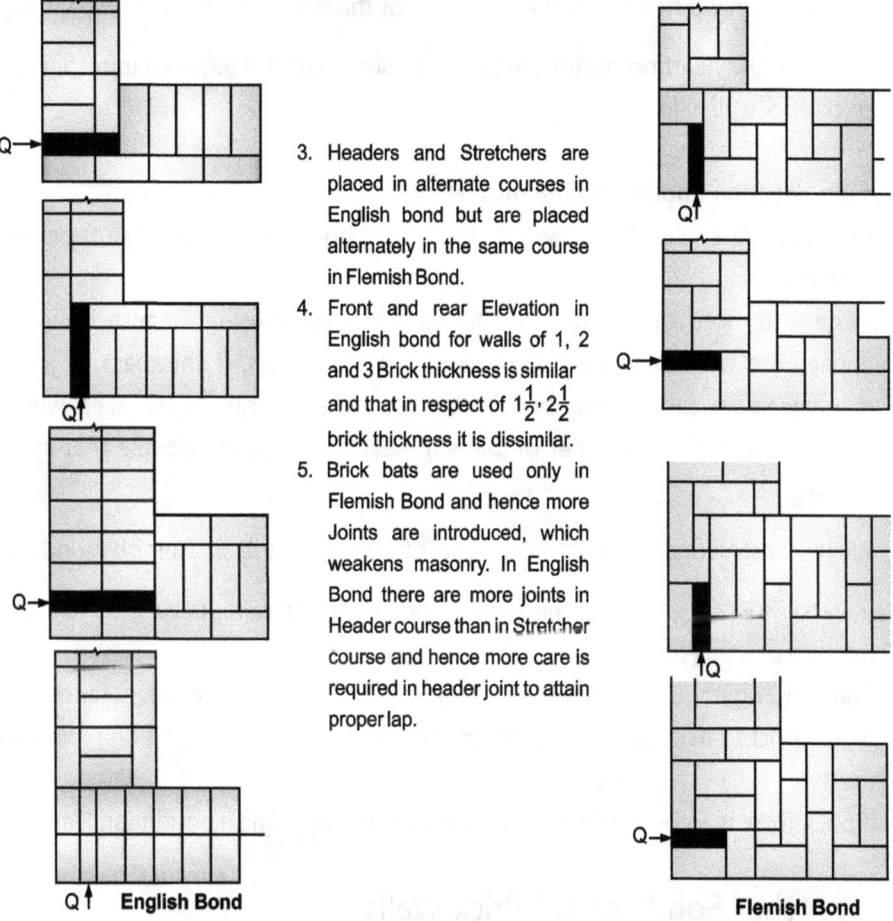

3. Headers and Stretchers are placed in alternate courses in English bond but are placed alternately in the same course in Flemish Bond.
4. Front and rear Elevation in English bond for walls of 1, 2 and 3 Brick thickness is similar and that in respect of $1\frac{1}{2}, 2\frac{1}{2}$ brick thickness it is dissimilar.
5. Brick bats are used only in Flemish Bond and hence more Joints are introduced, which weakens masonry. In English Bond there are more joints in Header course than in Stretcher course and hence more care is required in header joint to attain proper lap.

Fig. 3.11 (a) : Plans of alternate courses in English and Flemish bond for $1\frac{1}{2}$ and 2 brick thick walls

3.13.2 Flemish Bond

The following are the main features of this bond :

1. In this bond, in the same course, headers and stretchers are placed alternately.
2. As in English bond, Queen closer is placed next to Queen header.
3. Every header is centrally supported by a stretcher below; and hence gives pleasing appearance in elevation.
4. In English bond, in case of walls of thickness of 1, 2 or 3 bricks, only front and back elevation is similar; and is dissimilar in case of $1\frac{1}{2}, 2\frac{1}{2}$ thick walls. However, in Flemish

bond, walls of all thickness have similar elevation both in front elevation and rear elevation. Only difference is that, for walls of thickness of $1\frac{1}{2}$, $2\frac{1}{2}$ bricks, quarter bat is used in the hearting portion, whereas no such bats are required in respect of 2 or 3 brick thick wall.

Comparison between English and Flemish Bond :
1. Brick work in English bond having thickness 2 bricks and more, is stronger than that in Flemish bond.
2. In general more care is required to be taken while using Flemish bond. Pleasing appearance which can be had in Flemish bond is lost, if thickness of joint is not maintained. In case of English bond, more care is required to taken while laying header course, since number of joints in header course are double that in stretcher course.
3. While constructing $1\frac{1}{2}$, $2\frac{1}{2}$ walls, use of bats is made in Flemish bond. As such, material cost is less in Flemish bond. But strength is reduced due to increase in number of joints in Flemish.
4. Walls in English bond are monotonous bond have pleasing appearance. However, unless bricks have regular size, shape and sharp edges, Flemish bond should not be used.
5. If brick work is to be plastered, it is advisable to use English bond than Flemish bond.

3.13.3 Stretcher Bond For 1/2 Brick Walls

As name implies, all courses are laid as stretchers only; and that there are no headers. From plan and elevation, it is clear that, with this bond only 1/2 brick thick walls, (as in partition walls) can be constructed.

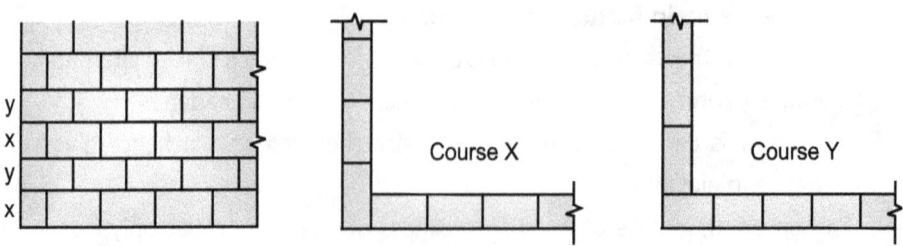

Fig. 3.11 (b) : Stretcher bond

3.13.4 Header Bond For 1 Brick Wall

In this bond, as the name implies, the bricks are laid with their ends towards the face of wall (like headers). There are no stretchers; and hence, wall of 1 brick thickness only can be constructed. The bond does not possess sufficient strength to transmit load, in the direction of the length of wall. However, with this bond, walls having curvature can be constructed as headers can be cut to suit curvature; whereas cutting of stretchers is quite inconvenient.

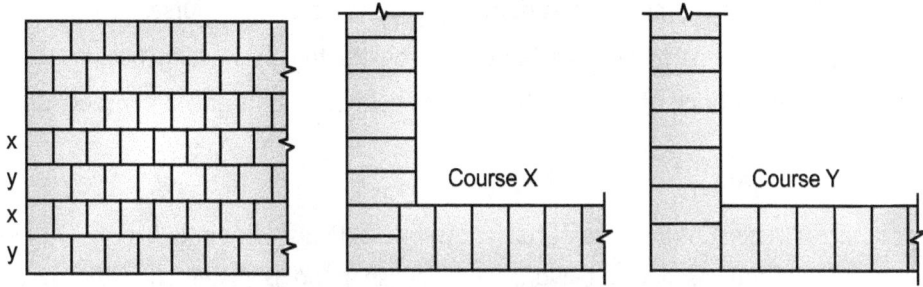

Fig. 3.11 (c) : Header bond

3.14 COLUMNS IN ENGLISH AND FLEMISH BONDS

Following are the features of square columns in English and Flemish bond :

(a) One Brick Thick Column :
  (i) In English bond, it can be constructed by laying two bricks side by side. Each of the next course is laid at right angles to the previous course.
  (ii) It may be noted that one brick pier in flemish bond is not possible.

(b) $1\frac{1}{2}$ Brick Thick Column :

(i) In English bond, it can be constructed either by laying 2 numbers of 3/4th bat side by side and 3 numbers of full bricks. It can also be constructed by using 6 numbers of 3/4th bats.

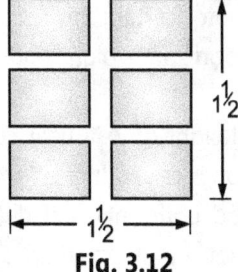

Fig. 3.12

However, columns constructed by using this second alternative, are not strong, hence are avoided.

(ii) In Flemish bond, $1\frac{1}{2}^{th}$ brick columns can be constructed by using 4 numbers of 3/4th bat and centrally placed half bat. This column in Flemish bond is comparatively weaker than that in English bond, since, more number of joints are introduced.

(c) 2 Brick Thick Column in English Bond :

(i) Here use of 6 bricks of full length and 4 Queen closers is made 2 brick thick column. Each of the next course is laid at right angles to the previous course.

(ii) Two brick columns in Flemish bond are constructed by making use of 10 pieces consisting of 4 brick of full length, 4 numbers of 3/4th bats and 2 numbers of queen closers.

It is clear that, as against 6 numbers of full length bricks, in English bond, use of 10 pieces in flemish bond is made. As a result, work with English bond is faster and stronger, when compared with the work in Flemish bond.

3.15 POINTS TO BE OBSERVED DURING THE CONSTRUCTION OF BRICK MASONRY

1. The bricks to be used in the work should be of appropriate quality as regards size, shape, burning, strength, efflorescence etc.
2. In order that brick do not absorb water from mortar, bricks should be soaked in water at least for 2 hours before use. This also helps in spreading of mortar uniformly, washing of kiln dust and proper adhering of mortar to bricks.
3. Next to quoin header, queen closer is placed.
4. Mortar is spread over the first course to a thickness of 1 cm. End stretcher is placed in position and hammered down till thickness of joint is one cm.
5. Corners of wall are built upto certain height first, and then by making use of reference monuments, "line dori" and "plumb bob", wall are constructed in line, level and in plumb.
6. When wall is built upto the height of wall near corner, brick work near the corner is raised further and construction is raised further and work proceeds further.
7. All the walls should be raised uniformly and difference between levels of any two portions of walls, should not be more than 1 metre. This will ensure uniform distribution of load and will avoid uneven settlement.
8. As work proceeds, joints in the brick work should be raked out to depth of about 1 cm. This will help in having proper key to plastering or pointing.

9. As far as possible double scaffolding should be provided, so as to avoid making holes in masonry to support cantilever scaffolding.
10. In order to have proper grip with previous brick work, either steps are provided or toothing is provided.
11. Previous days work is roughened and cleaned, while starting next day's work.
12. Brick work should be cured for 2 to 3 weeks.

3.16 COMPOSITE MASONRY

It is a masonry, in which facing wall and backing wall are constructed using two different types of masonry. Composite masonry is intended to
   (i) Reduce overall cost of construction.
   (ii) Provide maintenance free, durable and asthetically sound masonry.
Different varieties of composite masonry as listed below can be obtained :
   (a) Facing of stone slab and backing of concrete
   (b) Facing of brick work and backing of rubble masonry
   (c) Facing of brick work and backing of concrete
   (d) Facing of brick work and backing of hollow concrete
   (e) Facing of ashlar masonry and backing of rubble masonry of brick masonry.

Unless proper care is taken, composite masonry is likely to lead to unequal settlement, because number of mortar joints in the inside / backing masonry are more than those in facing masonry.

To guard against these defects, following measures are required to be taken :
   1. Facing and backing masonry should be constructed simultaneously.
   2. Backing work should be constructed using rich mortar.
   3. Connection joints between front and rear masonry can be obtained by use of cramps.
   4. Large sized tough stones should be provided.

Advantages :
- **New aesthetic possibilities :** An ability to mould complex, fluid and creative forms and produce more efficient geometric shapes.
- The ability to integrate special surface finishes and a wide variety of unusual effects including simulating traditional materials.
- Hugely significant weight savings – an advanced composite cladding model can typically weigh as little as 10% of its concrete equivalent.

- Rapid installation enabling time and cost savings on site – composite structures can cover much larger spans between support points, reducing the need for substructures dramatically. This has a positive effect on the cost and weight of the completed structure, as well as a significant reduction in installation time.
- Superior durability with reduced through life costs and less degradation.
- Improved thermal insulation and lack of cold bridging.

3.17 PARTITION WALLS

3.17.1 Partition Wall Aluminium

Aluminium Wall Partitions which find its wide application in various offices, restaurants, hotels and factories. These aluminium partitions are used to divide the room into various compartments in order to offer privacy to the people. These partitions find their place in offices to divide the cabins of employees. Available in various customizations.

Fig. 3.13

3.17.2 Timber Partitions

Timber partitions consist of wooden frame work, properly supported on floor and fixed to the side walls. This frame work, made of horizontal and vertical members can either be plastered or covered with boarding etc. from both the sides. Wooden partitions are light weight, but are costlier. It is likely to decay, or eaten away by termites. Also, it is not fire resistant. Its use is reducing day by day.

Two types of wooden partitions may be used :
(i) Common or stud partition.
(ii) Trussed or braced partition.

(1) Common or Stud Partition : It consists of a frame work of vertical members (called studs) and short horizontal pieces, called noggings. Horizontal pieces impart rigidity to studs. A stud of short length, such as the one provided on an opening, is called *puncheon*. The upper and lower horizontal members of the frame are known as head and sill respectively. The studs 10 cm × 5 cm in section, are spaced 30 to 45 cm apart. Nogging pieces are cut tightly and fixed between the studs and nailed. The head and sill are 10 cm × 75 mm in section.

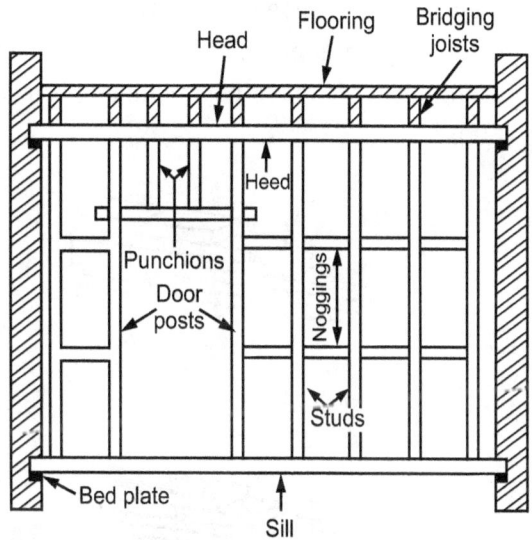

Fig. 3.14 : Common or stud partition

(2) Trussed or Braced Partitions : Such partitions are provided where there is no means of supporting the partition except at their ends. The frame work is similar to the stud partition, but inclined members called braces, and steel straps and bolts are additionally used. Sometimes, such partitions carry floor load also, in addition to its own weight. For more rigidity and strength, an additional horizontal member, known as inter-tie is provided between head and sill, as shown in Fig. 3.14. The ends of head and sill are made to rest on stone template embedded in the wall. Because of trussed action, tension may be developed at some joints. Hence, steel straps or steel bolts are provided at all joints.

3.17.3 Brick Partitions

Brick partitions are quite common since they are the cheapest. Brick partitions are of three types :
1. Plain brick partitions.
2. Reinforced brick partitions.
3. Brick nogging partitions.

(1) Plan Brick Partitions : Plain brick partitions are usually half brick thick. The bricks are laid as stretchers, in cement mortar. Vertical joints are staggered alternate blocks. The wall is plastered on both the sides. The wall is considerably strong and fire resistant.

(2) Reinforced Brick Partitions : These are stronger than the ordinary brick partitions and is used when better longitudinal bond is required and when the partition wall has to carry other superimposed loads. The thickness of the wall is kept equal to half brick (10 cm). The reinforcement consists of steel meshed strips, called *Exmet*, made from thin rolled steel plates which are cut and stretched (or expanded) by a machine to a diamond network. Such a strip is known as expanded metal and is provided at every third course. Another form of meshed reinforcement, called *Brichtor* is made of a number of straight tension wires with binding wires (Refer Fig. 3.14).

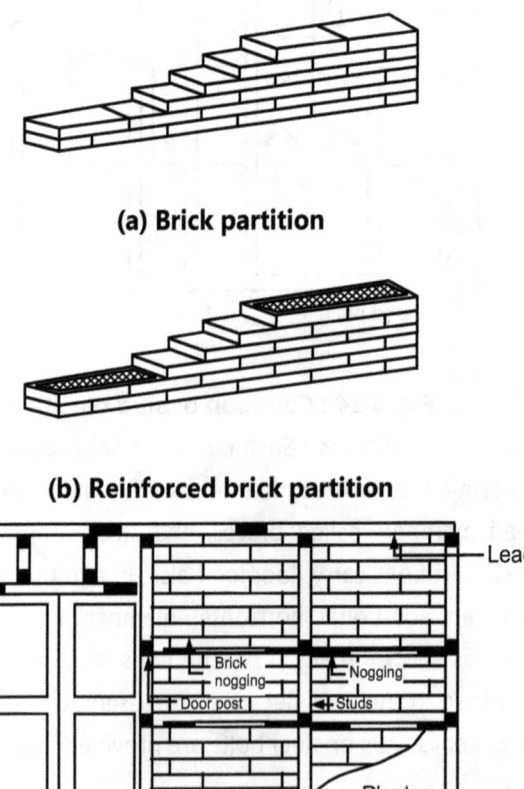

(a) Brick partition

(b) Reinforced brick partition

(c) Brick nogging partition

Fig. 3.15 : Brick partition walls

(3) Brick Nogging Partitions : Brick nogging partition wall consists of brick work (half brick thickness) built up within the frame work of wooden members. The timber frame work consists of (i) sill, (ii) head, (iii) vertical members called *studs* and (iv) horizontal members called *nogging pieces*. The vertical members or studs are spaced at 4 to 6 times the brick length. The nogging pieces are housed into the studs at vertical interval of 60 to 90 cm. The frame work provided stability to the partition against lateral loads and vibrations caused due to opening the adjoining door. The brick work is plastered on both the sides. The bricks are usually laid flat, but they may be laid on edge also. Cement mortar, 1 : 3 is used. The surfaces of the timber frame work coming into contact with brick work is coated with coal tar.

3.17.4 Clay Block Partition Walls

The blocks used for such partition wall are prepared from clay or terra-cotta and they may be either solid or hollow. For light partitions, hollow clay blocks are commonly used. They are good insulators for heat and sound. They are also fire resistant. The hollow clay blocks are usually 30 cm long, 20 cm high and 5 to 15 cm wide (Refer Fig. 3.16). The blocks are provided with grooves on top, bottom and sides. Grooves provide rigid joints, and serve as key to plaster. The blocks are laid in cement mortar.

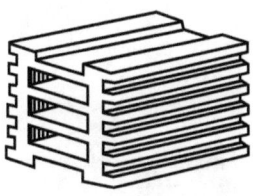

Fig. 3.16 : Hollow clay block

REVIEW QUESTIONS

1. Explain with neat sketch the uncoarsed rubble masonry.
2. Differentiate between :
    (a) Random rubble and Uncoarsed rubble.
    (b) Coarsed rubble and Uncoarsed rubble.
    (c) English bond and Flemish bond.

3. Write short notes on :
   (a) Stone masonry
   (b) Ashlar masonry
   (c) Carry over
4. Explain the brick partition wall.
5. Explain the aluminium wall.
6. Explain the timber wall.

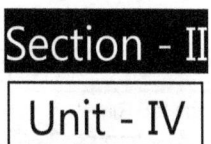

Chapter 4

ARCHES AND LINTELS

4.0 INTRODUCTION

The openings for doors, windows, ventilators, cupboards, wardrobes etc. are invariably required in a wall. These openings are bridged by provision of either a lintel or an arch. Thus, both lintel as well as arch are structural members designed to support the loads of the portion of the wall situated above the openings and then transmit the load to the adjacent wall portions (Jambs) over which these are supported.

The study of arches and lintels in this chapter will be made under the following sub-heads :

Part I : Arches
1. Various terms related to openings
2. Stability of arches
3. Types of arches
4. Method of construction of arches.

Part II : Lintels
1. Types of lintels
2. Details of R.C.C. lintel and chajja

4.1 DEFINITION OF ARCH

An arch may be defined as a mechanical arrangement of wedge - shaped units which mutually support each other and in turn, the entire arch is supported at the ends by piers or abutments. Wedge - shaped blocks are joined generally with rich cement or lime mortar. Arches of cement concrete, R.C.C. and steel are not built in wedge - shaped units but in form of a single unit.

4.2 TECHNICAL TERMS

Most of the technical terms used in connection with the arch work are illustrated in Fig. 4.1 and are described as follows :

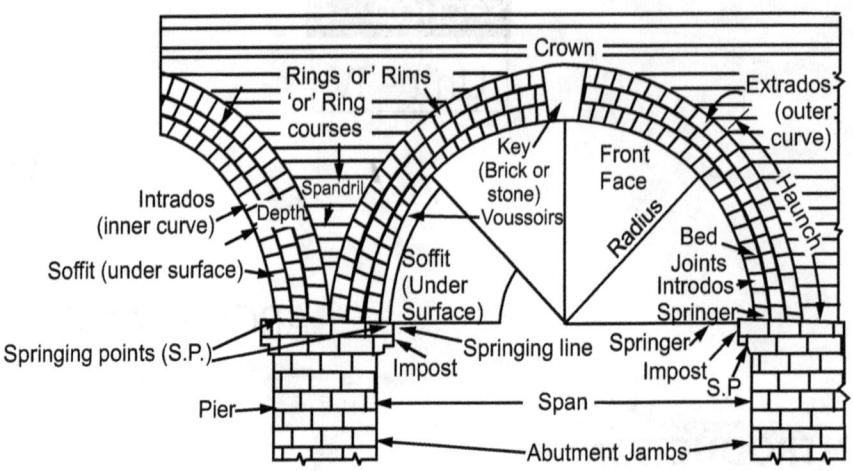

Fig. 4.1 : Semi-circular arch

1. **Abutments :** These are outermost support of an arch, from which arch springs.
2. **Piers :** These are intermediate supports of a series of arches or an arcade.
3. **Arch Ring :** This is the curved ring of masonry forming the arch.
4. **Voussoirs :** These are the wedge shaped or tapered units of bricks, stones or precast concrete blocks, forming the courses of an arch.
5. **Arcade :** This is a series or row of arches supporting a wall above and being supported by piers.
6. **Skew-backs :** These are the inclined or splayed surfaces of the abutments or piers, prepared to receive the arch. Arch work actually starts from skew back.
7. **Springing Points :** These are the points of the intersection between the skew-backs and the intrados and from these points only, the curve of an arch springs are commences.
8. **Springing Line :** This is the imaginary horizontal line joining the two springing points.
9. **Intrados :** The inner curved surface of the arch is known as **intrados**.
10. **Extrados :** Outer curved surface of the arch ring is known as **extrados**. It is also known as back of the arch.
11. **Soffit or Bottom :** This is the inner or under surface of the arch. Soffit and Intrados terms indicate same thing.

12. **Crown :** The highest point of extrados of arch.
13. **Key Stone :** This is the uppermost or central voussoir of an arch. It is sometimes made prominent by making it larger and projecting it above and below the outline of an arch. This is inserted in the centre of many types of arches to improve the appearance but it does not carry structural significance.
14. **Span :** Clear horizontal distance between the supports is known as **span of the arch**.
15. **Depth or Height :** This is the perpendicular distance between the intrados and extrados.
16. **Thickness (Breath of the Soffit) :** The horizontal distance measured perpendicular to the front and back faces of an arch is known as **breather thickness of soffit**.
17. **Rise :** It is the clear vertical distance between the springing line and the highest point on the intrados.
18. **Centre (or Striking Point) :** This is the geometrical centre point of the curve of an arch.
19. **Springers :** These are the extreme or lowest voussoirs of an arch, which are placed at springing level on either side immediately adjacent to the skew-backs.
20. **Haunch :** This is the lower half portion of the arch between the crown and the skew-back or springer.
21. **Spandril :** This is the triangular space formed between the extrados and the horizontal line drawn through the crown.
22. **Jambs :** These are the sides of the abutments or piers below the springing line.
23. **Import :** The projecting course at the upper part of a piers or an abutment to stress the springing line.
24. **Bed Joints :** These are the joints between the voussoirs which radiate from the centre.

4.3 STABILITY OF AN ARCH

An arch transmits the super-imposed load to the side walls (or abutments) through friction between the surfaces of voussoirs and the cohesion of mortar. Every element of arch remains in compression. It has also to bear transverse shear. An arch may therefore fail in the following four ways :

1. **The Crushing of the Arch Material :** In this case, the compressive stress or thrust exceeds the safe crushing strength of the materials and the arch fail due to crushing of the masonry. The measures to avoid failure of arch due to this reason are as follows :
   (i) The material used for construction should be of adequate strength.
   (ii) The size of voussoirs should be properly designed to bear the thrust transmitted through them.

(iii) The height of voussoirs should not be less than $1/12^{th}$ of the span or as below. (for brick work in cement mortar, 1 : 4)

for span upto 1.5 m – 20 cm.

between 1.5 to 4 m – 30 cm.

between 4.0 to 7.5 m – 40 cm.

(iv) For arch work, only first class blocks should be used, and in case of large spans the arches may be strengthened by steel reinforcement, so that safe crushing strength is not exceeded.

2. **Rotation or Overturning of some Joints about an Edge :** To prevent this following points are considered :
   (i) The line of resistance or thrust at any section should be within the middle - third of the arch.
   (ii) The thickness of the arch and its curve are so designed that the line of resistance atleast falls within the section and crosses each joint away from the edge.
3. **Sliding of Voussoirs :** To safeguard against sliding of one voussoir or another, the following points are considered :
   (i) All the bed joints should be perpendicular to the line of least resistance.
   (ii) The depth of voussoirs should be adequate to resist the tendency of the joints to open and slide upon the another.
4. **Uneven Settlement of Abutment or Pier :** The secondary stresses in the arch are developed due to the uneven settlement of the support of arch and to avoid such conditions, the following precautions should be taken.
   (i) The arch should be symmetrical so that unequal settlement of the two abutments or abutment and pier are minimised.
   (ii) The supports should be strong enough to resist the thrust of the arch due to self weight and superimposed loads.

4.4 TYPES OF ARCHES

An arch can be classified according to (1) Shape, (2) Number of centres, (3) Workmanship and (4) Materials of construction.

(I) Classification of Arches According to Shape :

According to shape, the arches are classified as follows :

1. **Flat Arch (or Straight, Square or Camber Arch) :** In flat arch, the extrados is horizontal and the intrados is given a slight rise or camber of about 10 to 15 mm per metre width of the span. The angle of skew backs with the horizontal is usually 60°. Flat arches are not very strong and hence they should be limited to span upto 1.5 metres unless they are strengthened by steel reinforcement. (Fig. 4.2 (a)).

2. **Segmental Arch (Fig. 4.2 (b))** : This is the common type of arch used for buildings. The centre of arch lies below the springing line. The thrust transferred to the abutment is in an inclined direction.
3. **Semi-circular Arch (Fig. 4.2 (c))** : The shape of their arch soffit is a semi-circle and hence named as semi-circular arch. The centre of the arch lies on the springing line. The thrust transferred to the abutments is perfectly in vertical direction since the skewback is horizontal.
4. **Horse shoe Arch (Fig. 4.2 (d))** : The arch has the shape of a horse shoe, incorporating more than a semi-circle. Such type of arch is provided mainly from architectural considerations.
5. **Pointed Arch (Fig. 4.2 (e))** : This is also known as Gothic arch. It consists two arcs of circles meeting at the apex. The triangle formed may be equilateral or isosceles; in the latter case it is known as Lancet arch.

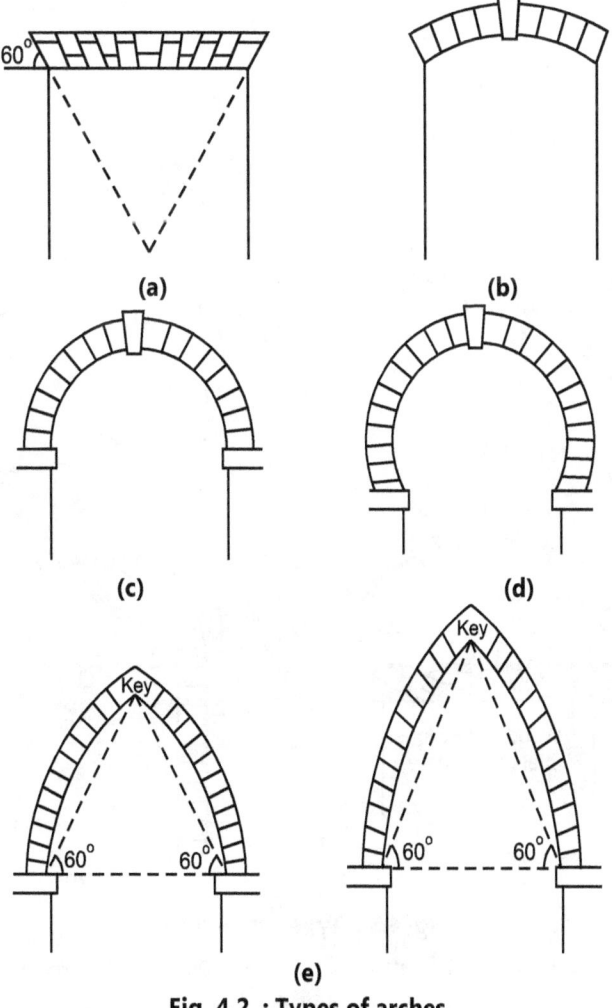

Fig. 4.2 : Types of arches

6. **Venetian Arch (Fig. 4.3 (a))** : This is another form of pointed arch which has deeper depth at crown than at springings. It has four centres, all located on the springing line.
7. **Florentine Arch (Fig. 4.3 (b))** : This is similar to venetian arch except that the intrados is a semicircle. The arch has, three centres, all located on the springing line.
8. **Relieving Arch (Fig. 4.3 (c))** : This arch is constructed either on a flat arch or on a wooden lintel to provide greater strength. The ends of the relieving arch should be carried sufficiently into the abutments. The relieving arch makes it possible to replace the decayed lintel later, without disturbing the stability of the structure.
9. **Stilted Arch (Fig. 4.3 (d))** : It consists of a semi-circular arch with two vertical portions at the springings. The centre of the arch lies on the horizontal line through the tops of the vertical portions.

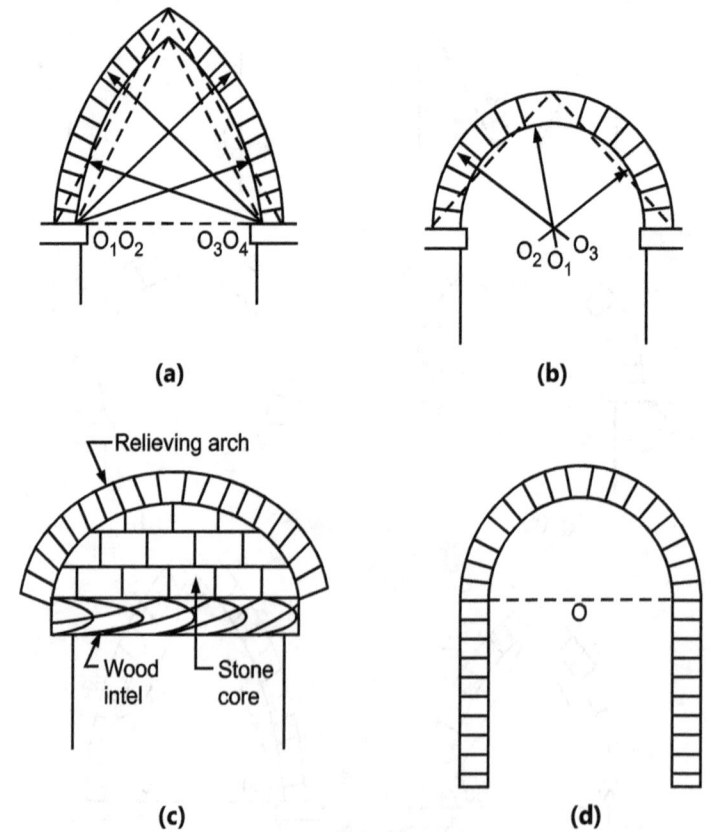

Fig. 4.3 : Types of arches

10. **Semi-Elliptical Arch (Figs. 4.5 and 4.6)** : This type of arch has the shape of a semi-ellipse and may have either three centres or five centres.

(II) Classification Based on Number of Centres:

The arches may be classified as (i) One-centered arch, (ii) Two-centered arch, (iii) Three-centered arch, (iv) Four-centered arch and (v) Five-centered arch.

1. **One-centred arches**: Segmental arches, semi-circular arches, flat arches, horse-shoe arch and stilted arches come under this category. Sometimes, a perfectly circular arch, known as bull's eye arch is provided for circular windows, as shown in Fig. 4.4.

Fig. 4.4

2. **Two-centred Arches**: Pointed arches, semi-eliptical arches and florentine arches come under this category.
3. **Three-centred Arches**: Eliptical arches come under this category. Fig. 4.5 shows a three-centered arch.

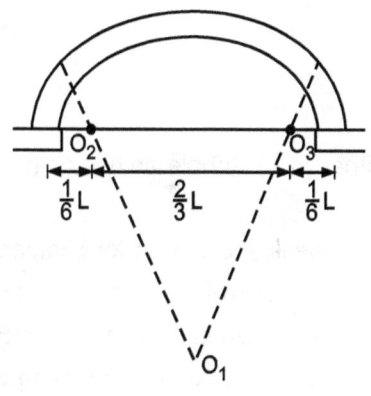
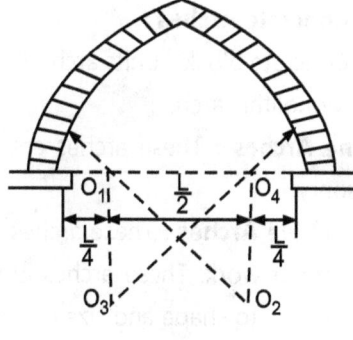

Fig. 4.5   **Fig. 4.6**

4. **Four-centred Arch**: It has four centres. Venetian arch is a typical example of this type. (Fig. 4.6)

5. **Five-centred Arch :** This type of arch, having five centres, gives a good semi-eliptical shape. (Fig. 4.7)

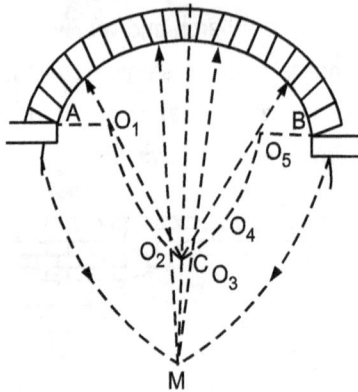

Fig. 4.7

(III) Classification Based on Material and Workmanship :

On the basis of material of construction and workmanship, arches may be classified as follows :

1. **Stone Arches :**
   (i) Rubble arch
   (ii) Ashlar arch
2. **Brick Arches :**
   (i) Rough arch
   (ii) Axed or rough - cut arch
   (iii) Gauged arch
   (iv) Purpose made brick arch.
3. **Concrete Arches :**
   (i) Concrete block - units arch
   (ii) Monolithic arch.

1. **Stone Arches :** These arches are constructed either in (i) Rubble arches or (ii) Ashlar masonry.

   (i) **Rubble Arches :** These arches are comparatively weak and is used for comparatively inferior work. These arches are made of rubble stones which are hammer dressed, roughly to shape and size of voussoirs of the arch and fixed in cement mortar. Rubble arches are used for limited span (upto 1.0 m). They are also used as relieving arches, over wooden lintels. Upto depth of 37.5 cm, these arches are constructed in one ring. For greater depths, rubble stones are laid in alternate course of header and stretchers.

(ii) Ashlar Arches : These are constructed of stones which have been properly cut and dressed to their true wedge shapes i.e. voussoirs. Upto depth of 60 cm, the voussoirs are made of full thickness of the arch. For determining the wedged shapes of voussoirs, it is preferable to set out the arch on a level platform, marking on it the keystone and voussoirs along with radial mortar joints. Fig. 4.8 shows some details of semicircular, segmental and flat arches of ashlar stones.

2. **Brick Arches :** Brick arches may be classified as rough brick arches, axed or rough cut brick arches, gauged brick arches and purpose made brick arches, depending upon the nature of workmanship and quality of bricks used.

   (i) Rough Brick Arches : These arches are constructed with ordinary bricks, without cutting these to the shape of voussoirs. In order to provide the arch curve, the joints are made wedge-shaped, with greater thickness at the extrados and smaller thickness in intrados. These types of arches, though cheap, yet lack in strength as well as appearance.

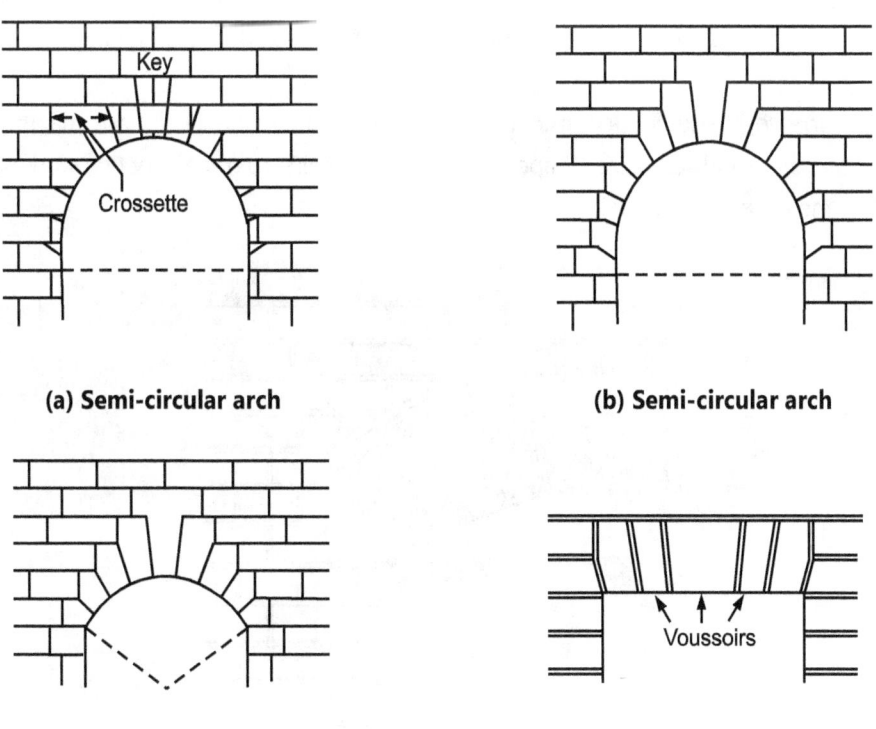

Fig. 4.8 : Ashlar stone arches

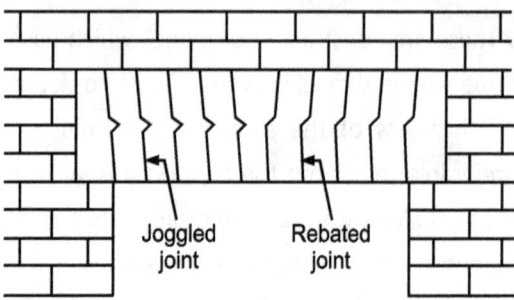

Fig. 4.9 : Joggled and rebated joints in flat arch of ashlar stones

(ii) **Axed Brick Arches :** In this arch, the bricks are cut wedge-shaped with the help of brick axe. Due to this joints are of uniform thickness along the radial line. However, the appearance of the arch is not very pleasant because the bricks cut to wedge shapes are not finely dressed.

(iii) **Gauged Brick Arch :** This type of arch is constructed of bricks which are prepared to exact size and shape of voussoirs by cutting it by means of wire saw. For this, only soft bricks (called rubber bricks) are used. The joints formed in gauged bricks are thin (1 to 1.5 mm) and truly radial. Lime putty is used for jointing. (Fig. 4.12 (a) and (b))

(iv) **Purpose made Bricks Arch :** In this type of arch, the bricks are manufactured, matching with the exact shape and size of voussoirs, to get a very fine workmanship. Lime putty is used for jointing.

Fig. 4.10 : Segmental rough brick arch

Fig. 4.11 : Axed brick arch

3. **Concrete Arches :** Concrete arches are of two types : (i) Precast concrete block arches and (ii) Monolithic concrete arches.

   (i) **Precast Concrete Block Arches :** Such arches are made from precast concrete blocks, each block being cast in the mould to the exact shape and size of voussoirs. Special moulds are prepared for voussoirs, key block and skew-backs. Because of exact shape and size of blocks, good appearance of the arch is achieved. Also, joints, made of cement mortar are quite thin. However, casting of blocks is costly, and such work is economical only when the number of arches is quite large. Cement concrete of 1 : 2 : 4 mix is usually used.

   (ii) **Monolithic Concrete Arches :** Monolithic concrete arches are constructed from cast-in-situ concrete, either plain or reinforced, depending upon the span and magnitude of loading. These arches are quite suitable for larger span. The arch thickness is 15 cm for arches upto 3 m span. Form work is used for casting the arch, and is removed only when the concrete has sufficiently hardened and gained strength. Curing is done for 2 to 4 weeks.

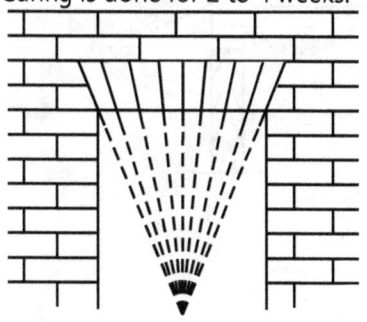

(a) Flat arch   (b) Semi-circular arch

Fig. 4.12 : Gauged brick arches

4.5 METHODS OF CONSTRUCTION OF ARCHES

The complete construction of arches, whether of brick, stone or concrete, involves basically the following three steps :

1. Installation of centering or form work for arches,
2. Actual laying of arch - work or courses and
3. Striking or removal of centerings.

1. Installation of Centering for Arches :

A temporary structure is required to support brick, stone or concrete arches during their construction. This is known as the centering which is usually of timber but may be of mild steel if so desired. The upper surface of the centering corresponds to the shape of intrados of the arch. Mild steel truss centering is used either for large spans or where large number of arches of similar nature is to be prepared.

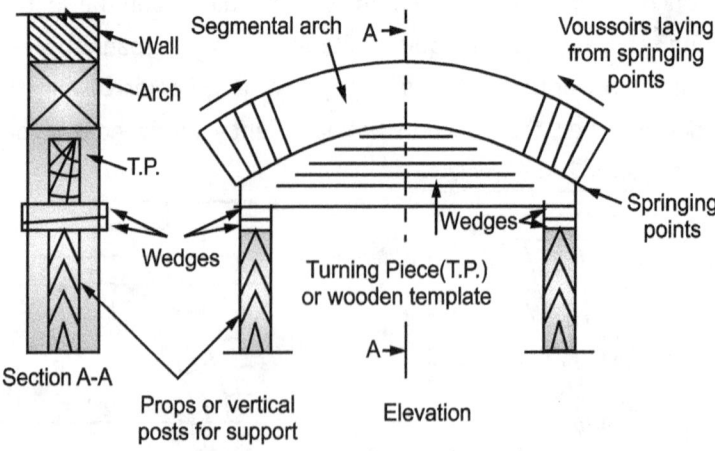

Fig. 4.13 : Centering for small spans and thinner soffit (upto 10 cm thickness) arches

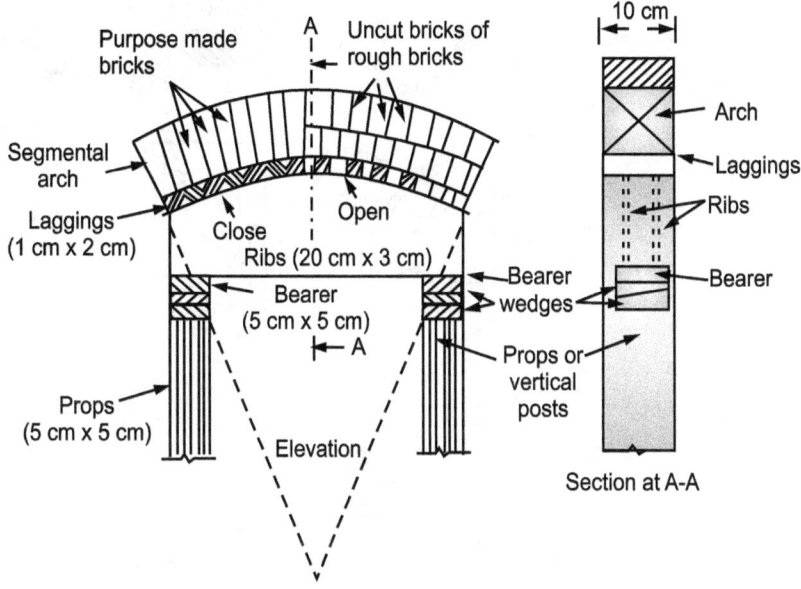

Fig. 4.14 : Centering for small spans but thicker soffit (more than 10 cm)

Arches (or simple Ribbed Centering)

Timber centering is most common in arch construction as it is easy in installation and removal, and also economical.

In simplest type of centering used for small spans with a thinner soffit (width = 10 cm) consists of a horizontal frame of timber known as "turning piece" or "wooden template". Fig. 4.13 shows a thick wooden plank, with horizontal bottom and the upper surface shaped to the underside of the soffit.

If the soffit is wider than 10 cm, two ribs, suitably spaced and suitably shaped at top may be used. These ribs may be connected by 4 × 2 cm wooden sections called laggings. At the ends the ribs are supported by bearers, wedges and posts as shown in Fig. 4.14.

For wider soffits and for large span, a built up centering of cut wood ribs is used. The upper surface of the ribs is given the shape of soffit of the arch. Laggings are nailed across the ribs at close intervals to support the voussoirs at its top. The ribs (25 to 40 mm thick with width varying from 20 to 30 cm) are connected by braces and struts to strengthen them. The ribs are supported on bearers and a pair of folding wedges is provided at the top of each prop to tighten or loosen the centering. (Fig. 4.15)

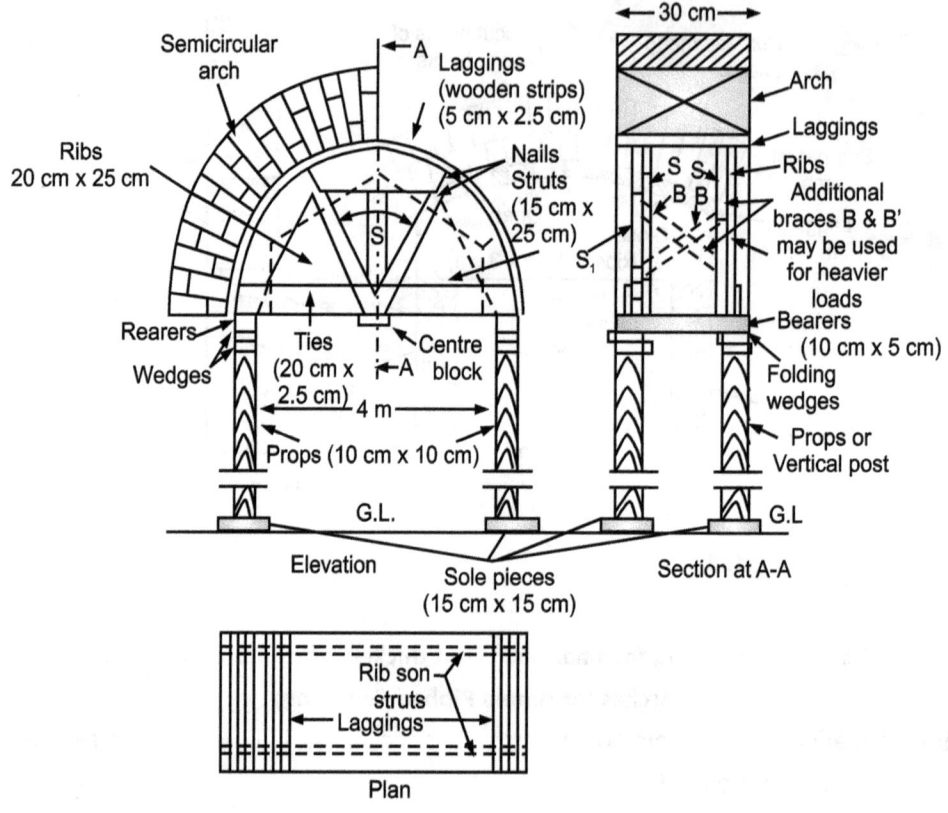

**Fig. 4.15 : Centering for large spans and very wide soffits.
Semi-circular arches (or Ribbed - Truss Centering)**

2. Actual Laying of Arch Work :

After the proper installation or erection of centering in position, skew backs are first prepared. Voussoirs are then arranged, starting from skew backs and proceeding towards the crown. Key stone is finally inserted to lock all the voussoirs in position. The voussoirs are bedded or laid in definite courses in sequence with radial joints to ensure stability and strength of the arch.

3. Removal of Centering :

When the arch has developed sufficient strength, the centering can be removed. The centering must be eased (i.e. slightly lowered) two days before its removal so that the voussoirs may close in and compress the mortar. No load should be placed on the arch unless the centering has been removed.

For small spans, the removal of centering is done by slightly loosening the folding wedges. When the span is more than 7.5 m, sand box method can be used for loosening, so that shocks are avoided. A sand box, shown in Fig. 4.16 is placed below the prop. Sand is filled in the box with a plugged hole at its bottom. Prop rests on steel plate placed on the top of sand. In order to lower the centering, plug is taken out due to which the sand flows out and lowers the prop gradually.

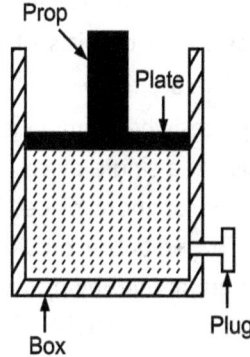

Fig. 4.16 : Sand box method

4.6 DEFINITION OF LINTEL

A lintel is a horizontal structural member which is placed across an opening viz. doors, windows, recesses etc. to support the portion of the structure above it. Though the lintels perform exactly the same function as arches, but they are preferred to arches due to the following reasons :

(i) The arches require more head room to span the openings, like doors, windows, etc.

(ii) The arches require strong abutments (walls) to withstand the arch thrust.

(iii) Lintels are more stable as they support the load by beam action and transfer the loads vertically to the walls.

(iv) The lintels are simpler in construction.

The ends of lintels are built into the masonry and thus, the load carried by lintels is transferred to the masonry in jambs. In general, it should be seen that the bearing of lintel i.e. the distance upto which it is inserted in the supporting wall, should be the minimum of the following three considerations.

(i) 10 cm; or

(ii) height of lintel; or

(iii) one - tenth to one - twelfth of the span of lintel.

4.7 TYPES OF LINTELS

On the basis of materials used in construction, the lintels are classified into the following types :

1. Wooden Lintels
2. Stone Lintels
3. Brick Lintels
4. Steel Lintels
5. Reinforced Concrete Lintels, and
6. Reinforced Brick Lintels.

1. **Wood or Timber Lintels :** These lintels consists of pieces of timber which are placed across the opening. The timber lintels are the oldest type of lintels and they have become obsolete except in hilly areas or places where timber is easily available.

   Wooden lintels may either consist of a single piece of timber usually for small spans or may be of built-up sections of two or more pieces held together by bolts at suitable intervals as shown in Fig. 4.17. The bolts are provided through the packing pieces as shown. If the timber lintels are strengthened by provision of mild steel plates at their top and bottom, they are known as the flitched lintels.

   The important features of wooden lintels are as follows :

   (i) Wooden lintels should be made of sound and hard timber, like teak wood, sal etc.

   (ii) The amount of bearing of lintel should be adequate (usually 15 to 20 cm) and lintel should rest on mortar to have a firm and uniform support.

   (iii) The depth of lintel should be $\frac{1}{12}$th of span or 8 cm, whichever is greater. The width of lintel is taken equal to the thickness of the opening.

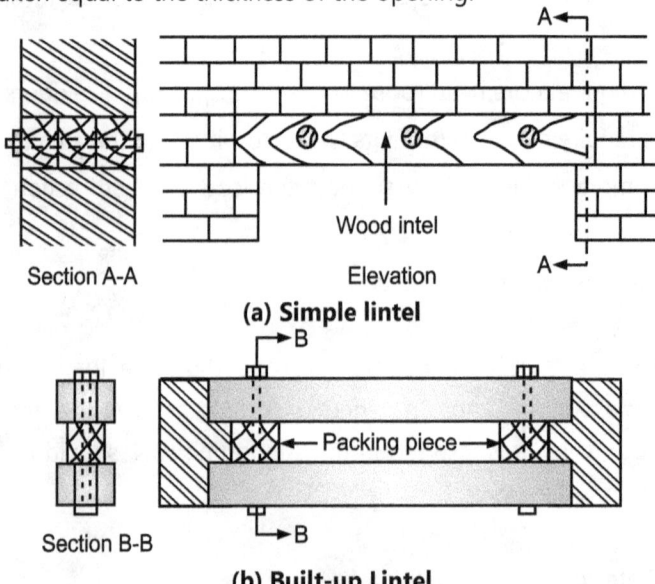

(a) Simple lintel

(b) Built-up Lintel

Fig. 4.17 : Wooden lintel

2. **Stone Lintels :** The use of stone lintels is recommended only in places where stone is available in abundance and the structure is made of stone masonry. These lintels consist of slabs of stones of sufficient length in single piece or combination of more pieces. The thickness of stone lintel should be 80 cm or 4 cm for every 30 cm of span, whichever is more.

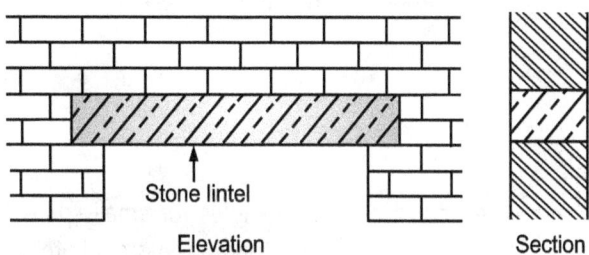

Fig. 4.18 : Stone lintel

The use of stone lintels in general is not recommended because of the following reasons :

(i) Stone, being poor in tensile strength, cannot withstand the transverse stresses.

(ii) It is difficult to obtain the slabs of stones of sufficient length and depth, free from defects or flaws.

3. **Brick Lintels :** Brick lintels generally consist of bricks which are normally laid on end and occasionally on edge as shown in Fig. 4.19.

The important features of brick lintels are as follows :

(i) The bricks should be well burnt, hard, free from defects such as lumps, cracks, flaws etc. and with sharp and square edges.

(ii) A temporary wood support known as a turning piece, is used to construct a brick lintel.

(iii) In order to maintain the appearance of brick work, a brick lintel should have a depth equal to multiple of brick courses.

(iv) Brick lintels are used to span small openings (less than one metre) with light loading.

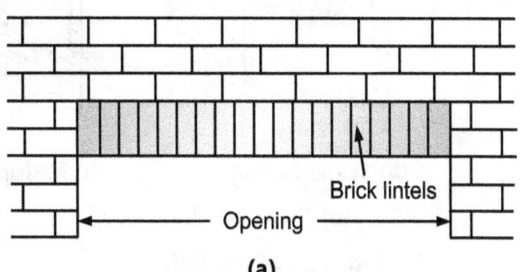

(a)

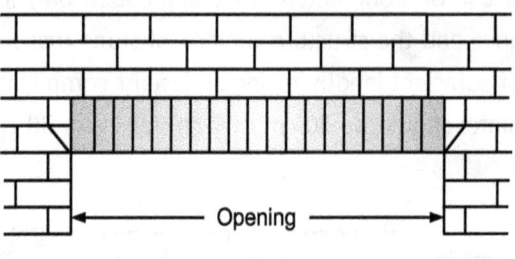

(b)
Fig. 4.19 : Brick lintel

4. **Steel Lintels :** These lintels consist of steel angles for small spans and light loading or rolled steel joints for large spans and heavy loading. A steel lintel becomes useful when there is no space available to accommodate the rise of an arch. The tube separators may be provided to keep the joints in position. The joints are embedded in concrete to protect the steel from corrosion and fire. (See Fig. 4.20)

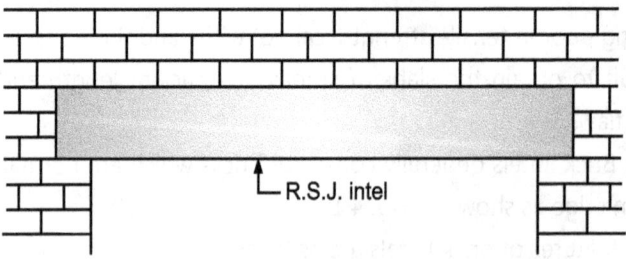

(a) Elevation

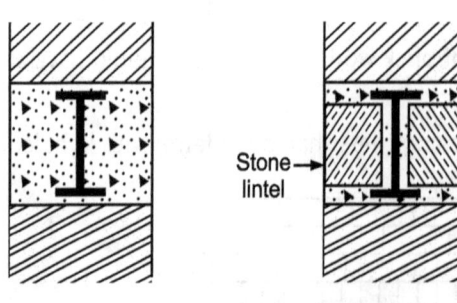
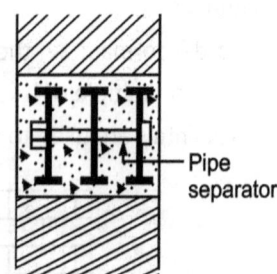

(i) **Concrete Embedment**   (ii) **Stone Facing**   (iii) **Multiple Units**

(b) Cross-section
Fig. 4.20 : Steel lintels

5. **Reinforced Cement Concrete Lintels :** Reinforced concrete lintels are extensively used and practically R.C.C. has replaced all other materials used for lintels. The R.C.C. lintels are fire-proof, durable, strong, economical and easy to construct. No relieving arches are necessary when the R.C.C. lintels are adopted. R.C.C. lintels may be either precast or cast in-situ. Precast R.C.C. lintels are preferred for small span upto 2 metres or so, and they are economical as the same mould can be used to prepare a number of lintels. The precast R.C.C. lintels increase the speed of construction and allow sufficient time for the curing before fixing. One precaution to be taken in case of precast R.C.C. lintels is that the top of lintel should be properly marked with tar or paint.

For large spans, the lintels should be cast in-situ. Details of lintels are as follows :

(i) **Depth of Lintel :** For ordinary loads, adopt 15 cm depth for span upto 1.2 m and add another 2.5 cm for every additional 40 cm span.

(ii) **Reinforcement in Lintels :** As a rule, for thickness of wall 10 cm (half-brick), adopt 2 bars and for every additional 10 cm thickness, one main bar should be added. The diameter of bar varies with the span and is adopted as follows, as a general rule (Alternative central bars are bent up).

$\qquad$ 6 mm φ for spans upto 1 metre
$\qquad$ 8 mm φ for spans upto 1 to 1.5 metres
$\qquad$ 10 mm φ for spans upto 1.5 to 2.0 metres
$\qquad$ 12 mm φ for spans upto 20 to 30 metres

(iii) **Concrete :** The usual concrete mix for R.C.C. lintel is 1 : 2 : 4.

For cast in-situ, R.C.C. lintels, the centering is prepared, reinforcement is placed and concreting is done as usual.

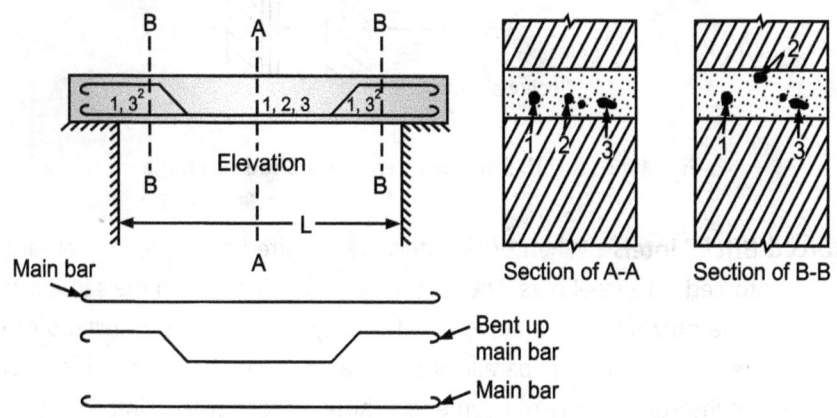

Fig. 4.21 : R.C.C. lintel - details for small spans (L < 2 metres)

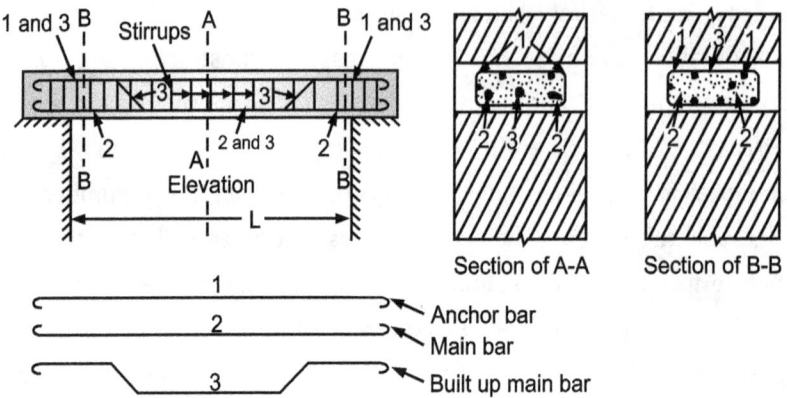

Fig. 4.22 : R.C.C. lintel - details for large spans (i.e. span > 2 metres)

The projection, in the form of weather shed Chajja can be easily taken out from R.C.C. Lintels, as shown in Fig. 4.23. The weather shed throws the rain water away from the wall.

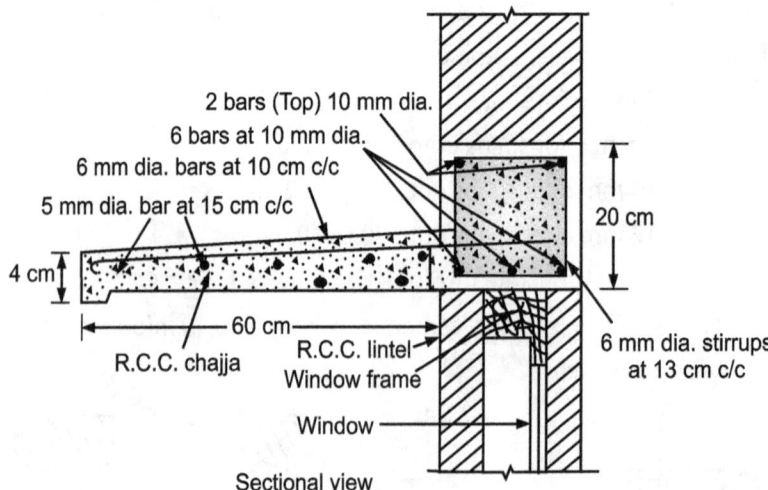

Fig. 4.23 : R.C.C. lintel with weather shed or chajja

6. **Reinforced Brick Lintels :** When brick lintels are required to be used over large spans, they are reinforced with steel bars. These lintels are constructed on the same principles as R.C.C. lintels, the only difference being good quality bricks are used instead of concrete. The bricks are so arranged in parallel rows that a 2 cm to 4 cm wide space is left lengthwise for inserting the reinforcements. These spaces with reinforcement are then filled with rich cement mortar or cement concrete.

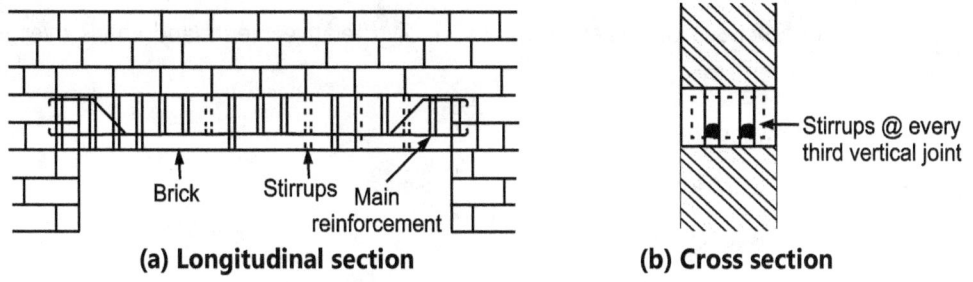

Fig. 4.24 : Reinforced brick lintel

REVIEW QUESTIONS

1. State the procedure of constructing a segmental arch for an opening of size 1.80 m × 2.40 m. Rise is one third of span.
2. Draw a labelled sketch of semi-circular arch and indicate the following :
    (a) Sprining line,
    (b) Key stone,
    (c) Spandril,
    (d) Voussior,
    (e) Rise,
    (f) Extrados.
3. Write down the methods of construction of arches and describe how arch opening is constructed in residential building.
4. Differentiate between arch and lintel. Give detailed sketch of lintel with weather-shed.
5. What are the functions of arches and lintels ? Give relative merits of lintel over the arches.
6. Explain the detailed procedure of installation of centering for arches.
7. Differentiate between lintel and arches. Explain stability of an arch.
8. Explain the detailed procedure of construction of an arch in monumental building.
9. Write short notes on :
    (a) Types of lintels
    (b) Weather shade necessity and types
    (c) Lintel necessity and types.
10. Give a detailed sketch of lintel with weather shed. Write down its functions.
11. To maintain the stability of arches, which points will you consider ?

12. What are the functions of arches and lintels ? Give relative merits and lintels over the arches.
13. Differentiate between the following :
    (a) Extrados and Intrados
    (b) Spandril and Haunch
    (c) Axed Arch and Gauged Arch.
14. "In modern times, R.C.C. lintels have practically replaced all other materials use for lintels. Comment on the axiom.

Chapter 5

DOORS AND WINDOWS

5.0 INTRODUCTION

To enter into a volumetric space of a room what we need is an openable barrier known as a **Door**. To provide light and ventilation and better vision what we need is a **Window** and when these are closed for partial or full privacy what we need is a **Ventilator**.

Location, positioning and total number of doors and windows have a great impact on planning of a building.

General Guidelines for Location and Number of Doors :
- The number of doors should be kept minimum so as to increase the circulation area thereby increasing utility of the space.
- Normally (preferably) the door be located near the corner of the room, at around 20 cm from it.
- If it is customary to have two doors for a room, place them in opposite walls, facing each other for good ventilation and free circulation within the room.
- Other governing factors for location, number and size are desired day light, desired vision of surrounding privacy, natural ventilation, heat loss and other local climatic factors etc.
- Also in today's context interior decoration is to be considered while positioning the doors.

For locating the windows and for deciding their number one must concentrate upon the following factors; climatic condition, floor area, distribution of light within the room, ventilation control, privacy, interior decoration, outside vision etc.

General guidelines :
- The windows should preferably be located in opposite walls, facing each other.

- Fresh air and continuous diffused daylight entry is achieved if northern side placement is worked out for windows.
- Windows should be located in prevalent wind direction.

Thumb Rules :
- For residential buildings the sill height ranges from 0.7 to 1.0 m from floor level.
- $B_W = \frac{1}{8}$ (Width of room + Height of room).
- Total area – $\frac{1}{10^{th}}$ (min.) to $\frac{1}{5^{th}}$ of floor area (max. in case of public buildings).
- Area of opening = Residential 1 sq. m for 30 to 40 cu. m of inside volume.
- For admittance of light → glazed panel area = 8 to 10% of floor area.

5.1 DOORS AND WINDOWS

(A) Doors :

1. A door may be defined as an openable barrier secured in a wall opening OR
2. It can also be defined as a movable barrier, secured in an opening, known as doorway through a building wall or partition, for the purpose of providing an access to the building or rooms of a building.

Purposes Served :

(a) Access,

(b) Connecting link for various sections specially in case of commercial buildings,

(c) Security and privacy as and when needed.

(B) Windows :

A window is a barrier secured in a wall opening.

Purposes Served :

(a) Admittance of natural light and air.

(b) For viewing outside scenario.

Materials Used : Wood, Glass, Steel, Plastic and combinations of these etc.

Designation of Door, Window and Ventilators : Frames are designated by symbols denoting width, type and height in succession.

Width : It is indicated by the number of modules of 10 cm; (initial number in the designation - Refer examples a, b, c).

Type : It is indicated by an abbreviated letter/alphabet (middle term).

Height : It is indicated by number of modules of 10 cm (final number).

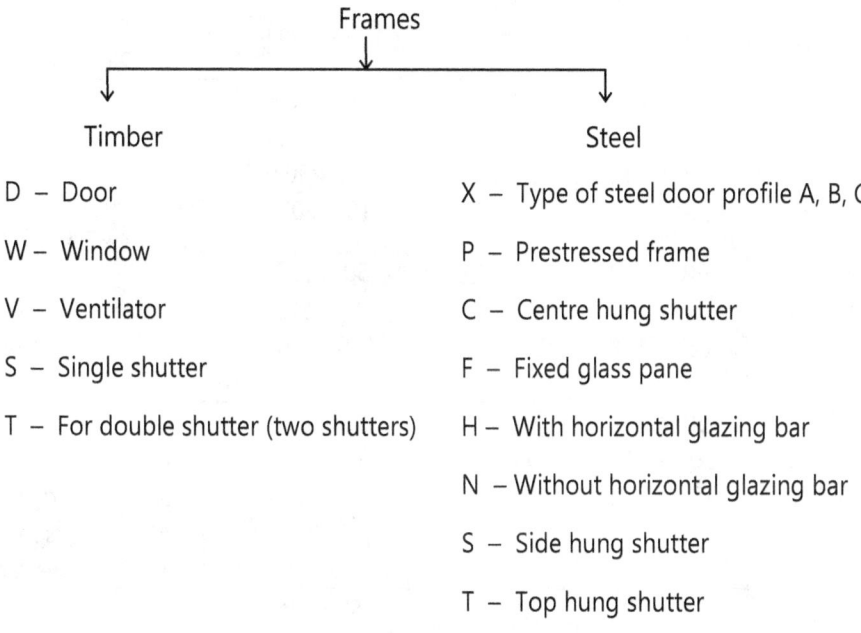

```
                          Frames
                            ↓
        ┌───────────────────┴───────────────────┐
        ↓                                       ↓
      Timber                                  Steel
```

Timber	Steel
D – Door	X – Type of steel door profile A, B, C
W – Window	P – Prestressed frame
V – Ventilator	C – Centre hung shutter
S – Single shutter	F – Fixed glass pane
T – For double shutter (two shutters)	H – With horizontal glazing bar
	N – Without horizontal glazing bar
	S – Side hung shutter
	T – Top hung shutter

Examples :

(a) 8 DS 20 indicates single shutter door with;

$$\text{Width} = (8 \times 10) - 1 = 79 \text{ cm}$$

$$\text{Height} = (20 \times 10) - 1 = 199 \text{ cm}$$

(b) 10 P X 20 indicates prestressed steel frame with, profile X (i.e. X – A, X – B or X – C).

$$\text{Width} = (10 \times 10) - 1 = 99 \text{ cm}$$

$$\text{Height} = (20 \times 10) - 1 = 199 \text{ cm etc.}$$

(c) 6 WS 12 indicates single shutter window with 60 cm as width and 120 cm height for opening.

∴

$$\text{Clear width} = (6 \times 10) - 1 = 59 \text{ cm}$$

$$\text{Clear height} = (12 \times 10) - 1 = 119 \text{ cm}$$

Table 5.1

Designation	Size of Opening	Frame Size	Shutter Size (Total)	Remark
8 DS 20	80 × 200	79 × 199	70 × 190.5	
9 DS 20	90 × 200	89 × 199	80 × 190.5	
10 DS 20	100 × 200	99 × 199	90 × 190.5	→ Each shutter 56 cm wide with 2 cm overlap.
12 DT 20	120 × 200	119 × 199	110 × 190.5	
8 DS 21	80 × 210	79 × 209	70 × 200.5	
9 DS 21	90 × 210	89 × 209	80 × 200.5	
10 DS 21	100 × 210	99 × 209	90 × 200.5	→ Each shutter 56 cm wide with 2 cm overlap.
12 DT 21	120 × 210	119 × 209	110 × 200.5	
6 WS 12	60 × 120	59 × 119	50 × 110	
10 WT 12	100 × 120	99 × 119	90 × 110	Shutter width 46 and 56 cm respectively with 2 cm overlap.
12 WT 12	120 × 120	119 × 119	110 × 110	
6 WS 13	60 × 130	59 × 129	50 × 120	
10 WT 13	100 × 130	99 × 129	90 × 110	Shutter width 46 (1st case) and 56 cm (2nd case) respectively with 2 cm overlap.
12 WT 13	120 × 130	119 × 129	110 × 120	
6 V 6	60 × 60	59 × 59	50 × 50	
10 V 6	100 × 60	99 × 59	90 × 50	
12 V 6	120 × 60	119 × 59	110 × 50	

Nominal sizes adopted – (Residential buildings) :

    External door   – 1.0 × 2.0 m

    Internal door   – 0.9 × 2.0 m

    Bath/W.C. doors   – 0.7 × 2.0 m/0.9 × 2.0

    Public buildings   – 1.2 × 2.25 m

    Garages etc.   – 2.5 × 2.25 m

Note : Minimum height should not be less than 1.8 m.

5.2 TECHNICAL TERMS

(A) Frame :

An assemblage of vertical members (post/upright/jambs/gramps) and horizontal members (Top - head, Bottom - sill) forming an enclosure, to which shutters are attached.

    Materials Used : (a) Timber, (b) Steel sections, (c) Aluminium sections, (d) Concrete, (e) Stone.

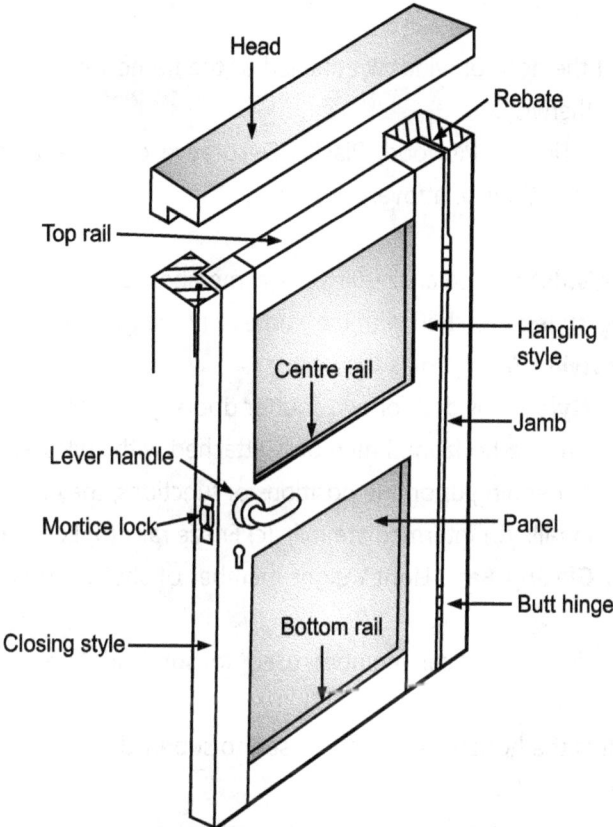

Fig. 5.1 : Parts of standard door

Details :
1. **Head :** The top horizontal member to be connected with vertical posts with horns on either side (15 cm in length beyond vertical members) for securing the frame with masonry.
2. **Sill :** The bottom horizontal member to be connected with vertical posts (in case of window).
3. **Jambs or Posts :** The vertical parts of the frame attached to head (and sill of window) with tenon and mortise joint. The shutter rests on jambs (inner side).
4. **Reveal :** The external jamb or right angles to the face of the wall. Hence, it represents a narrow cross surface of the wall on both sides of the opening on the outside of the frame.
5. **Rebate :** A cut or a recess made inside a frame all around on one side to which the shutter is attached through rivets/hinges.
6. **Holdfasts :** To provide additional fixity to the frame, M.S. flats 30 mm × 6 mm and 20 cm in length are provided, which remain embedded in the masonry.
7. **Threshold :** Wooden fixture, fixed to the floor under door frame, thereby enabling the door to be cut short enough to clear floor coverings on the inside.

(B) Shutters :

A movable barrier of the door or window attached to the frame with assembly of styles, rails, panels or planks or otherwise.

Materials Used : Timber, Plywood, Plastic, Decorative or plane glass, Pressed boards, Hard boards and combinations of above.

Details :
1. **Styles (style/stile) :** These are outer vertical members of shutter :
   (a) **Hanging style :** Attached with the frames with hinges, the door hangs on it.
   (b) **Closing style :** Which holds the latch.
   (c) **Meeting style :** Provided for two shutter doors, where they meet.
2. **Rails :** These are the horizontal members attached with styles at different levels and are classified depending upon the positions or functions, they are going to serve :
   Types : (a) Top rail, (b) Intermediate rail, (c) Frieze rail, (d) Lock rail, (e) Bottom rail.
3. **Sash Bar or Glazing Bar :** Light weight member of shutter receiving or holding the glass.
4. **Mullion :** It is the vertical member used to subdivide door or window shutter vertically.
5. **Transom :** It is the horizontal member used to subdivide the window or door shutter horizontally.
6. **Panel :** It is the area enclosed between the rails and styles. Glass or timber is usually used.
7. **Louver :** An inclined piece of wood or glass positioned in such a way to maintain privacy but ventilation is possible through number of louvers.
8. **Architrave :** This is a strip of wood, usually moulded or splayed, which is fixed round a door frame to improve its appearance at the joint with masonry, without leaving any reveal.
9. **Putty :** This is a mixture of linseed oil and whiting chalk. It is used for fixing glass panels.

5.3 INSTALLATION OF DOOR AND WINDOW FRAMES

The usual trend of materials used is mentioned earlier. Timber is most popular material of all as it can be moulded to required shape, size and made attractive. The drawback associated is attack by vermines, scarcity and thus costlier. Plywood can be used as covering material for flushed doors. Glass is invariably used where ornamental effect is essentially to be obtained and for admittance of more light. Steel confirming to IS 513, IS 1079 is in demand specially for windows but it can be easily subjected to dampness.

Hence, at places where above conditions are prevalent such as attack of vermines on timber and dampness, R.C.C. or dressed stone frames can be used.

Methods of Installation :

1. Built in Method : The frame is installed either before or during the construction of the wall. For the door frame three holdfasts on either side of the posts are provided whereas in case of window frame two holdfasts are provided. Horns are provided at the top and metal pins or wrought iron dowels are used to fix the frame to the floor. The frames are coated with thick coal tar or any such water proofing paint. The cross battens hold the frame in rectangular shape during construction.

In case of positioning, the windows, chalk line marking for head and sill levels is essential as against only head in case of door. Plumb line check for the posts is done to secure the frame exactly in vertical way.

2. Prepared Opening Method : The frame is installed after the construction of wall. The frame is less liable to distortion and moisture change as the opening is in finished state, hence superior type of frames can also be easily installed in this case.

The frames can be nailed to the already driven plugs which are flushed with jambs. In the end holdfast openings and the bottom pins are grouted with water proof grouting material.

5.4 FIXTURES AND FASTENINGS

To ensure the gripping of frame to the wall, shutter to the frame and to close the door or window various fixtures and fastenings are used. Material for them may be iron, brass or aluminium. Sharp edges for such items are to be avoided and the screws to be used are counter sunk.

Iron items are black enamelled or copper oxidized whereas brass fittings are oxidised, chromium plated with bright lustre. Aluminium fittings are normally anodised. Depending upon type, size, positions of different doors and windows, different shapes are suitably promoted.

(A) Hinges :

1. **Butt Hinges :** These are screwed to the edges of doors/windows and rebates in frame. Length is 1 to 20 cm. One flange is screwed to edge of shutter and other to rebate of frame with countersunk holes.
2. **Back Flap :** When shutters are thin these are placed on the backside of shutter and frame.

3. **Counter Flap :** As it is formed in three parts and two centres it allows folding of two leaves back to back.
4. **Rising Butt Hinge :** To clear the obstructions like carpets, mats these butts are used. The shutter is raised about 10 mm from floor level as they are provided with helical joint. Closing operation is automatic.
5. **T-shutter or Garnet Hinge :** Long arm is screwed to shutter, short plate to the frame. It can be used for heavy doors, gates, stable doors etc.

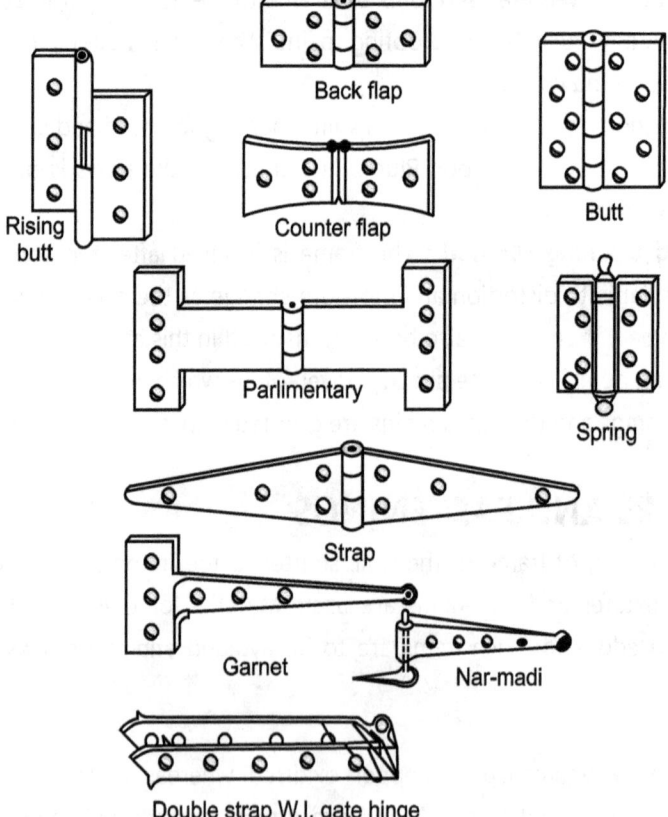

Fig. 5.2 : Various types of door hinges

6. **Nar-madi Hinge :** Used for heavy doors. The flange or strap is fixed to shutter and the pin on which strap rotates is fixed to the frame.
7. **Parlimentary Hinge :** Shutter rotates through 180° and leans against wall. Opening remains free i.e. with minimum obstruction.
8. **Pin Hinge :** This is to be used for heavy doors. The centre pin can be removed and two straps or leaves can be fixed separately.
9. **Strap Hinge :** A substitute to garnet hinge, it can be used for heavy doors.

10. Spring Hinge : Single or double acting hinges to be used in case of swinging doors. Single action indicates that the swing is only on one side whereas double action indicates swing is on either side. Closing operation is automatic.

Bolts :

1. **Hook and Eye :** When the window is open it remains at its place using hook (fixed to the sill of the frame) which is inserted in the eye fixed to the bottom rail of the shutter. It may be provided in case of doors as well.

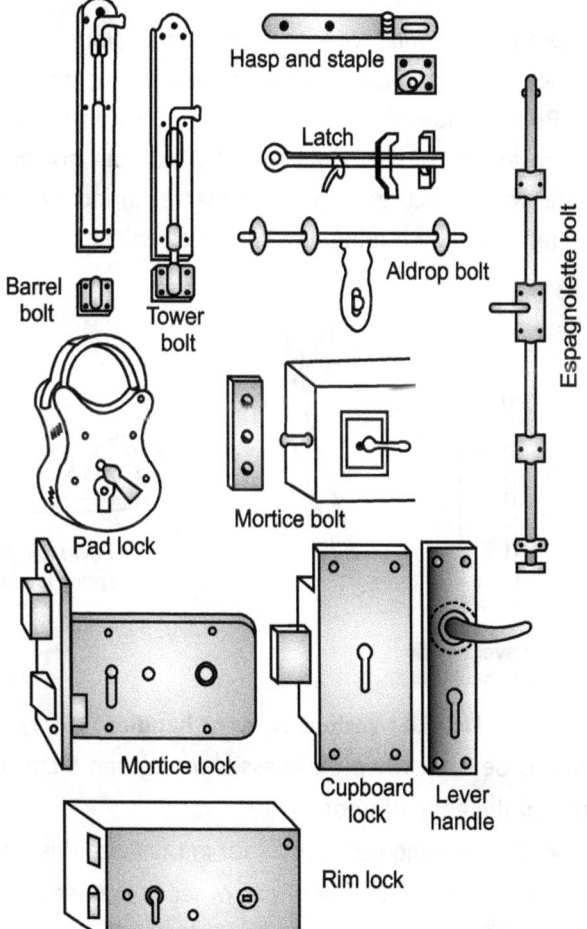

Fig. 5.3 : Various types of bolts, staples, latches, aldrops and locks

2. **Barrel Bolt :** Used for fixing back faces of external doors. Plate is screwed to the inside of shutter and the bolt engaged in barrel or socket fixed to the frame. Length varies between 10 to 40 cm.

3. **Tower Bolt :** Similar to barrel bolt with two or three steples provided with door frame instead of barrel.

4. **Flush Bolt :** When it is desired to keep the bolt flush with the face of the door this is used. Hence, it is let into the doors either upon a face or on the edge.
5. **Aldrop :** It is provided on external doors where padlocks are to be used. It is made up of iron.
6. **Norfold Latch or Thumb Latch :** Made up of malleable iron or bronze, consisting of lever pivoted at one end. Lever can be actuated by trigger passing through door and pivoted in upper part of a vertical bow handle. The latch can be released by pressing the trigger. It offers security to the door.
7. **Hasp and Staple Bolt :** Similar operation as that of aldrop. Hasp is fixed to shutter and staple to the door frame. It facilitates padlocking. It is made of iron.
8. **Espagnolette Bolt : Material :** Iron, steel, bronze. Extension bolt used for securing tall doors and casement windows the top of which can not be reached easily. Two long bolts, one which secures top and other securing bottom of the door are operated simultaneously by turning handle in the centre.

Locks :

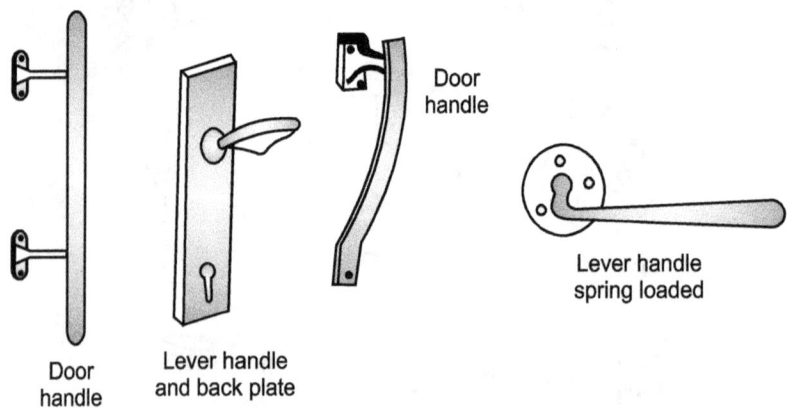

Fig. 5.4 : Various types of handles

1. **Mortise Lock :** To be used when thickness is more than 5 cm. The lock is fixed in a mortise formed on the edge of door.
2. **Cupboard Lock :** For securing doors of minor importance this is used.
3. **Padlock :** Securing for entrance door or any other as per need.
4. **Rim Lock :** It can be employed in case of thin doors. Fixed on edge with screw, such that it has projecting rim or flange.
5. **Lever Handle :** Normally to be employed for interior doors.

Handles : For facilitating opening or closing of doors handles are provided.

Types : Bow handles, lever handles, wardoble handles.

It adds to the aesthetic of door. Different metals or materials are used for handles and they are made very attractive.

5.5 CLASSIFICATION OF DOORS AND WINDOWS

Doors are generally classified on the basis of :

(A) Functional :
1. **Entrance Doors :** The door provided at the Principal entrances of a building are called **entrance doors**.
2. **Ordinary Doors :** The main function of which is to permit passage of persons are called **ordinary doors or exterior and interior doors**.
3. **Screen Doors :** The light doors which are provided in conjunction with main doors and mounted on the outside of the frames of exterior doors are called **screen doors**.
4. **Fire Doors :** The doors specially designed to resist the passage of fire are called **fire doors**.
5. **Wicket Doors :** A small size door provided within a large door to permit the passage without opening the large door.

(B) Operational :
1. **Swinging Doors :** Shutters are hung to the door frame with hinges on one side and they swing about a vertical axis. Type - single swing or double swing.
2. **Sliding Door :** Horizontal or vertical sliding action.
3. **Folding or Accordian Door :** Shutter leaves fold on one or either side.
4. **Revolving Door :** Door revolves around central pivot.
5. **Rolling Door :** Vertical rolling of shutter.
6. **Collapsible Door :** Door collapses on one side or on either side.

(C) Materials Used :
1. Timber/Wooden doors.
2. Plywood - Veneer - particle boards as types of timber.
3. Glazed doors.
4. Steel doors.
5. Aluminium framed doors etc.

Classification of Windows :

(A) Functional :
1. For admitting light only - fixed - glazed window.
2. For admitting light and air - ordinary windows.
3. For admitting air and maintaining privacy - louvered windows.
4. Projecting windows - outward/inward projections.
5. Ventilator - special category.

(B) Operational :
1. Side hung - hinges on sides.
2. Top hung - hinges on top.
3. Bottom hung - hinges at bottom.
4. Sliding - horizontal and vertical.
5. Folding - normally on either side.
6. Pivoted - horizontal and vertical pivots.

(C) Materials Used :
Wooden, Aluminium, Steel, Glazed etc.

5.6 TYPES OF DOORS

Following are the usual types observed in rural and urban areas in India.
1. Battened and ledged doors.
2. Battened, ledged and braced doors.
3. Battened, ledged and framed doors.
4. Battened, ledged, braced and framed doors.

(**Note :** Above types are becoming obsolete for many reasons such as - unpleasant elevation, scarcity of timber, it can be used only for narrow openings etc.)

5. Framed and panelled doors.
6. Glazed or sash doors.
7. Sliding doors.
8. Flush doors.
9. Collapsible doors.
10. Revolving doors.
11. Swing doors.
12. Rolling steel shutter doors.
13. Louvered doors.
14. Folding doors.
15. Plastic doors.

(A) Framed and Panelled Doors :
Characteristics : These are commonly used as their appearance is pleasing and tendency of shrinkage is reduced. Also if the panel area is partially occupied by glazing it admits additional natural light inside the room. The ratio of glazed to panelled portion is 2 : 1. The styles run vertically for the whole height and are most important as all other parts are connected to it. If the width is more, then additional vertical member, mullion is also provided to give additional strength.

Scaffolding

Arcade With Semicircular Shape

Arch With Key Stone

Dormer Window Projecting from Inclined Roof

Stair

Spiral Stair with
Winders Hand Rail & Balusters

Escalator

Steel stairs

Stairs at Public Place

Minimum number of rails is three i.e. top rail, lock rail and bottom rail. The available space between styles and rail is termed as panel. The minimum width of style is kept as 100 mm and for bottom and lock rail it is 150 mm. The thickness of shutter depends on various factors such as size of the door, type of work, position of door, number of panels, moulding size etc. Usually, it ranges from 30 mm to 50 mm. Internal edges are grooved to receive the panels and mortised-tenoned joint is preferred for framework. Total number and pattern of panel depends upon designer's aspect or owner's choice.

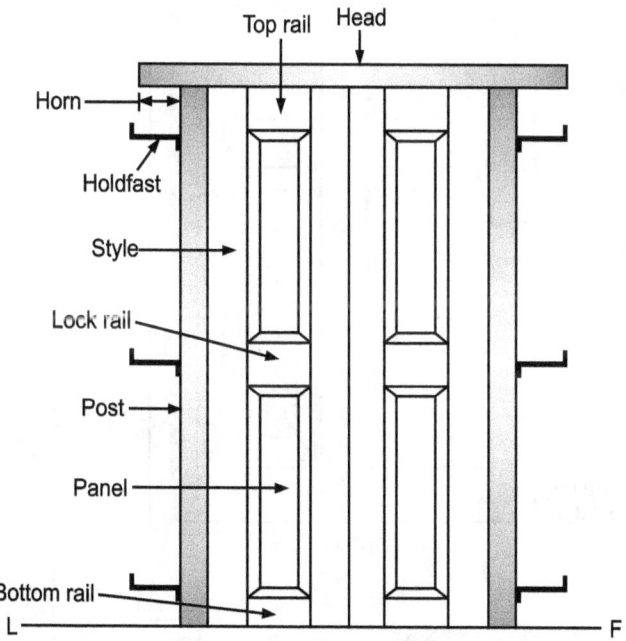

Fig. 5.5 : Doors frame and panelled shutters

(B) Glazed and Sash Doors :

If employed, this door gives very good effect, hence specially provided for private bungalows or in case of public buildings such as hospitals, colleges, libraries, showrooms etc. For fully glazed door, a single glass panel (plate glass) is received into the rebates along the inner edge of styles and secured by nails and putty or by wooden beads. Sometimes the glazed area is subdivided into number of small areas by providing sash bars. The glass panes are secured in the rebates of framework of sash bars.

To increase the area of glazing, width of style above lock rail is sometimes reduced. These reduced dimensioned styles are known to be diminished or gunstock styles.

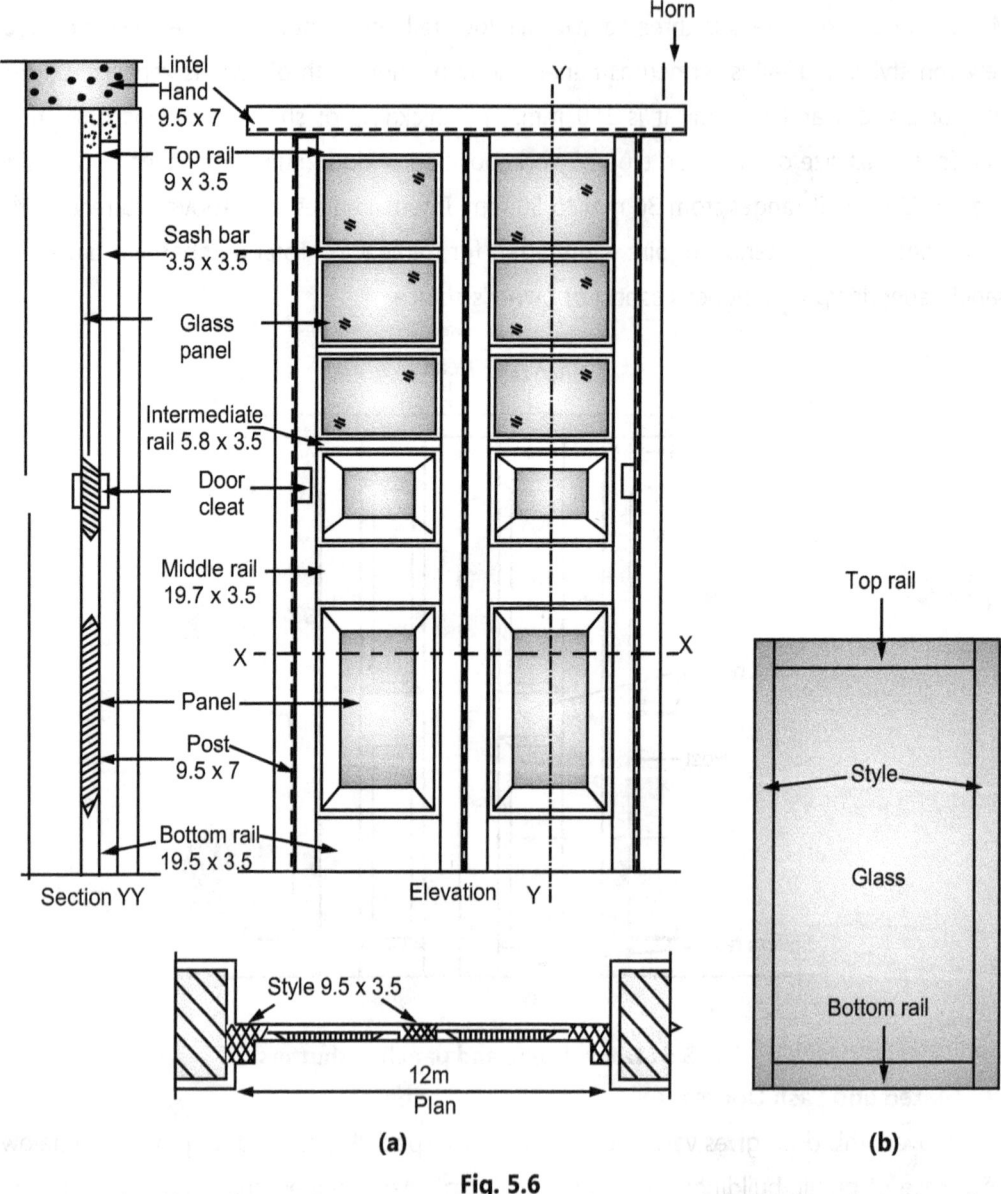

Fig. 5.6

(C) Sliding Doors :

The rotational movement about the hinges is completely avoided in this door as they are sliding parallel to the wall. They occupy less space as the support is provided at top and bottom. Through runners or guides, lateral movement of the door is restricted. These are used for entrances of godowns, sheds, shops, showrooms, offices and sometimes in residential buildings where the room area is less.

The door may have more than one panel (leaf) and may have sliding tendency on one side or on either side as shown. (Refer Fig. 5.7). For receiving the leaves either the cavities are provided in the thickness of the wall or the shutters lie against wall.

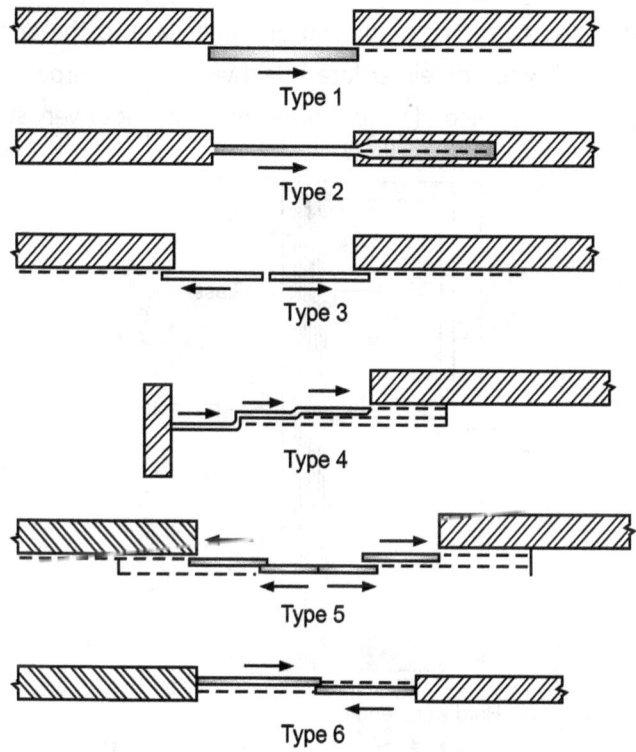

Fig. 5.7 : Plan showing arrangements of side sliding arrangement

(D) Flush Doors :

Use of plywood and block board increases the pleasing appearance of the flush door. Also it is simple to built or construct and has better weathering qualities. It provides plane surface for the shutter, hence economic, easy to clean, durable and less affected by moisture attack.

IS 2191 - 1962 and IS 2202 categorises the flush door as :
- (1) Solid core flush door.
- (2) Cellular core flush door.
- (3) Hollow core flush door.

1. Solid Core Flush Door (Laminated flush door) : As the name suggests, no hollow portion or space is left while forming the core thereby indicating heavy weight and consumption of more material.

Core is made of strips of wood (laminee) glued together with width not less than 20 mm, under great pressure and placed edge to edge, within a framework of styles, top rail and bottom rail with width not less than 75 mm. For forming core, laminated strips can be replaced by particle board, block board or a combination of these two. Cross bands are laid with grains at right angles to the core, running on either face to the extreme edge of the shutter. Face veneer or plywood on either face is laid with grains perpendicular to the cross band. This placement or positioning of various layers make the door very strong and durable.

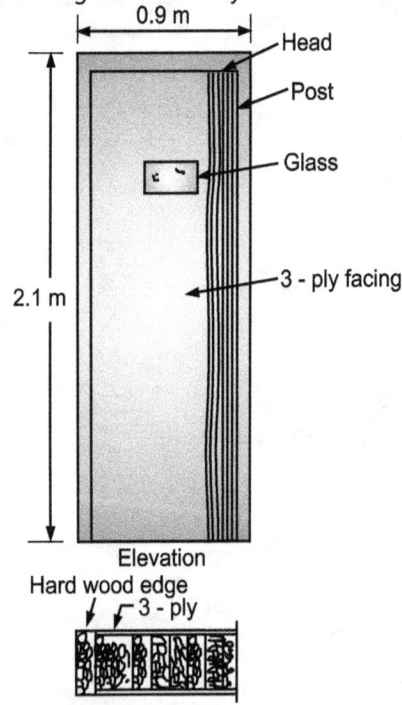

Fig. 5.8 : Solid flush door

2. **Cellular Core Flush Door :** The vertical and horizontal battens or ribs, not less than 25 mm wide, made up of strips of wood, plywood or blocks of compressed wood are so fixed that a grid of area not more than 25 sq. cm is formed with total void content not more than 40% of volume of core. Otherwise positioning of cross band and face ply is same as in case of solid core flush doors; with framework of style, top, intermediate and bottom rails.

Characteristics : Comparatively lighter, cheap and weaker in section.

3. **Hollow Core Flush Door :** A hollow core flush door consists of frame made up of styles, top and bottom rails and minimum two intermediate rails with width not less than 75 mm. The vertical battens with width not less than 25 mm are so placed such that they form void with area not more than 500 sq cm. Sometimes granulated cork is placed within the hollow portion. For free circulation of air ventilating holes are provided.

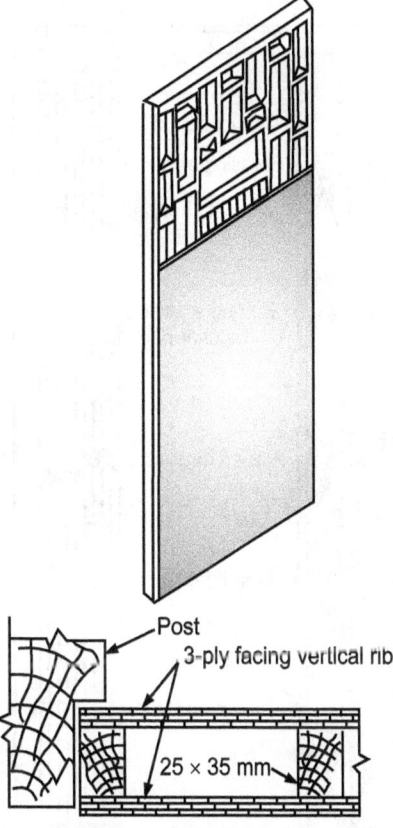

Fig. 5.9 : Hollow flush door

(E) Collapsible Doors :
At the entrances for residential buildings, public buildings, sheds, workshops, godown etc. these doors are usually provided. These doors provide safety and are made up of single or double shutters, depending upon the width of the opening.

It can be opened by giving a horizontal push to the shutter. The door is fabricated from vertical, double M.S. channels 16 mm to 20 mm wide (usual sizes being 18 × 9 × 3 mm, 20 × 10 × 2 mm), joined together with hollows inside to form a vertical gap of 12 to 20 mm. These units are placed 100 to 120 mm centre to centre and joined together by means of iron flats 16 to 20 mm wide and 5 mm thick and placed diagonally. Diagonal allows the movement of assembled channels. Shutter rolls up horizontally and causes no obstruction to the motion. End channels are usually embedded in the masonry work leaving hollow space as it is or fixed to the wall. Two horizontal rails or runners are fixed at lintel and floor level. Lateral movement of the door is avoided.

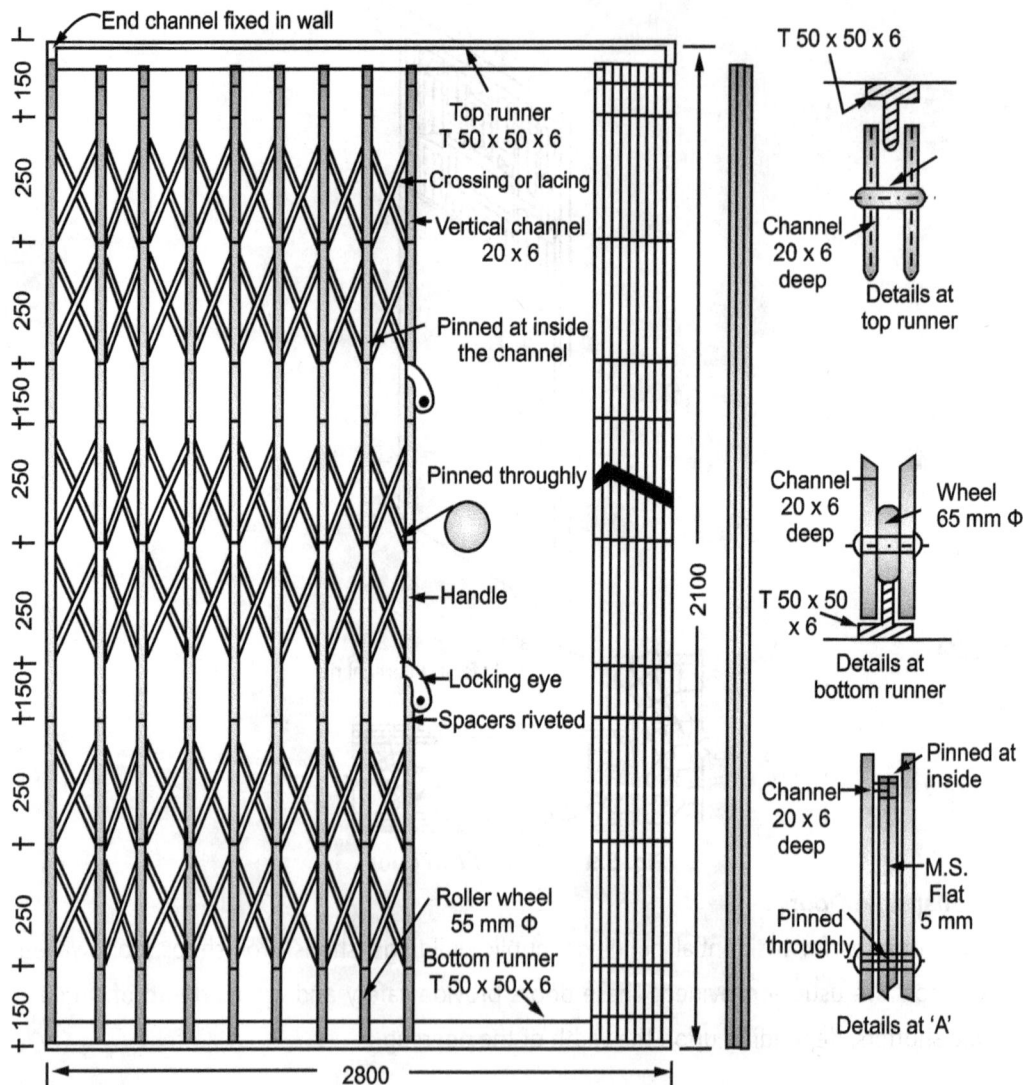

Fig. 5.10 : Collapsible door

(F) Revolving Doors :

In case of some of the public buildings, such as hospitals, big hotels, offices, banks etc. where predominant pedestrian traffic is utilizing the door way, revolving door proves to be most efficient as entry and exit is possible simultaneously.

The door consists of a central pivot and four radiating shutters or leaves attached to central mullion, and which are fully panelled, fully glazed or partly panelled and partly glazed. The four rubbing ends of the shutters carry projecting pieces of rubber for preventing draught of air. When not in use, the door is automatically closed and during peak hours even the shutters or wings can be folded.

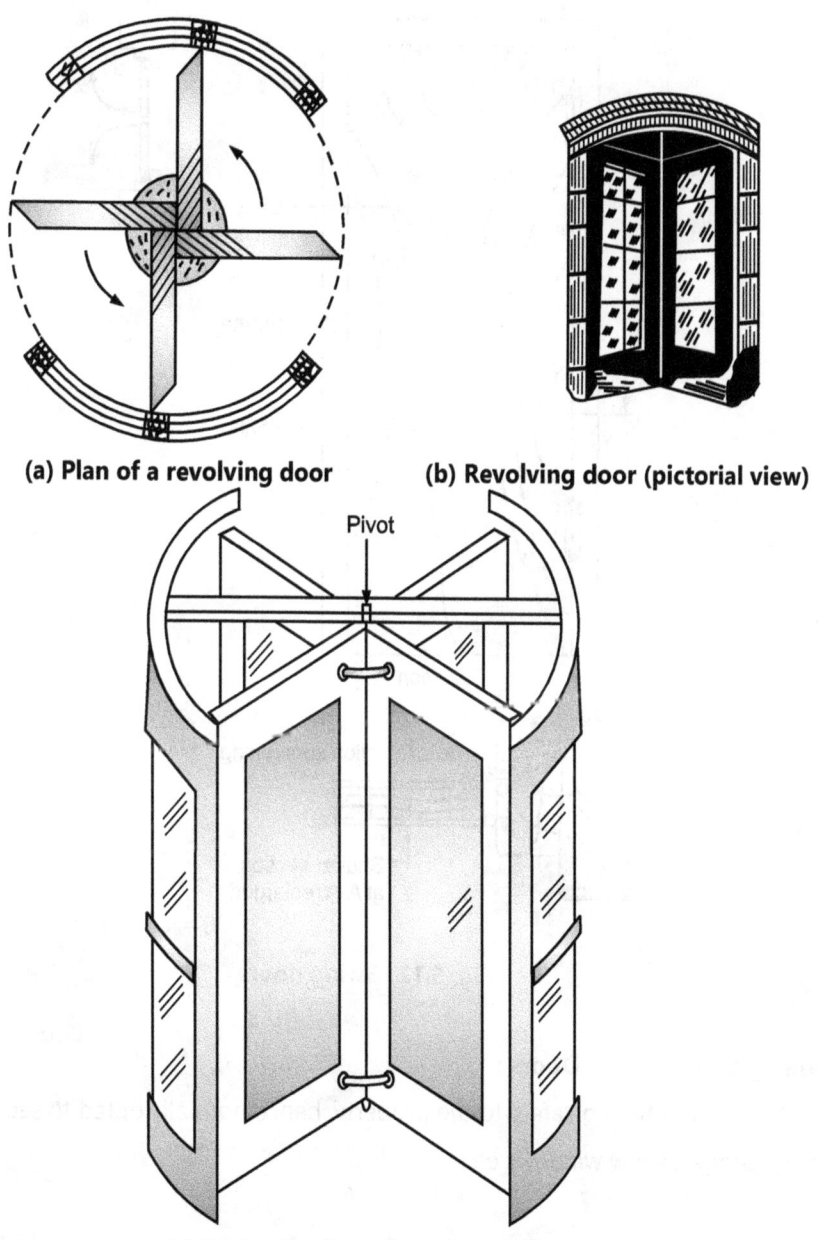

(a) Plan of a revolving door (b) Revolving door (pictorial view)

(c) Isometric view of revolving door

Fig. 5.11

(G) Swing Doors :

It has single or double shutter arrangement with double action spring hinge provided for the fixation. A gentle push opens up the shutter and it returns back to its position with spring force. To avoid accident, partial glazing is provided to see the person pushing it for entry. The doors have meeting style without rebate.

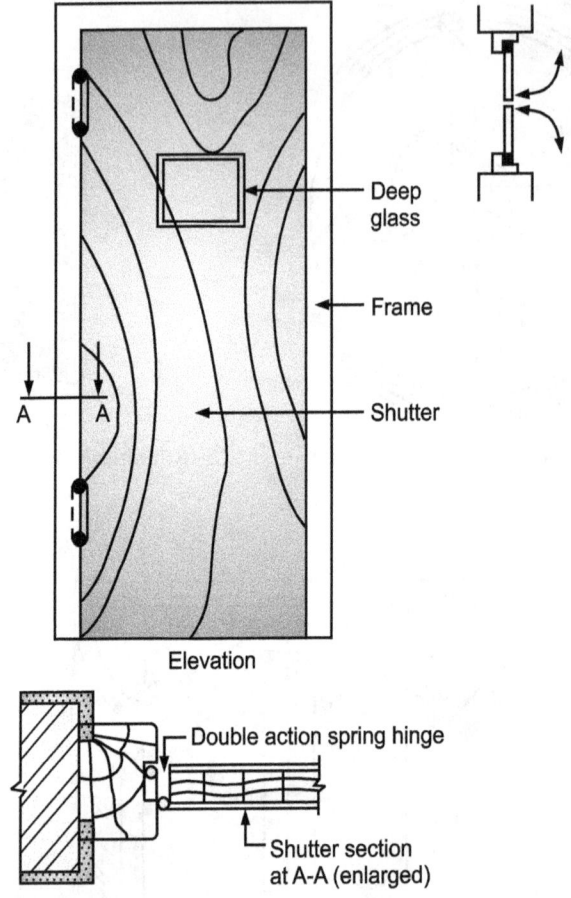

Fig. 5.12 : Swing doors

(H) Rolling Steel Shutter Doors :

Sufficiently strong, offering safety to the property, hence normally opted to secure big shops, godowns, garages, show windows etc.

Assembly for door consists of a frame, a drum and a shutter of thin steel plates (laths or slates) about 1 - 1.25 mm thick and interlocked together. Shutter moves within steel guides of the frame and coils around the drum (with diameter 200 to 300 mm).

Door is counterbalanced by means of helical springs enclosed in drum. Hood of steel protects the drum. Size of rolling shutter is specified as W × H mm (clear opening).

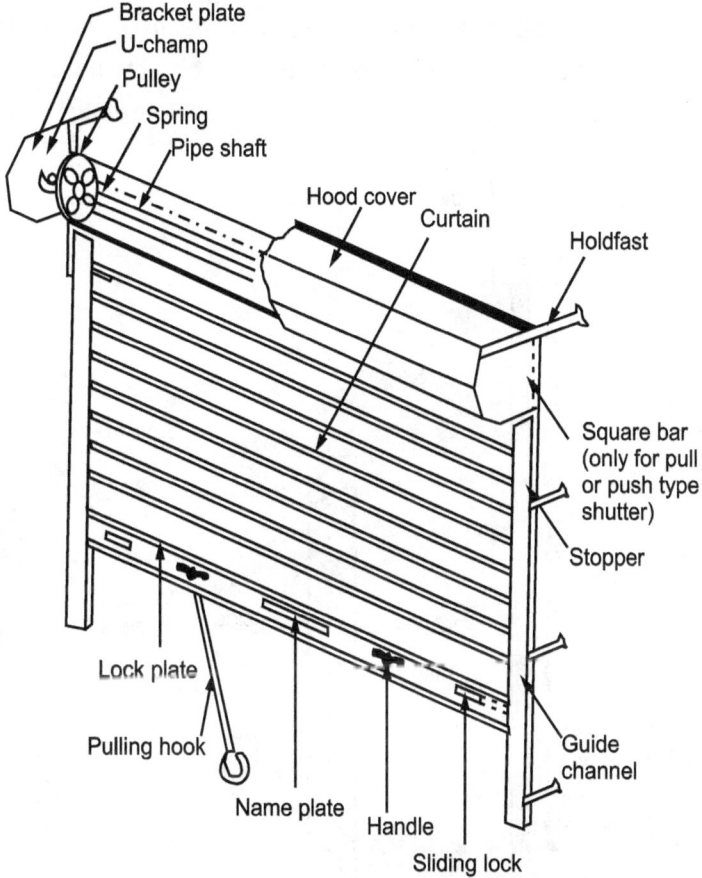

Fig. 5.13 : Component parts of self coiling - rolling shutter

Operation of Door Shutter :

1. **Self coiling :** Pull-push force application is responsible for opening the shutter. The force can be applied manually, directly or indirectly by pulling hook. It shall be used for maximum 8 m² clear areas without ball bearing or 12 m² with ball bearings.

2. **Gear operated - (Mechanical type) :** Ball bearing mounted shutter is operated by a bevel gear box and crank handle space (upto 25 m²) and with chain wheel and endless chain mounted on worm shaft (upto 35 m² area).

3. **Electrically operated :** If the shutter area is more (of the order of 35 m² to 50 m²) then the shutter operation is carried out electrically.

(I) Louvered Doors (Venetained Doors) :

These doors allow free passage of air when closed and are responsible for maintaining the privacy. Cleaning process is difficult as they harbour dust. However, at places like latrines, bathrooms of the buildings these may be suitably provided.

Louvers may be for full height or partially and may be fixed or movable type. The arrangement is worked out at such an inclination that it obstructs horizontal vision. Upper back edge of any louver is higher than lower front edge of the louver just above it.

In case of movable type, the up - down motion is carried out by pivots. Louvers may be of timber or glass.

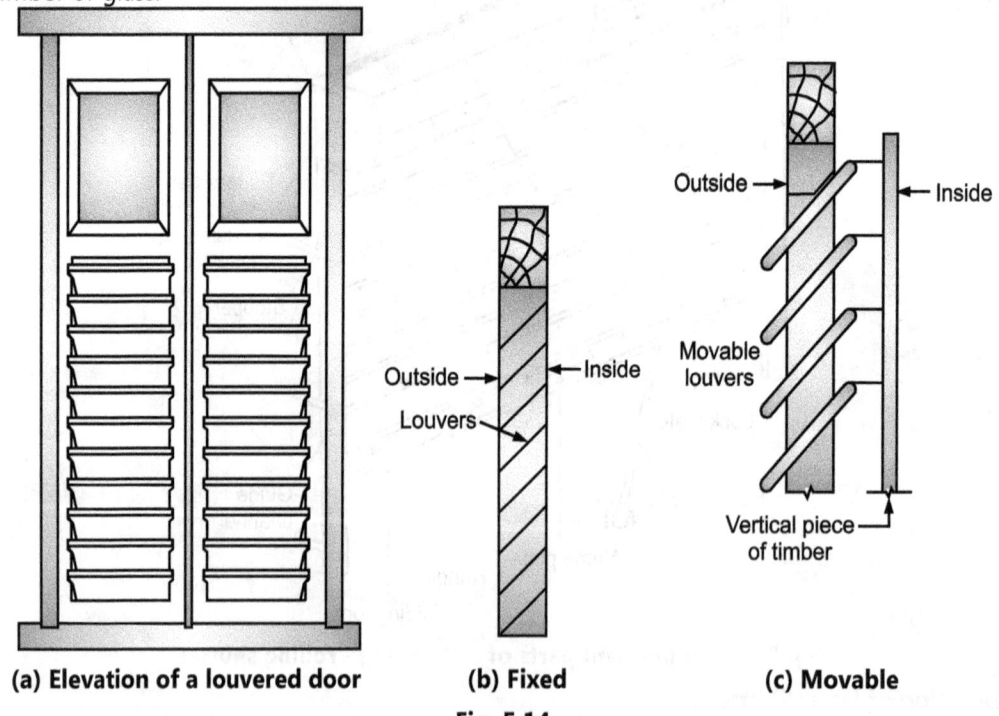

(a) Elevation of a louvered door   (b) Fixed   (c) Movable

Fig. 5.14

(J) Wire-Gauged/Doors :

To avoid nuisance of flies, insects, mosquitoes etc. these doors are provided; specially in case of refreshment areas, kitchens, sweet shops, hotels etc. The shutter is made up of styles and rails and the galvanized, fine wire mesh is nailed to the frames with peripheral wood beading. This is the outer door in case of two door entry, and opens inside of the room.

(K) Folding Door :

The character differs according to the type of building. In case of public buildings such as educational institutes etc. larger entrance area is provided. Here the elevational treatment may not be that important, hence 4 folded shutters are provided, central two of which carries locking arrangement. 1st and 4th is joined to frame by hinges and 2nd and 3rd are hinged to them respectively.

But in case of residential bungalows or lavish apartments elevation has got more importance, hence panelled door with 4 shutters may be fully glazed, fully panelled or partly glazed and partly panelled is provided to have access to attached terrace, garden or even these are located for main entrance.

Costlier in case of residential areas as special treatment is to be provided for enhancing the appearance.

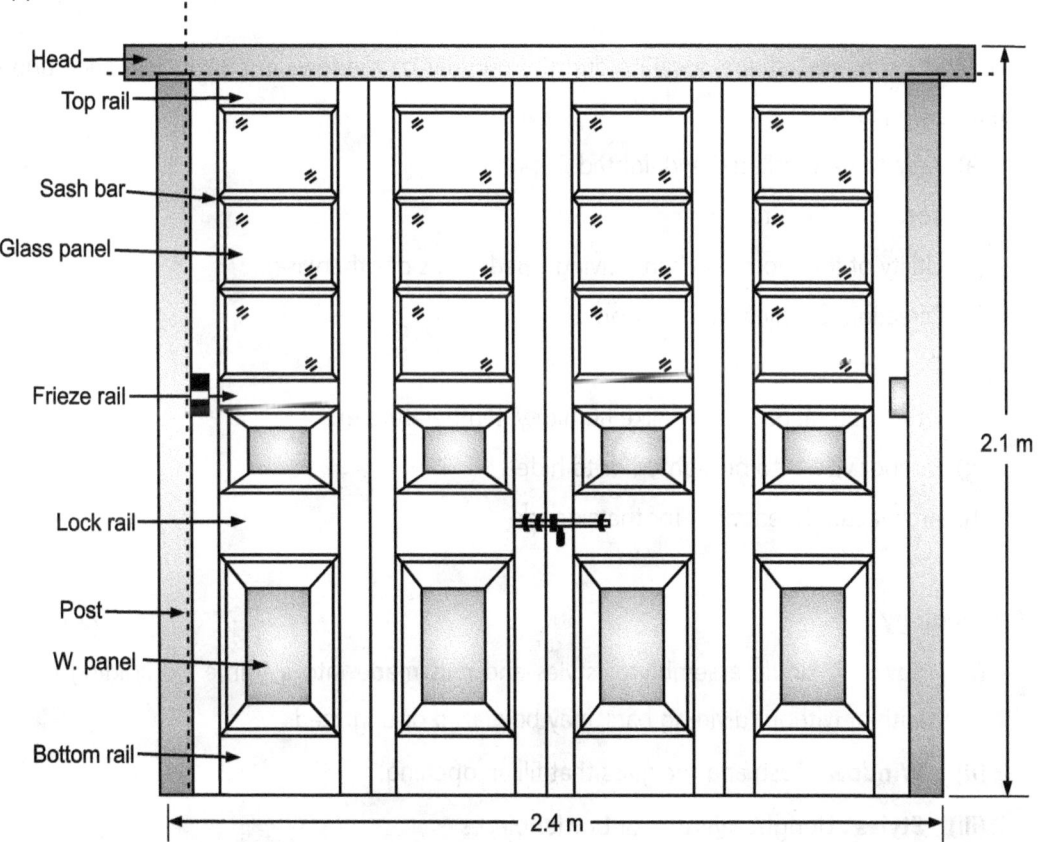

Fig. 5.15 : Detailed elevation of a folding door partly glazed and panelled

(L) Plastic Doors :

Light in weight, ease in cleaning, water proof; hence these can be provided in case of bathrooms, toilets etc. for any type of building. The colour scheme of the area plays an important role in deciding the colour of plastic door.

The durability depends upon the thickness of the door. Shutter is attached to the frames by means of nails built in with shutter.

5.7 WINDOWS

Depending upon various natural agencies deciding the climatic pattern at a particular place the window area in % of floor area will vary with a minimum of $1/10^{th}$ (10%) of floor area.

Continuous sash or one large window in a room gives better light distribution, than separated narrow windows.

The selection of size, shape, location and the number of windows in a room depends upon the following factors :
- (a) Area to be ventilated and lighted.
- (b) Location of the room.
- (c) Utility of the room (Kitchen - Living - Bedrooms or otherwise).
- (d) Direction to which window fronts.
- (e) Direction of the wind.
- (f) Other natural parameters like humidity, temperature etc.
- (g) Exterior views (to be sighted or to hide).
- (h) Architectural treatment for the exterior.

Terminology :
- (i) **Sash :** A single assembly of styles and rails made into a frame for holding glass, with or without dividing bars, may be glazed or unglazed.
- (ii) **Window :** Sash and the glass that fill an opening.
- (iii) **Styles :** Upright - vertical or border pieces.
- (iv) **Rails :** Cross-horizontal pieces.
- (v) **Bar :** Member that extends in height and width of an opening to be ventilated.
- (vi) **Muntin :** A short light bar.
- (vii) **Mullion :** A vertical member dividing the window (Please refer other details with door section.)
- (viii) **Transom :** A horizontal dividing member.

Types of Windows :

1. Casement Windows :

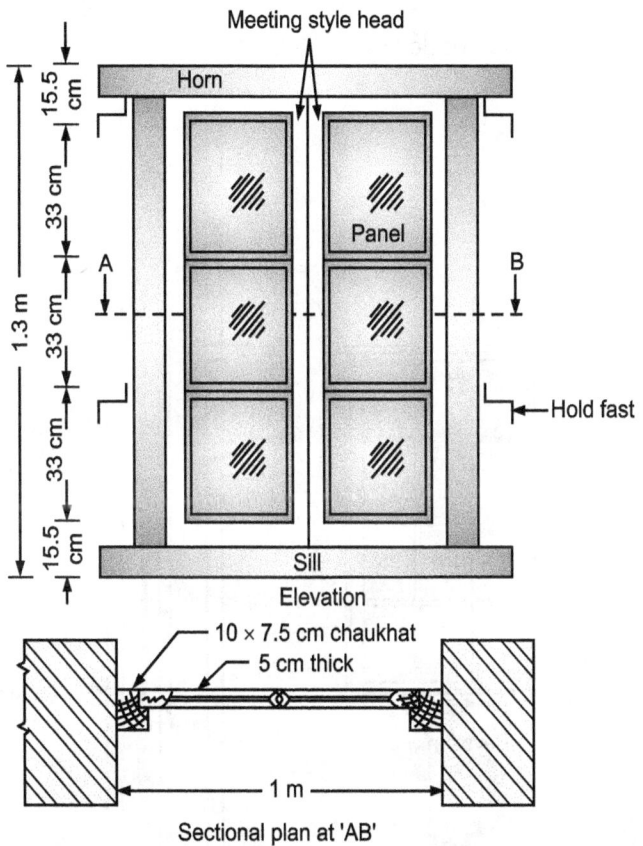

Fig. 5.16 : Casement window

Members : Shutter with styles, rails, sash bars, panels (glazed, unglazed or partially glazed). Frame with jambs, head, sill and sometimes with mullion and transomes.

Material : Timber, metal.

Sometimes a combination of door, window and ventilator is also provided specially at the entrance to enhance appearance and to check for unwanted entries.

Construction Method : Construction method is same as door, side hinged opening part of window with glass panes is known as casement and hence the name.

2. Double Hung Window : This window consists of a pair of shutters sliding vertically with upper shutter moving in downward direction and vice versa. They slide in two grooves made two posts. Two metallic weights are connected to each shutter by a cord or chain passing over pulleys. Chain is attached to style. When the weights are pulled, shutter can be opened to any extent half way in upward or downward direction.

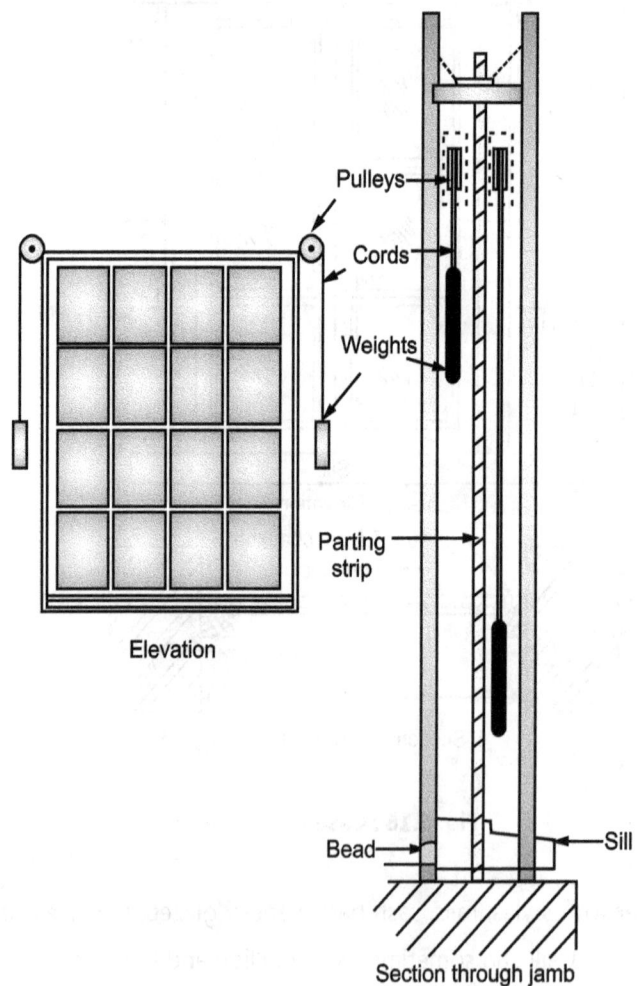

Fig. 5.17 : Double hang steel window

3. Pivoted Window : Shutters swing around the pivots provided either horizontally or vertically. Frame is without rebates.

Advantages : More light admittance, easy to clean but for security a special box type grill is to be provided additionally so as to facilitate rotation. Grills are not close to window frame.

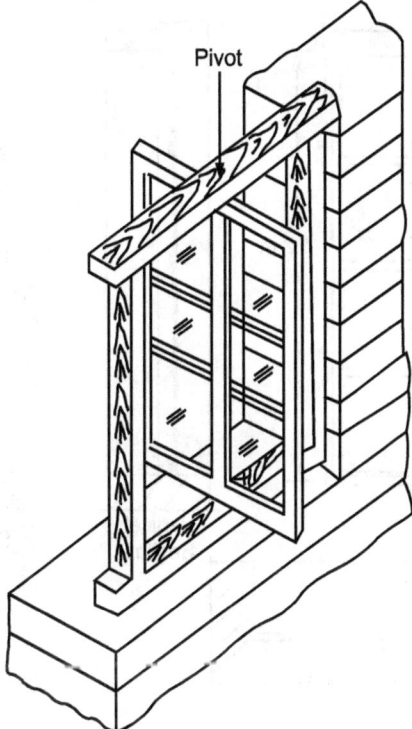

Fig. 5.18 : Pivoted window (vertical)

4. **Sliding Window :** Working or operational principle is exactly same as in case of sliding doors. Motion of shutters is either horizontal or vertical. The openings or grooves or cavities are provided in the frames or walls to receive the shutters. Usual occurrence - Buses, trains, shops, bank counters. Now-a-days aluminium sliding window with tinted glass pane and mosquito resistant jali is normally provided in residential buildings as well.

5. **Louvered or Venetian Window :** This provide free passage to air and sufficient light even when closed. The economical angle of inclination of the louvers is 45°C. The construction of this window is similar to louvered doors and as it also maintains privacy it is provided in W.C. rooms for all buildings with opaque glass louvers, timber or metal louvers. Sometimes, venetian shutters are provided with movable louvers.

6. **Metal Window :**

Materials : Mild Steel (M.S.), Aluminium (Al), Bronze etc. are used for the purpose. Most commonly used in public buildings is M.S.; as it is cheapest with angle sections, channel sections, Z-sections (for frame) and T-sections (sash bars). A slight modification may be adopted as per the requirement. Aluminium windows are rust proof, durable, hence very little maintenance is required and no paint is required.

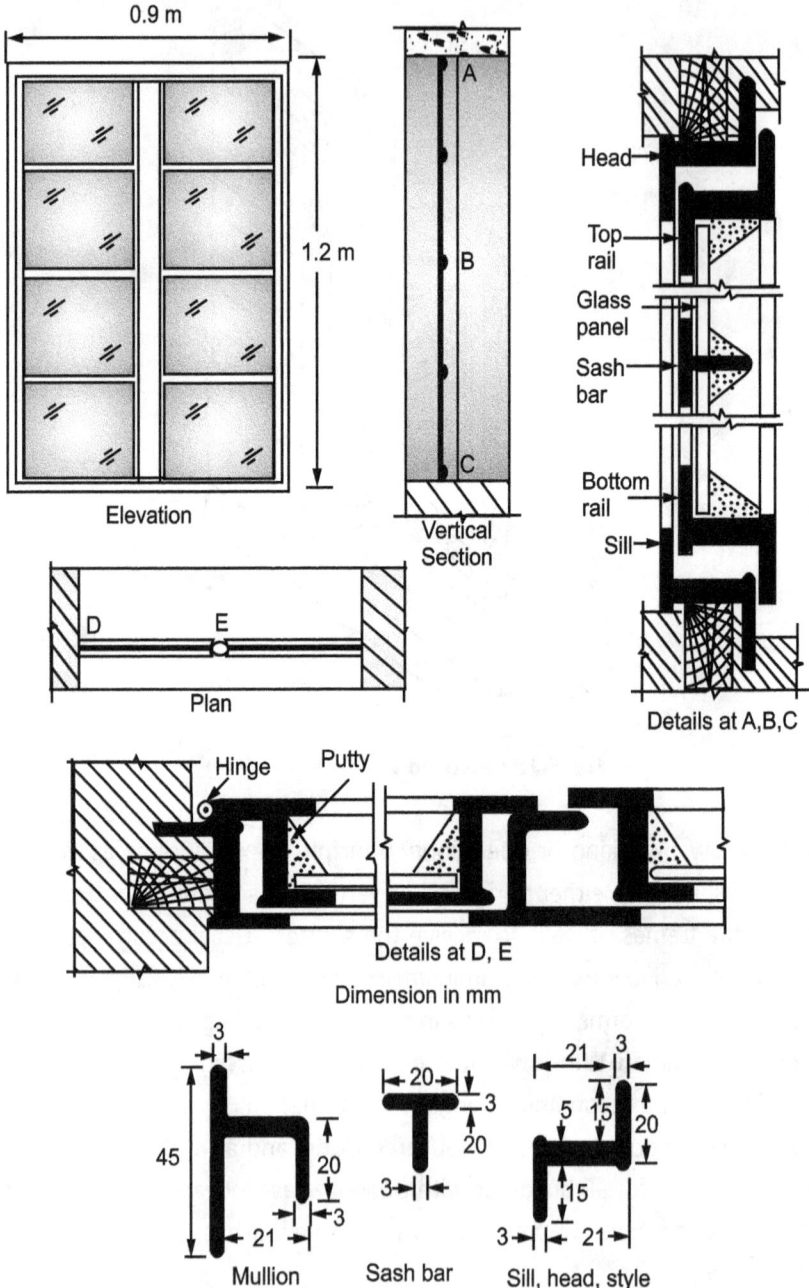

Fig. 5.19 : Elevation and other details of a steel window

During construction of any building window openings slightly more than frame size are left. Entire frame unit along with shutters can be fixed directly into the wall opening or through wooden frame. After the masonry work is over and lintels are casted above the openings, the framework is to be placed so as to ensure that no structural load is transferred onto the window frame.

Fixation Method :
1. If the frame is to be fitted directly in the brick or hollow concrete block masonry, the positions of fixing holes are marked on the jambs. Holes are cut in the masonry (5 cm sq. and 5 to 10 cm deep) and steel hold fasts or lugs are fixed in them tight with the help of cement concrete or otherwise.
2. If the window is to be fixed in R.C.C. work or structural steel work, the holes for fixing the window are left in the correct position in the opening during construction work period.
3. In case of window to be fixed in a wooden frame, the wooden frame is rebated to fix the steel window. Window unit is set within it with the help of wooden wedges and fixed to wooden frame with galvanized screws. One has to ensure that there is slight gap between actual opening and window frame.

The frames are made from light rolled steel sections. The glazing is fixed within the frame with the help of putty. First coat of primer should be applied to steel windows before they are installed at its place. Second coat is after fixing and a final coat is applied after the glazing is fixed.

Advantages :
(a) Manufactured in factories with great precision and better quality control.
(b) Elegant appearance.
(c) Stronger and durable.
(d) No contraction or expansion due to weather effects.
(e) Rot proof and termite proof.
(f) Fire resistant.
(g) Easy to maintain at negligible cost.

7. Sash or Glazed Window : Sash is a special type of frame of a lighter section designed for carrying the glass panes within styles and rails. Sometimes further division of shutter into small panels is achieved by providing transome, mullion as per the opening area. Categories under sash are casement window, double hung, sliding, pivoted. Horizontal and vertical sash bars are rebated to receive glass panes (with ribet width – 15 mm and depth – 5 mm). Fixation of glazing is achieved by putty, fillets or timber beads (known as glazing beads).

8. Bay Window : If the window is provided in the projected area of the room it is termed as Bay Window. It gives increased area of opening thereby admitting more light and provides more ventilation to a particular room area. It beautifies the elevation of the building.

The shape may be half square, splayed, (semi-hexagonal) semi-octagonal or semi-circular in shape. It is provided for full height from floor to lintel or from sill to lintel level.

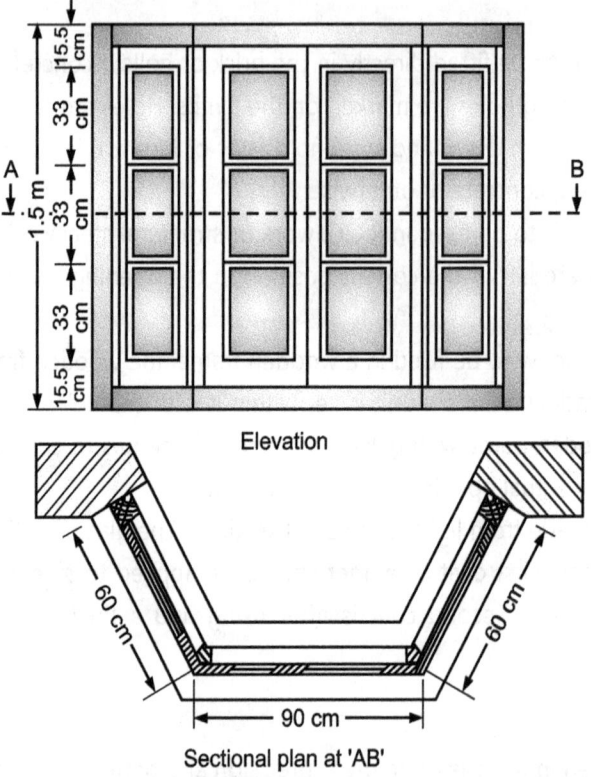

Fig. 5.20 : Bay window

9. Corner Window : If the position of the window is in the corner of the room then it is known as Corner window. It admits light and ventilations from two sides at 90° to each other.

It improves the elevation of the building. The central or corner jamb piece is heavier than the sides as it has to receive shutter from either side. Special lintel casting has to be carried out.

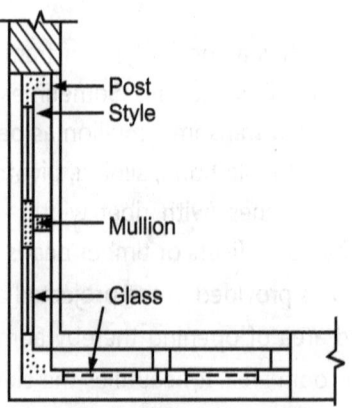

Fig. 5.21 : Corner window

10. Dormer Window : In case of old bungalows with sloping roofs or even Government buildings or quarters these dormer windows are seen, improving the elevation of the building. The vertical windows built on sloping sides of a pitched roof is known as Dormer Window. These are provided to admit light and air to the rooms or the enclosed space below the roof slopes.

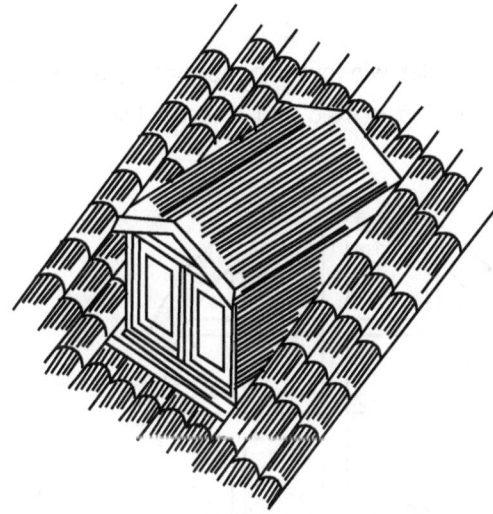

Fig. 5.22 : Dormer window

11. Gable Window : This serves the purpose of admitting light and ventilation from gable end of a pitched roof.

12. Skylight Window : A window i.e. provided in a sloping roof parallel to the pitch (means the angle of inclination) of the roof. Exclusively these are used to admit light, hence the panels are fixed-glazed panels.

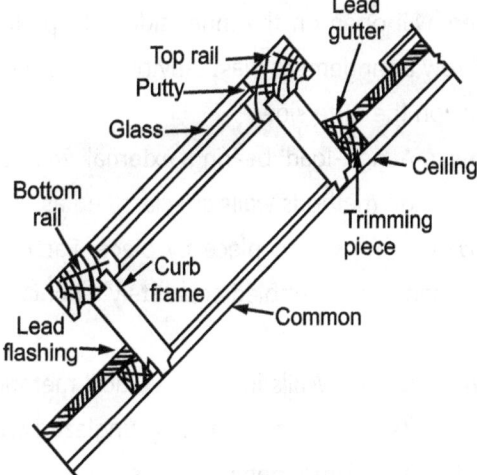

Fig. 5.23 : Skylight window

The framework supporting glass is made of trimming pieces, curb frame, top-bottom rails and lead flashings/gutters to ensure water proofing.

13. Circular Window : Following are the categories :

(a) The windows provided at greater heights, circular in elevation and providing light and ventilation when main windows are closed (horizontal pivots are usually provided).

(b) Full dimensioned circular window for improvising the elevation with framework of timber and some portion is fixed and glazed while the remaining is with openable shutters.

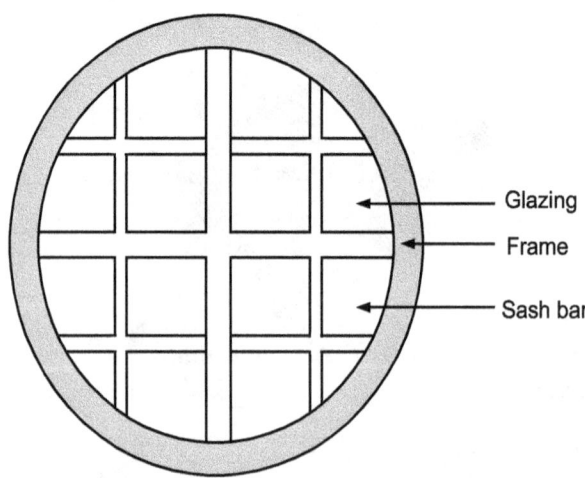

Fig. 5.24 : Circular window, Glazing - partially

14. Mosquito Proof Window/Wire Gauzed Window : Wire gauze is provided on fixed outer side whereas shutters will open on the inner side with parliamentary hinges. Now-a-days with the help of welcrow arrangement plastic-nylon nets are provided on the inner side as well if the window opens on the outerside.

15. Curtain Wall Window : A non-load bearing external wall is known as Curtain wall. Depending upon field installation methods walls are classified as :

(i) **Stick system :** Walls are installed piece by piece. Each principal framing member with windows and panes is assembled separately - hence more parts and joints are seen.

(ii) **Mullion and panel system :** Walls in which vertical members (mullions) are erected first and then wall units usually incorporating unglazed windows. A cover strip can be added to cap the vertical joint between units.

(iii) **Panel systems :** It consists of horizontal and vertical members.

Sometimes to have partial privacy a curtain wall is provided and there fixed glazed window admitting light partially is provided. Hence, it indicates a designer's view and owner's choice put together.

16. Clere-storey Window : Horizontally pivoted window near top of main roof. Suitable for ventilation and light, if front verandah blocks the light/ventilation. Upper part of window opens inside whereas lower part opens on outer side.

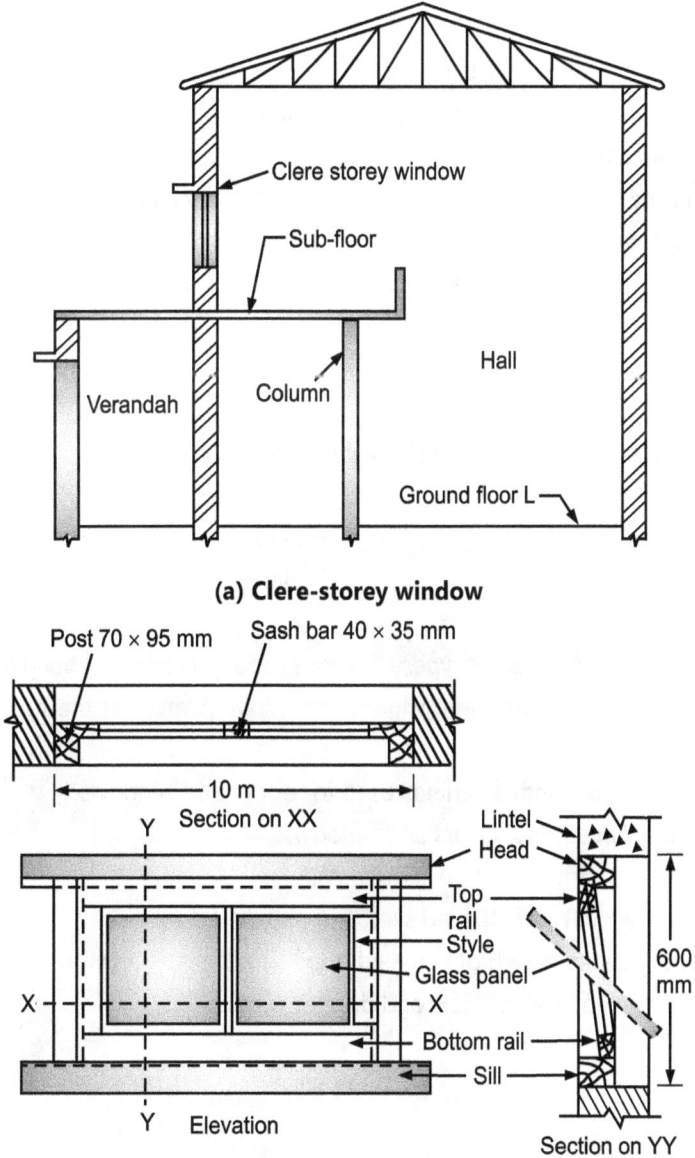

(a) **Clere-storey window**

(b) **Details of clere-storey window**

Fig. 5.25

REVIEW QUESTIONS

1. Explain the designation 10 DT 20. Draw the sectional plan of above said door. State advantages and limitations of different materials used for door frames and shutters.
2. Draw a labelled line sketch of a steel window for a wall opening of 1.50 × 1.20 m. Explain method of fixing glazing. Draw cross-sectional detail plan. State different sections used for fabrication of steel window. State checks to be carried out for fabrication accuracy before installing window in position.
3. Draw labelled sketch of solid core flush door for opening of size 0.9 m × 2.0 m. Give dimensions of frame members and thickness of shutter. State all fixtures and fastening used for the flush door.
4. Explain with a neat sketch sliding, single shutter door management. State the situations favourable for type of door.
5. State different fixtures and fastenings used for doors and windows. Describe any two types of locks with neat sketches.
6. State different fixtures and fastenings used in doors and windows. Explain any four hinges with sketches.
7. Draw a detailed sketch of door and show the following terms :
    (a) Panel,
    (b) Horn,
    (c) Hold fast,
    (d) Meeting style,
    (e) Lock rail,
    (f) Mullion,
    (g) Reveal.
8. Explain the sketches of different types of hinges used in residential building.
9. Draw a neat sketch of a basement window having ventilators at the top to illustrate the different parts of a window.
10. Explain various fixtures and fastenings used for doors and windows.
11. Write a note on : Location of doors and windows.
12. Describe collapsible door with labelled sketch.
13. Define door. Draw neat and labelled sketch of panelled door.
14. Draw neat and labelled sketch of panelled door. Give sizes of any four components.
15. Differentiate between : Bay window and dormer window.

Unit - V

Chapter 6

STAIRS

6.0 INTRODUCTION

A successful functioning of a multistorey building needs circulation of traffic in normal use and in emergency requirement. For proper appreciation of building design, a due care should be required for selection of type of vertical circulation, their location, number of units required and design and arrangement. Vertical circulation between the various floors is possible by different structures such as stairs, lifts, escalators, ladders and ramps.

A stair is a set of steps arranged for the purpose of connecting various floors and to provide means of ascent and descent between various floors of a building. Stairs can be made up of various materials such as wood, stones, bricks, steel, P.C.C., R.C.C. etc.

The location of staircase in a building is very important. It should be located in such a way that, it should give maximum benefit to its user. In public building, it should located near the main entrance and in residential building it should provided centrally. So as to provide easy access from all the rooms and to maintain privacy.

6.1 TECHNICAL TERMS

1. **Baluster :** It is a vertical member of wood or any metal supporting the hand rail.
2. **Balustrade :** The combined frame work of hand rail and baluster is known as balustrade.
3. **Flight :** A series of steps without any platform, break or landing in their direction.
4. **Step :** It is the portion of a stair which consists of riser and tread. This allows ascent and descent from one floor to another.
5. **Tread :** It is the upper horizontal portion of each step on which the foot is placed while ascending or descending.
6. **Rise :** This is a vertical distance between the upper surface of the two successive treads.

7. **Going** : It is the width of the tread between two successive risers.
8. **Landing** : It is the platform provided between two flights. It allows facility for change of direction and provides a resting place in between ascends and descends.
9. **Nosing** : It is the projecting part of the tread beyond the face of the riser. It is generally rounded to give pleasing appearance.
10. **Scotia** : It is a moulding provided under the nosing to improve the beauty of the step.
11. **Soffit** : It is the under surface of a stair.
12. **Winders** : These are tapering steps used for providing for change of the direction of a stair.
13. **String** : It is the sloping member which supports the steps in a stair.
14. **Newel Post** : It is the vertical post provided at the top and bottom ends of flights supporting the hand rails.
15. **Head Room** : This is the minimum clear height from a tread to overhead construction.

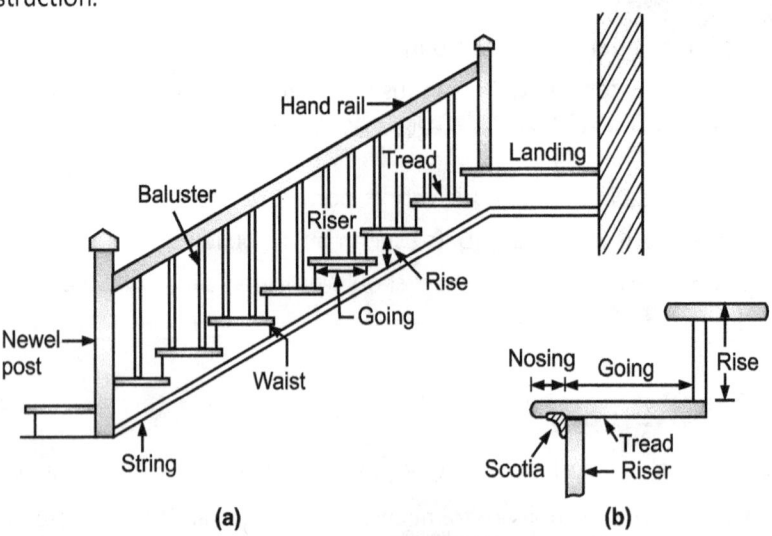

Fig. 6.1 : Terms used in stairs

6.2 REQUIREMENTS OF A GOOD STAIRCASE

1. Stair should be so located as to provide easy access to the occupants, there should be proper light and ventilation directly from the exterior and it should be so located as to have approaches convenient and spacious approaches.
2. It should have sufficient stair width to accommodate number of persons in peak hours. In residential building 90 cm wide stair is sufficient. While in public building 1.5 to 1.8 m width may be provided.

3. The number of steps in a flight should generally be, maximum of 12 and minimum of 3 from comfort point of view.
4. Sufficient head room should be provided to avoid head injury to tall people. At the same time it should give a feeling of spaciousness. Vertical clearance should not be less than 2.15 m.
5. Risers and treads should generally be proportioned from comfort point of view. Treads should be 25 to 30 cm wide and rise should be 17.5 to 18.5 cm in height. Generally, the following thumb rules are used.
   (i) (2 × Rise in cm) + (Tread in cm) = 60.
   (ii) (Rise in cm) + (Tread in cm) = 40 to 45.
   (iii) (Rise in cm) × (Tread in cm) = 400 to 450.
6. The minimum width of landing should be equal to the width of the stairs.
7. The pitch of stair or slope of the stair should never exceed 45° and should not be flatter than 25°.
8. The material used for the construction of stair should have sufficient strength and should be fire resistant.

6.3 TYPES OF STAIRS

Generally, stairs are of the following types :
   (1) Straight stairs,
   (2) Dog legged stairs,
   (3) Open newel stairs,
   (4) Geometrical stairs,
   (5) Circular stairs,
   (6) Bifurcated stairs,
   (7) Open well stairs,
   (8) Half turn stair,
   (9) Quarter turn stair.

1. **Straight Stairs :** These are the stairs which run straight between the two floors. These stairs are generally used for small houses where there is restriction for the width. These stairs may consist of either single flight or more than one flight with a landing as shown in Fig. 6.2.

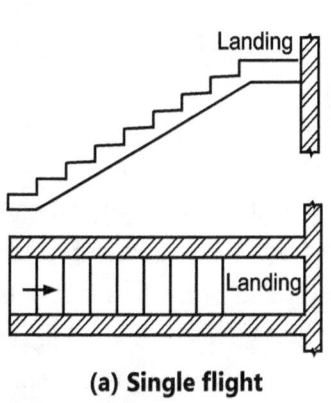
(a) Single flight

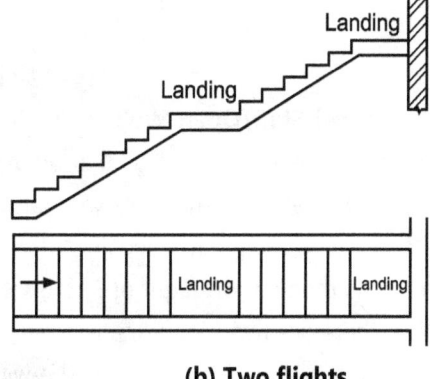
(b) Two flights

Fig. 6.2 : Straight stairs

2. **Dog Legged Stair :** It consists of two straight flights of steps with abrupt 180° turn between them. In this type, a level landing is placed between the two flights at the change of direction. This type of stair is useful where the width of the staircase hall is sufficient to accommodate two widths of stairs.

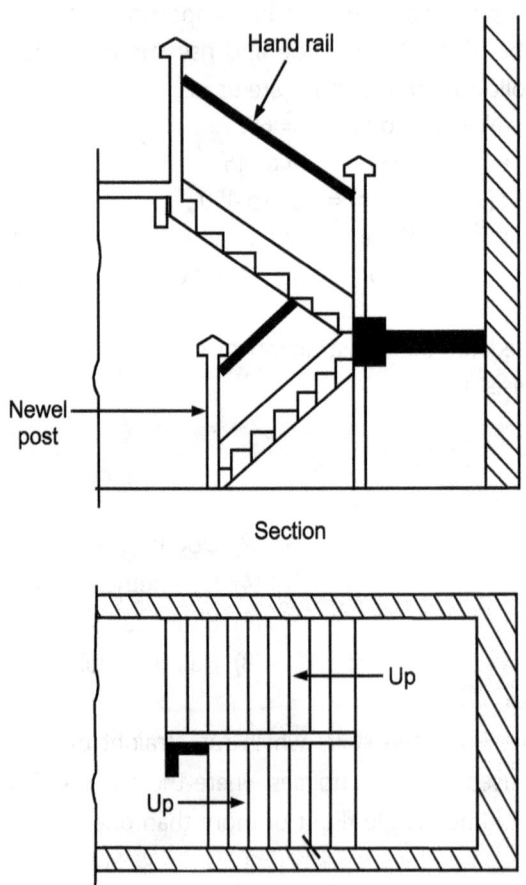

Fig. 6.3 : Dog legged

3. **Open Newel Stair/Open Well Stair :** It has a space or well between the outer strings. It consists of two or more flights arranged in a such manner that a clear space known as well occurs between the backward and the forward flights. When the width of the staircase hall is such that it becomes difficult to accommodate the number of steps in the two flights then a short flight of 3 to 6 steps may be provided along the width of the hall. In this, there are two type : one is open well half turn and second is open well stair with quarter space landing. Sometimes the width of well is so adjusted as to accommodate a lift in between.

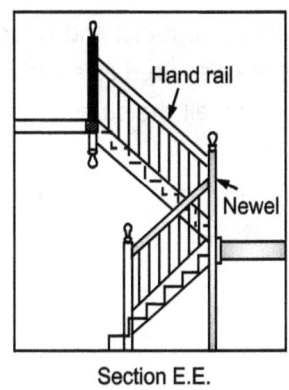
Section E.E.

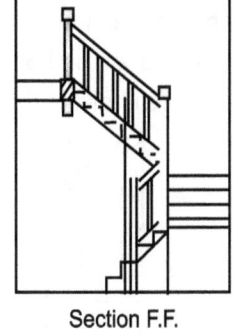
Section F.F.

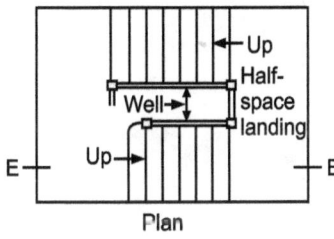
Plan

(a) **With half space landing**

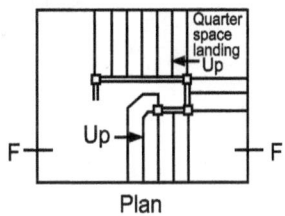
Plan

(b) **With quarter space landing**

Fig. 6.4 : Open newel stair

4. **Geometrical Stair :** This is similar to the open well stair only the difference is that the shape of the open well between the forward and the backward flight is curved. In this type of stair, there is no landing and the change in direction is obtained by providing winders.

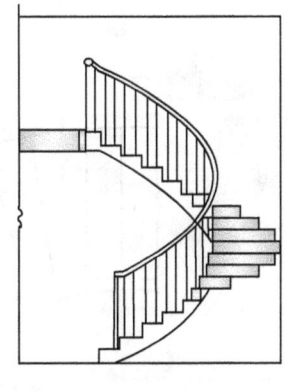

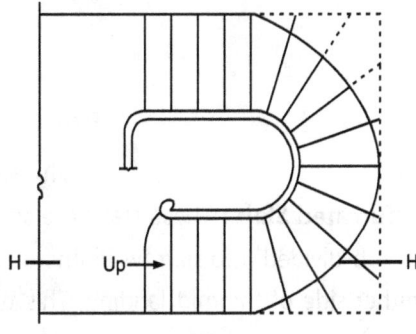

Fig. 6.5 : Geometrical stair

5. **Circular Stair :** Circular stair is usually constructed of R.C.C. or metal and is located at a location where there are space limitations. These stairs are also used as emergency stairs and are provided at the back side of building. In this stair, all the steps radiate from a newel post or well hole, in the form of winders.

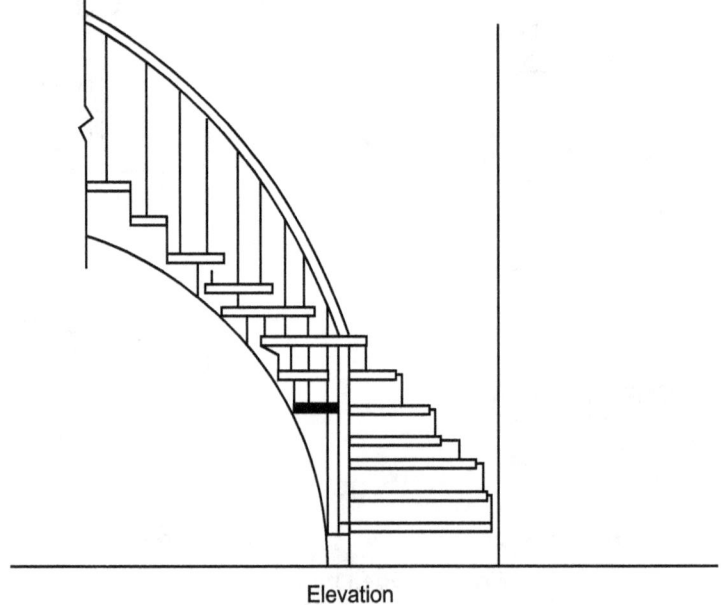

Elevation

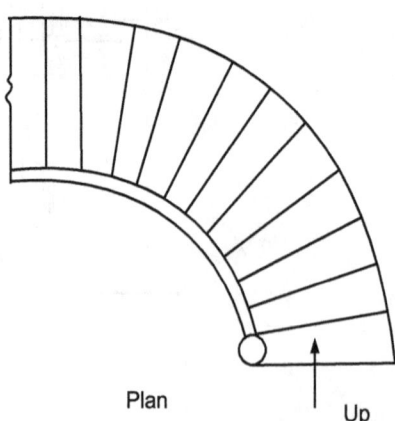

Plan　　Up

Fig. 6.6 : Circular stair

6. **Bifurcated Stair :** These stairs are so arranged that there is wide flight at the start which is sub-divided into narrow flights at the mid-landing. The two narrow flights start from either side of the mid-landing. This type of stair is commonly used in public building at the entrance.

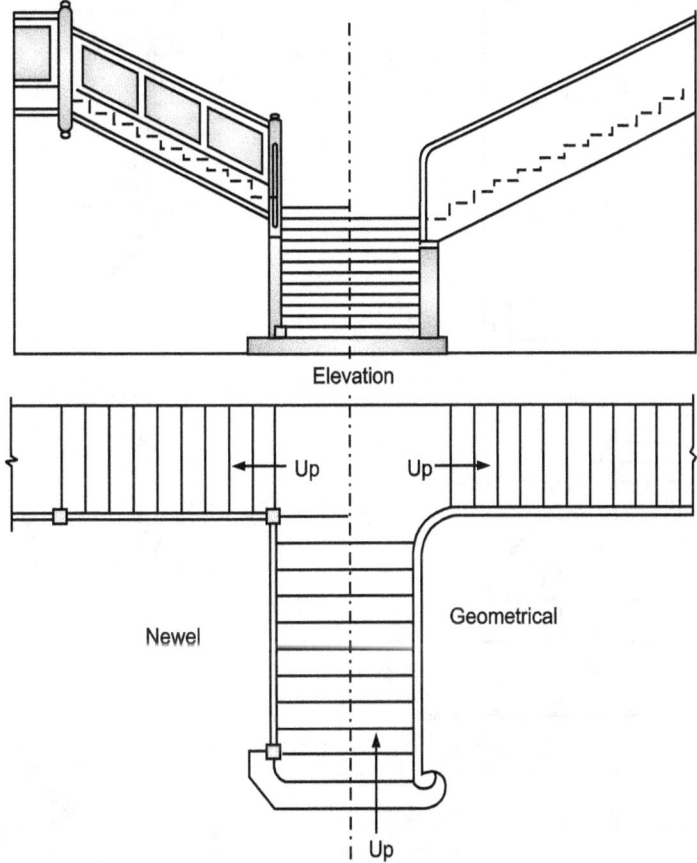

Fig. 6.7 : Bifurcated stair

7. **Turning Stairs :** Types of turning stairs are as follows:
   (a) **Quarter Turn Stairs :** In this type of stairs, flight changes its direction by 90°, either to the left, or to the right. At the quarter turn, either a quarter space landing may be provided or winders may be provided.

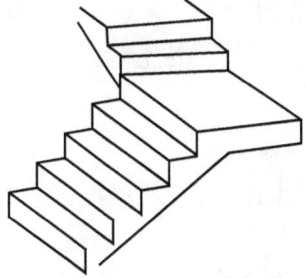

Fig. 6.8 : Quarter turn stairs

In a newel quarter turn stair, newel posts are provided at either end of each flight.

In geometrical quarter turn stairs, the stringer as well as the hand rail are continuous with no newel posts at the landings.

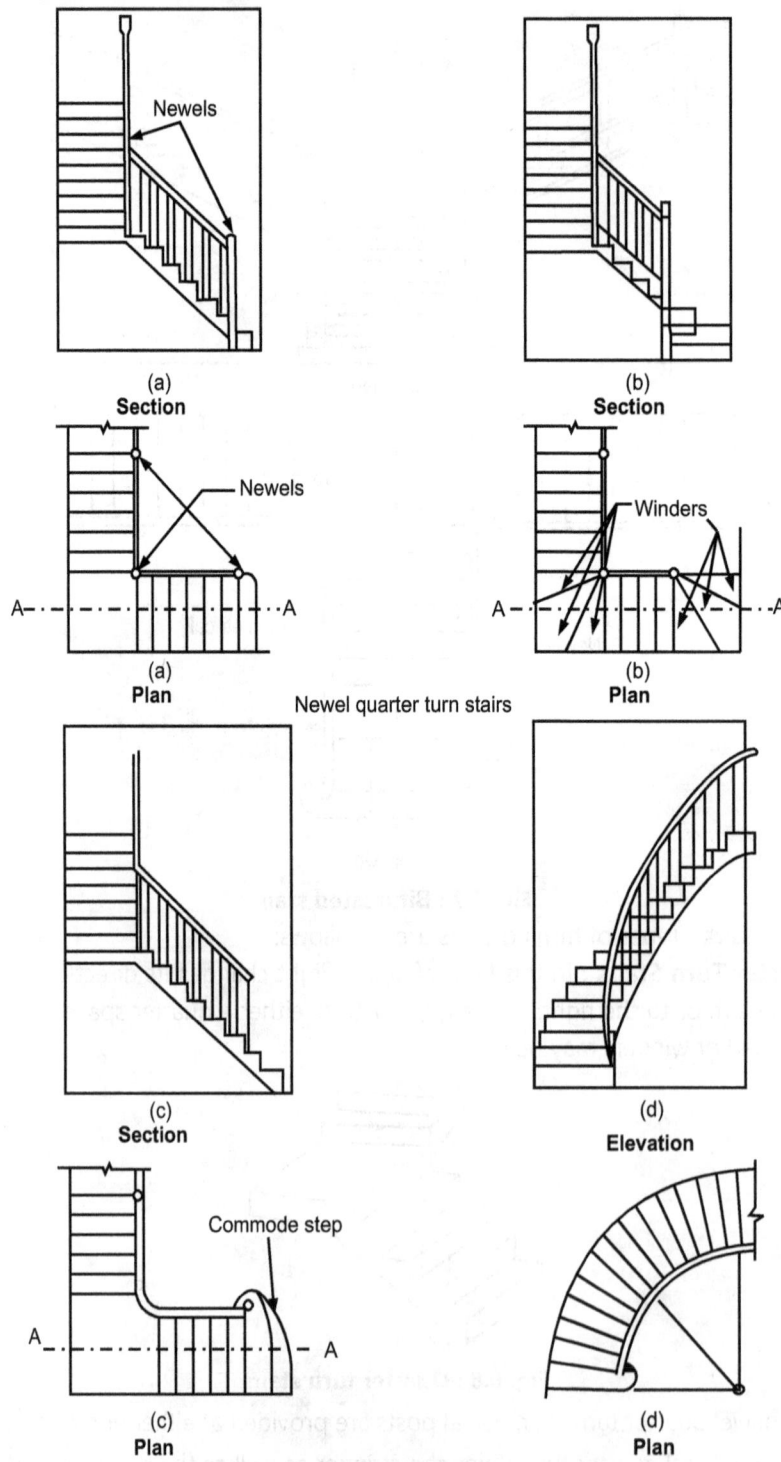

Fig. 6.9 : Geometrical quarter turn stairs

(b) Half Turn Stairs : In this type, the direction of succeeding flights is reversed. A dog legged staircase is a case of half turn stair in which there is no gap between the strings of the two flights.

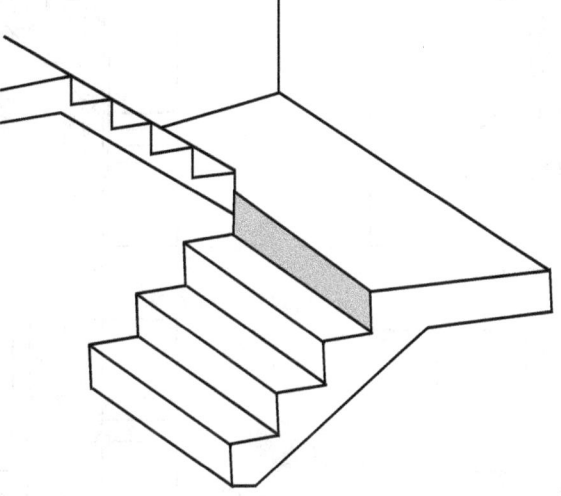

Fig. 6.10 : Half turn stair

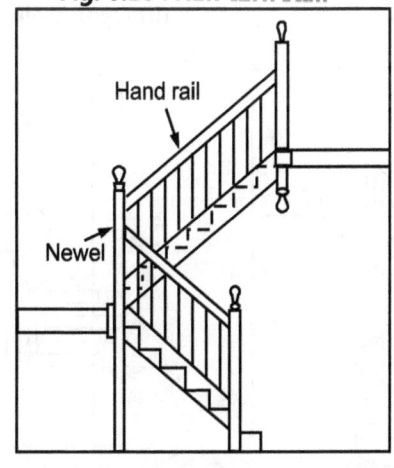

Section E.E.

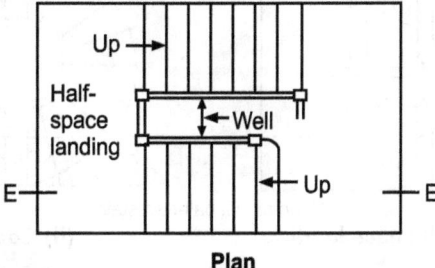

Plan

Fig. 6.11 : Open well with half space landing

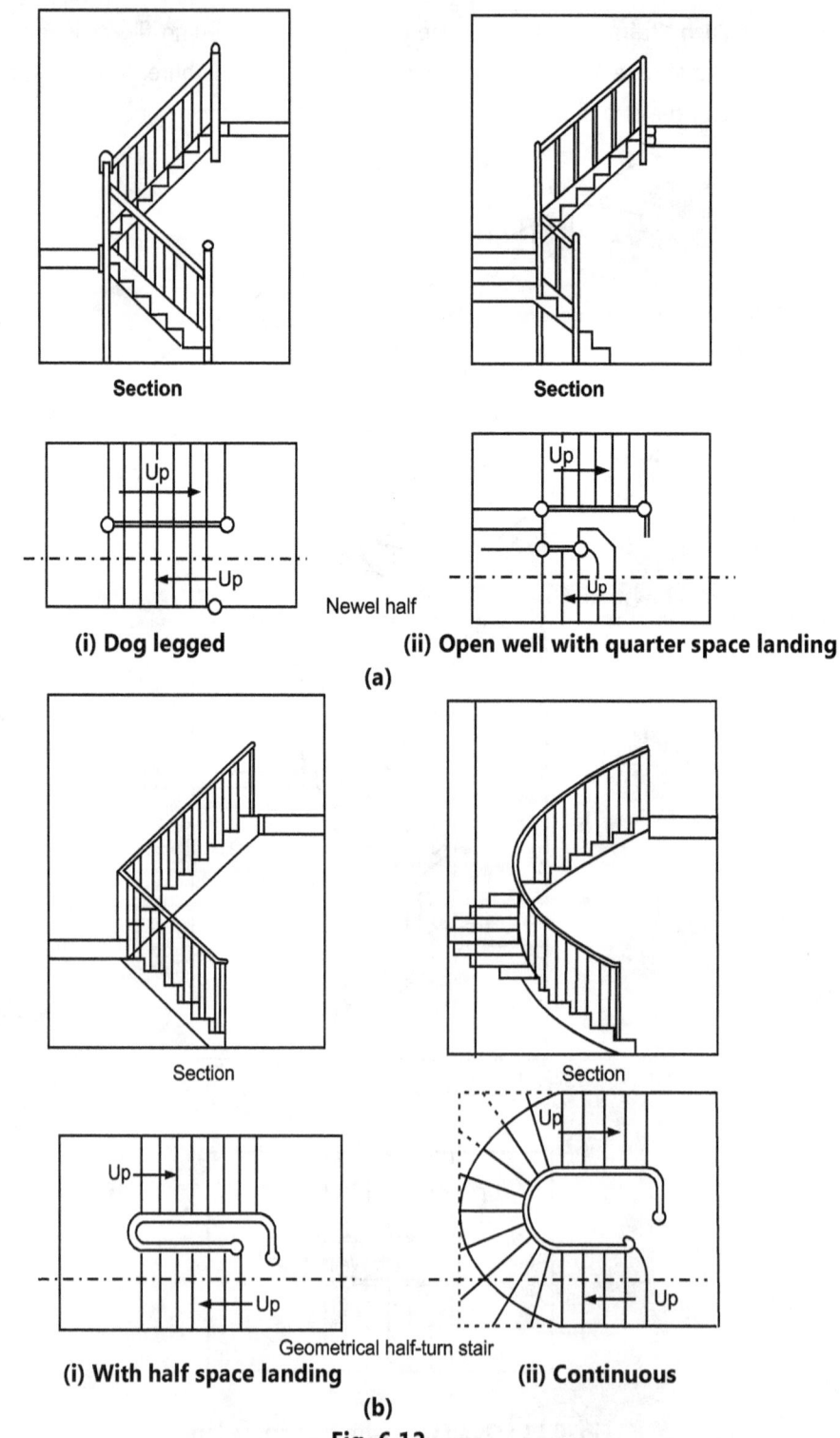

Fig. 6.12

In an open newel half turn stair, there is a rectangular well or an opening between the previous and the next flights. The landing between the two flights may be continuous, the gap between the two flights is more, then few steps may be introduced on the narrow side of the well with two quarter space landing one on either side.

A geometrical half turn stair is one in which the stringer and the hand rail are continuous without any newels in between. The well hole is curved and there may be half space landing or winders radiating from the centre of curvature of the curve between the flights.

(c) **Three Quarter Turn Stairs :** In this case, the direction of flight changes thrice with its upper flight crossing the bottom one.

(d) **Bifurcated Stairs :** In this type, the bottom flight, which is wider, bifurcates into two upper flights of smaller widths, each flight being on either side of the bottom flight.

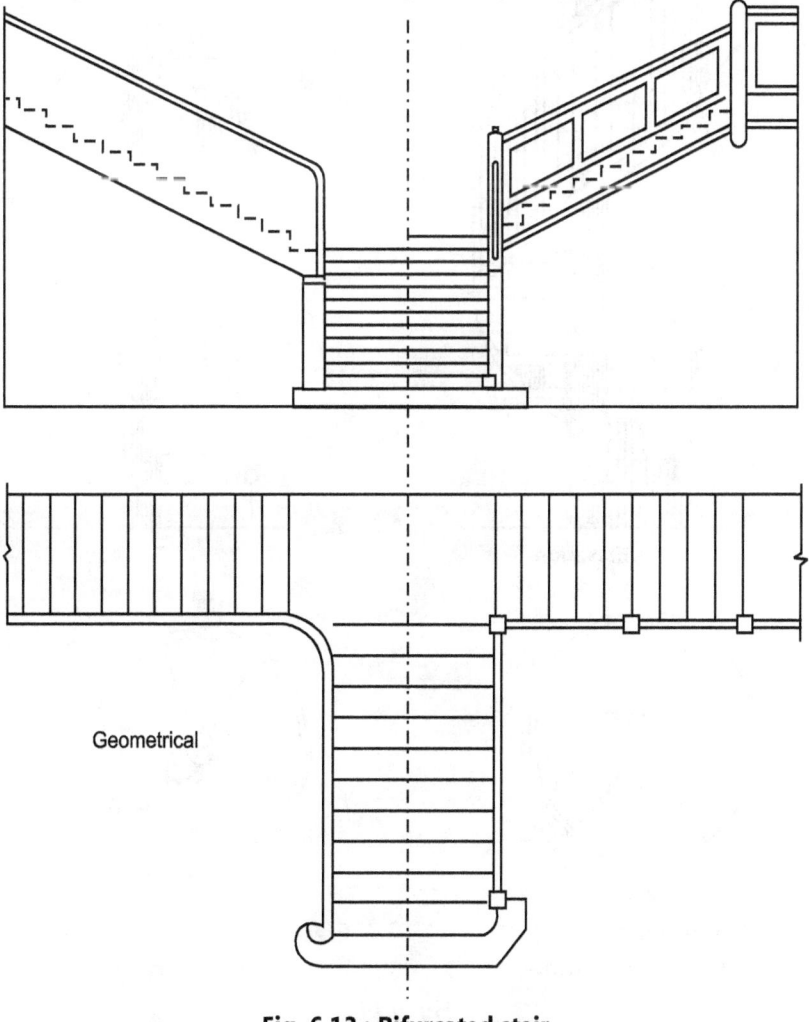

Fig. 6.13 : Bifurcated stair

(e) Spiral Stairs : These do not have any landing and are therefore continuous type of stairs. Such staircases are normally of R.C.C. or steel. All steps are winders, hence not very convenient to use.

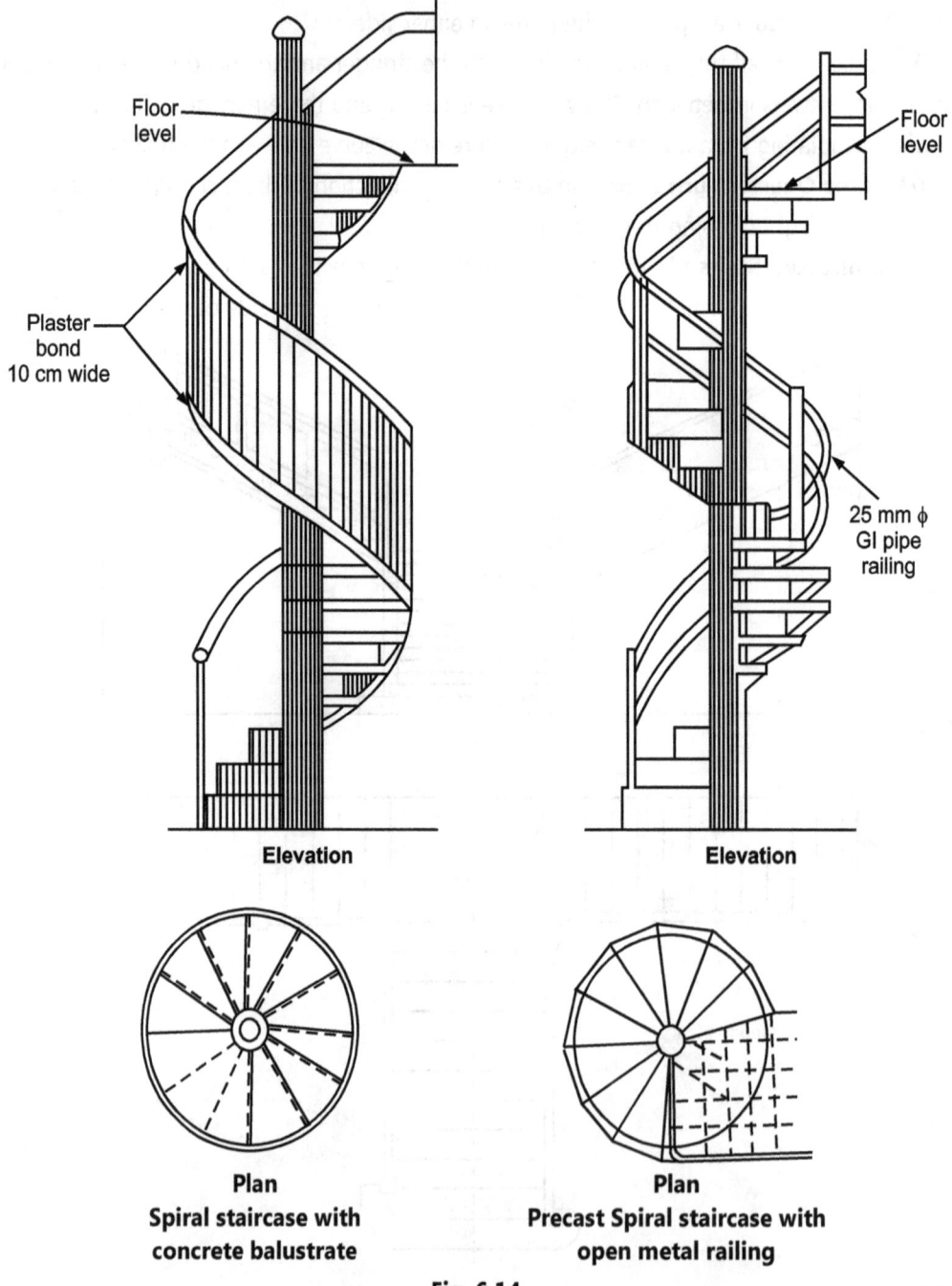

Fig. 6.14

6.4 MATERIALS USED FOR CONSTRUCTION OF STAIRS

The commonly used materials in the construction of stairs are wood, stone, steel cast-iron, plain cement concrete, reinforced cement concrete, precast concrete and bricks.

1. **Timber or Wooden Stairs** : Timber stairs are light in weight and easy to construct, but they have very poor fire resistance. These stairs are generally used for small residential buildings. Timber stairs are cheap, easy in construction and maintenance and light in weight. These stairs are constructed from fire resisting hard wood such as oak, teak, mahogany, Babul, Neem etc. In wooden, stairs the thickness of tread should not be less than 32 mm and that of the riser as 25 mm. The risers and the treads are connected by tongue and grooved joints and the joints are nailed or screwed.

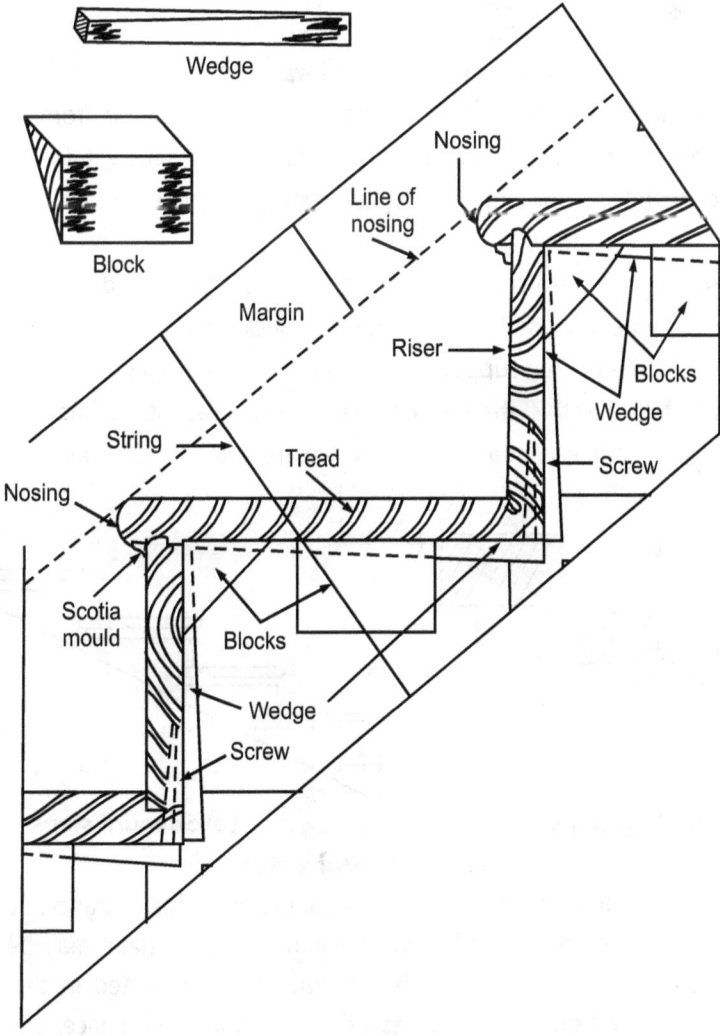

Fig. 6.15 : Wooden stair

The treads and risers are supported on one or more stringer beams. The upper edges of beams are cut to receive the riser and treads. Stringers are supported on transverse beam known as headers. To add rigidity, blocks are glued between the stringer and the treads and the treads and risers.

2. **Stone Stairs :** Stone stairs are widely used at places where ashlar stone is abundantly available. Stone used for the construction of stairs should be hard, strong and resistant to wear. These stairs are commonly constructed in workshop, warehouses and other public buildings.

In residential building, these stairs are generally restricted to outside stairs at the entrance. Being heavy in weight, stone stairs require stable support to avoid the danger of settlement of supporting walls.

The main types of stone stairs are as described below :

(a) **Rectangular steps :** These are the simplest type, prepared from solid stone into square or rectangular blocks of uniform size. In its simplest form, the steps are arranged with the front edge of one step resting on the upper back edge of the steps below.

(b) **Built-up steps :** These consists of treads and risers prepared from thin stone slabs. These are generally used as a facing for brick or concrete steps. The minimum thickness of tread, when supported at end is restricted to 5 cm.

(c) **Spandril steps :** In this, the steps are cut to give plain soffit. These steps are nearly triangular in shape except at the ends which are built into the wall.

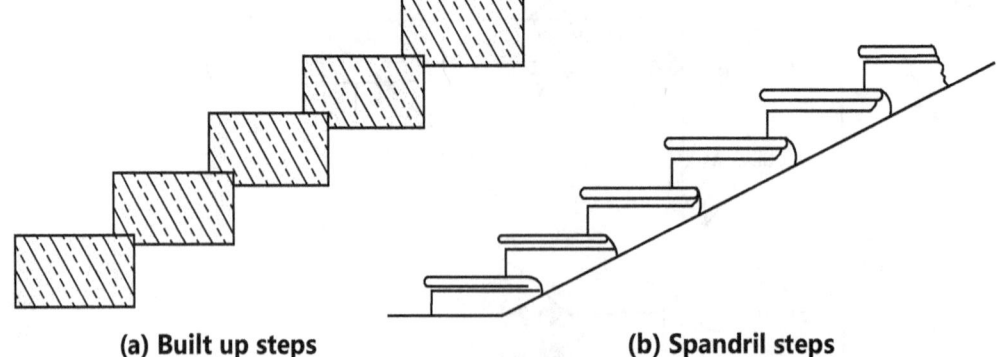

(a) Built up steps   (b) Spandril steps

Fig. 6.16 : Stone stair

3. **Brick Stairs :** Brick stairs are not very common, except at the entrance. Sometimes brick stairs of single flight are constructed in village houses. These stairs may be built of solid masonry construction or arches and cupboards may be constructed in the lower portion which reduces masonry work and increases utility of underneath space. These steps need frequent maintenance. Hence, these may be faced with various types of stone slabs.

4. Metal Stairs : These stairs are made of mild steel or cast iron. These are generally used in factories, godowns, workshops etc. In its simplest form, a steel stair consists of rolled steel stringers of channel section, to which angle sections are welded and steel plates are used as treads. Generally metal balusters with hand rails of pipe are used for these stairs.

5. R.C.C. Stairs : R.C.C. stairs predominate the stairs made from other materials. This is because of various advantages of R.C.C. over the other materials. R.C.C. stairs are the one which are widely used for residential, public and industrial buildings. They are strong, hard wearing and fire resisting. These are usually cast in situ.

Advantages of R.C.C. stairs :

    (i) R.C.C. stairs can be moulded in any desired shape to suit the requirement of the architect's design.

    (ii) These stairs are durable, strong, pleasing in appearance and non-slippery.

    (iii) These stairs can be designed for greater widths and longer spans.

    (iv) These stairs can be easily cleaned, and are fire resistant.

    (v) The maintenance cost of these stairs is almost nil.

SOLVED EXAMPLES

Planning of typical R.C.C. stairs :

Example 1 : Plan a dog legged stair for a building with the following data :

    (i) Vertical distance between the floors = 3.6 m.

    (ii) Size of stair hall = 2.5 m × 5 m.

    (iii) Thickness of the floor slab = 140 mm.

    (iv) Thickness of the waist slab and landing slab = 100 mm.

Solution : Assume, Rise = 150 mm

and Tread = 250 mm

$$\text{Width of the flight} = \frac{2.5}{2} = 1.25 \text{ m}$$

$$\text{Height of each flight} = \frac{3.6}{2} = 1.8 \text{ m}$$

$$\therefore \text{Number of risers required} = \frac{1.8 \times 1000}{150}$$

= 12 in each flight

Number of treads in each flight = 12 − 1 = 11

∴ Space required for treads = 11 × 250 = 2750 mm

∴ Space left for passage = 5 − 1.25 − 2.75 = 1.00 m

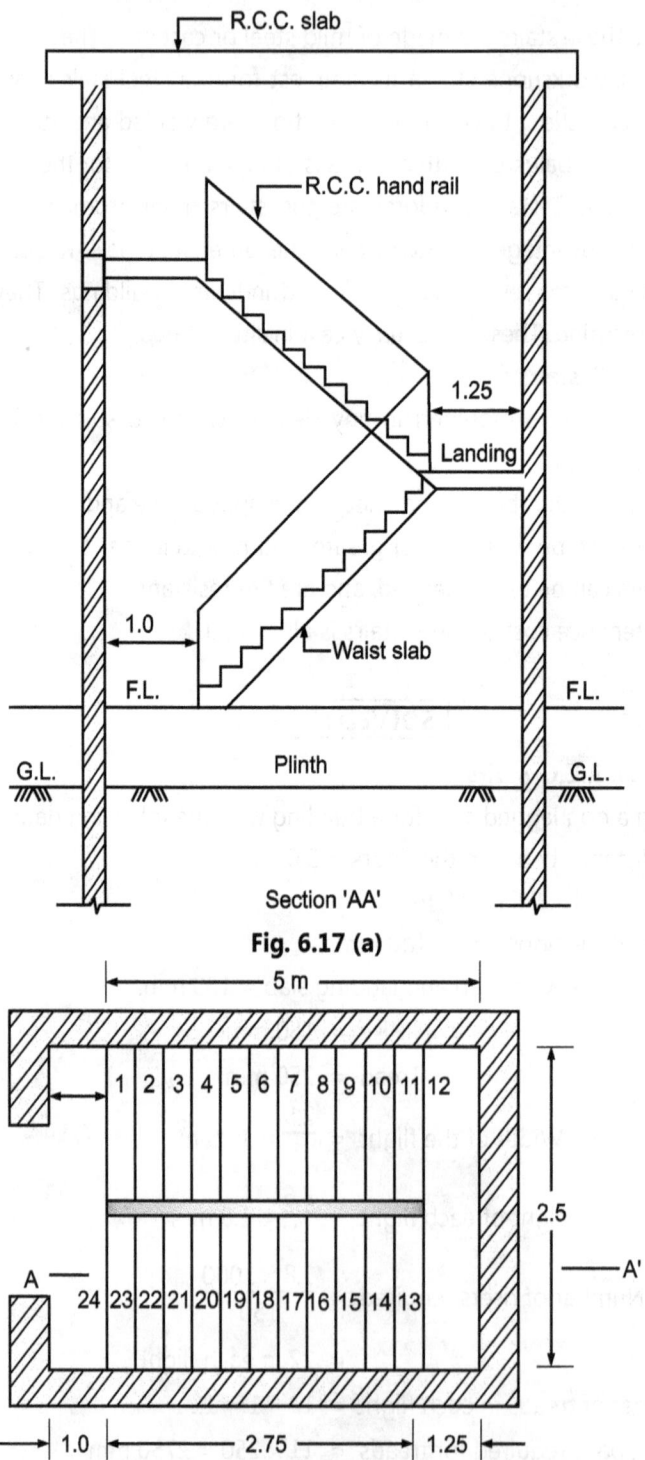

Fig. 6.17 (a)

Fig. 6.17 (b): Arrangement of risers in staircase, when total risers are divisible by 4

Example 2 : Calculate numbers of risers and treads in each flight for dog legged stair, floor to floor height is 3.3 m and riser is 150 mm. **[P.U. Nov. 2007]**

Solution : Given data :

$$\text{Floor to floor height} = 3.3 \text{ m}$$
$$\text{Riser} = 150 \text{ mm}$$
$$\therefore \quad \text{Total number of risers} = \frac{3300}{150} = 22$$

Assuming two flights, number of risers in each flight = 11 number and number of treads in each flight = 11 – 1 = 10 number.

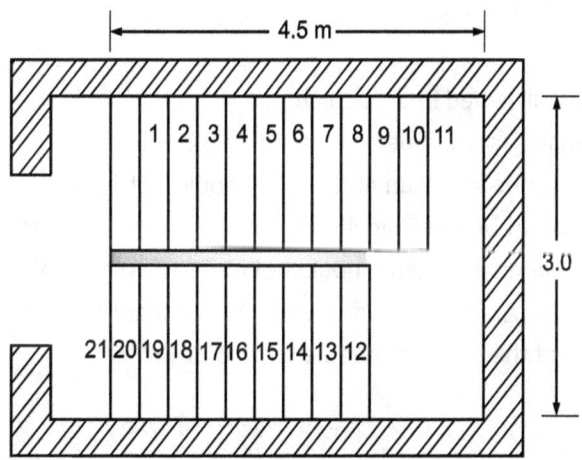

Fig. 6.18: Arrangement of risers in staircase, when total risers are even, but not divisible by 4

Example 3 : Plan a staircase for a residential building in which the vertical distance between each floor is 3.36 m. The size of the stair hall is limited to 4.5 × 3 m.

Solution : Given data :

(i)   Floor to floor height = 3.36 m

Let,   Width of landing = 1.5 m = Width of stairs.

Assume,   Rise = 16 cm

$\therefore$ Total number of risers = $\frac{3.36 \times 100}{16}$ = 21 risers $\Rightarrow$ 11 in first flight, 10 in second flight

Provide 11 risers in each flight.

$\therefore$ Number of treads in first flight = 11 – 1 = 10

                 in second flight = 10 – 1 = 9

6.5 ESCALATORS

A power driven, inclined, continuous stairs, used for ascending or descending, is known as an **Escalator**. It has continuous automatic operation, hence does not need any operator. Escalators are used when there is need to move more number of people from one floor to another. They have large capacity with low power consumption. The main components of an escalator are a steel trussed framework, hand rails and an endless belt with steps.

The arrangement of escalators in each floor may be either parallel or criss-cross. Escalators are more preferable at places where movement of large number of people is involved e.g. Airports, Molls, Exhibition halls, Railway stations etc.

Important points to be observed in an escalator :
1. Angle of inclination should be between 30 to 32°.
2. Tread should not be less than 40 cm, rise should not be more than 20 cm and width of steps should not be less than 45 cm and should not be more than 105 cm.
3. The rate of movement of steps should not be 30 to 40 m/min.
4. Escalators are generally installed in pair. One of them is used for carrying on upper floor people and the other for people moving down.

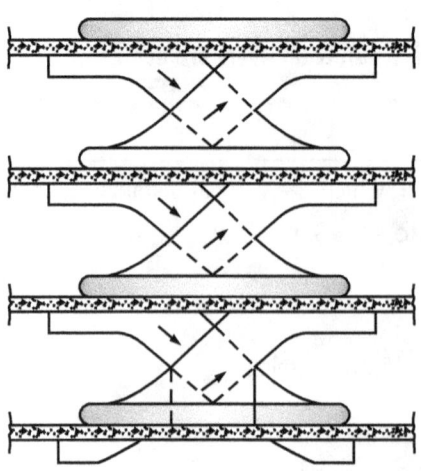
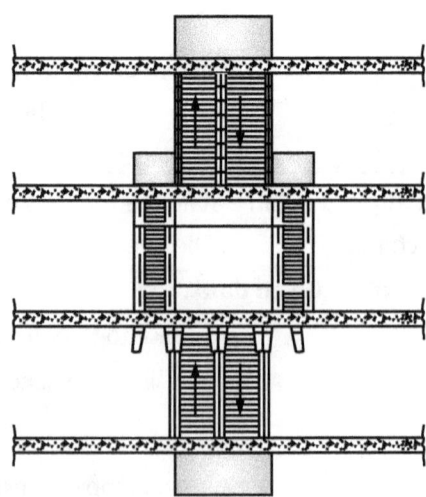

(a) Criss-cross arrangement of escalators　　　(b) Parallel arrangement of escalators

Fig. 6.19

6.6 RAMPS

Ramps are the inclined surfaces used for the easy movement between different floors. These are essentially useful when more number of people or vehicles has to move from one floor to another. Ramps are usually provided in Hospitals, Garages, Railway station, Town halls, Stadiums, Office buildings, Exhibition halls, Schools of physically handicapped children etc. They must be constructed with non-slip surfaces. They may be straight or curved.

Some essential requirements for the construction of ramps :
1. Slope for the ramp should be 10 to 15%.
2. For pedestrian traffic, minimum width of ramp should be 75 cm and maximum 2 m.
3. For carrying vehicles and machinery, width of ramp should be 4 m to 8 m with slope of 10%.
4. Hand rails must be provided on either side of ramp.
5. For powered ramps, slope should be 8 to 11° and speed in between 47 to 60 m/min.

6.7 LIFT

For multi-storeyed buildings, the installation of lift is must, to avoid fatigue in climbing up the stairs and for quick vertical circulation.

Elevators or lifts are used in buildings having more than four storey height. The provision of lifts in the structure is a highly specialised job. Some provisions are required to be made in the building the layout to accommodate lift and other accessories like operating devices. A vertical shaft with opening at the floor level is provided. The shaft is located at a suitable place such as by the side of the stair or within the open well of the stair.

Open Well of the Stair :
The various components of electric driven lifts are car or cab, hoist wire ropes, driving machine, control equipment, counter weight, hoist way rails, penthouse etc. The car is a cage of light weight metal which is supported on a structural frame. The wire ropes attached at the top of car raises or lowers the car in the shaft. They pass over a grooved motor driven sheave and are fixed to the counter weights. The path of counter weight and the car is controlled by set of T-shaped guide rails. The control and operating machinery may be located at top of the lift shaft. Safety springs or buffers are located at basement. Depending upon function, lifts may be classified as passenger lifts, goods lifts and service lifts.

6.8 LADDER

Ladders may be of fixed type or moveable type. They may be of wooden or cast iron. Pitch in ladder vary from 75 to 85°, there is no hand rail provided to the ladder. Fixed ladders are similar to stairs except that they are usually of metal and are used as a means of access to roofs. Ladders are also used to have access to water tank, wells, sewer pipes, septic tanks, basements and mezanine floors.

REVIEW QUESTIONS

1. Explain the situation in which the following means of vertical circulation are favoured :
   (a) Escalators
   (b) Ramps
   (c) Elevators
   (d) Spiral stairs
2. Explain the concept of head room and state its value. State normally used values of rise and treads for a commercial building.
3. State the requirements of good stair with respect to :
   (a) Pitch
   (b) Head room
   (c) Location
   (d) Rise and tread
   (e) Number of steps in a flight
   (e) Width of stair.
4. Design a stair for stair case of size 2.40 m × 4.60 m. Floor to floor height is 3.15 m state number of risers, value of rise, width of landing, height of baluster, value of going and number of risers in each flight.

   Hint: Assume riser of 15 cm. Therefore, total risers = $\frac{3.15}{0.15}$ = 21. Proceed as per solved example 3. Fig. 6.18.
5. Draw a typical cross-section illustrating arrangements in a lift well. State the function of each component.
6. Write a short note on Escalators.
7. Write down the thumb rules used in design of stair. Explain the following terms with sketch :
   (a) String
   (b) Newel post
   (c) Rise
   (d) Riser
8. Write down types of stairs as per geometric design and describe any one in detail.

9. As a site incharge, if demolition of building in congested area is to be carried out, what preventive measures or precautions you will take ?
10. What is Elevator ? Explain important terms used in it.
11. Explain the following terms :
    (a) Baluster
    (b) Nosing
    (c) Head room
    (d) Pitch.
12. Design a suitable staircase for a residential building, using the following data :
    (a) Size of the stair hall – 4.80 × 2.40.
    (b) Floor to floor height – 3.40 m.
    (c) Thickness of slab – 120 mm.
    Assume suitable data if necessary. Draw a detailed designed plan only.
    Hint: Assume risers of 17 cm. Therefore, total risers = $\frac{3.40}{0.17}$ = 20. Proceed as per solved example 1. Fig. 6.17.
13. Write down essential requirements for Escalators.
14. Give the plan of dog legged stair. Explain the design procedure for dog legged stair in detail.
15. Write a short note on lift.
16. State the requirements of a good vertical circulation.
17. State the different types of stairs based on materials of construction. Explain any one in detail.
18. Explain the following :
    (a) Tread, (b) Going, (c) Riser, (d) Header, (e) Nosing, (f) Balustrade.
19. What is vertical transportation ? What are ramps and escalators ?
20. What special consideration should be kept in view while designing stair cases ?
21. State the different means of vertical circulations. Explain escalators in detail.
22. Name the different types of stairs and draw a dog-legged stair.
23. Write notes on : (a) Steel stairs, (b) Bifurcated stair.
24. Design a R.C.C. dog-legged staircase and draw a detailed plan for an office building, a staircase room available is 3 m × 5 m with the outer wall thickness of 0.23 m. Height of the ceiling is 3.6 m. The thickness of R.C.C. slab is 0.10 m.
25. Write down the essential requirements of escalators.
26. Write a short note on ramps.

BUILDING CONSTRUCTION AND MATERIALS   STAIRS

27. Discuss the various considerations that are made in planning of staircases. Illustrate the different types of staircases generally used, indicating their suitability for specific use.
28. What are the limitations on different types of staircases in regard to their rise and tread ? How would you choose them for :
    (a) House   (b) School
    (c) Hospital   (d) Railway Station
29. What shall happen –
    (a) If the slope of the staircase is less than 25° and more than 40° with the horizontal ?
    (b) If a straight flight stair is erected to reach first floor without any midlanding.

Unit - VI

Chapter 7

ROOFS AND ROOF COVERINGS

7.1 INTRODUCTION

Roofs form important part of superstructure and serves the following functions :
1. It should offer adequate protection against natural forces like heat, sound, rain, etc.
2. It should sustain various stresses due to dead load, wind load, etc.
3. It should also enhance aesthetic sense of building.
4. It should be easy to maintain and durable.
5. It should be economical.
6. Roofs constructed out of materials of inferior quality, bad workmanship and inadequate attention to safety practices often leads to permanent source of nuisance and maintenance. Hence, it is essential that adequate steps are taken to guard against the same.

This chapter deals with these aspects.

7.2 GALVANIZED CORRUGATED IRON SHEETS

These sheets are extensively used as a roof covering material in factories, workshops, sheds, cheap buildings etc. Actually, these sheets have been superseded, particularly for superior work, by asbestos cement sheets. Though galvanized corrugated iron sheets do not have an attractive appearance but still they are widely used as they are very durable, fire-proof, light in weight and require no maintenance. These sheets are manufactured in a form which have the corrugations (i.e. a series of parallel depressions) from one end to another. These sheets are laid with corrugations running down the slope of the roof. The purpose of corrugations is to impart additional strength to thin iron sheets and to discharge the water quickly away from the sheet. The iron sheets are galvanized with zinc to protect them from the rusting action of wet weather. Sometimes, these sheets are covered with ordinary half-round country tiles so as to maintain the inside coolness of the building by preventing the transmission of heat through roofing.

7.2.1 Laying and Fixing of Galvanized Corrugated Iron Sheets

It is explained as follow :

(i) These sheets are light in weight, so it can be fixed easily.

(ii) It is generally 0.6 to 0.76 m wide, 1.37 m to 3.6 m long and of 1.625 to 6.559 mm gauge.

(iii) The sheets are fixed to timber purlins at intervals about 0.8 m apart with special galvanized screws and washers driven through holes drilled in the crowns of corrugations.

(iv) The sheets may also be fixed to steel angle purlins by means of hook bolts.

(v) All bolts should be in white lead.

(vi) The lap of 15 cm in its length should be provided. The side lap should extend one and a half corrugations.

(vii) Wind ties should be fixed along the eaves of the roof and the ventilators. Slot holes should be provided for expansion and contraction.

Special sections are available for covering hips, ridges and valleys.

It is shown in Fig. 7.1.

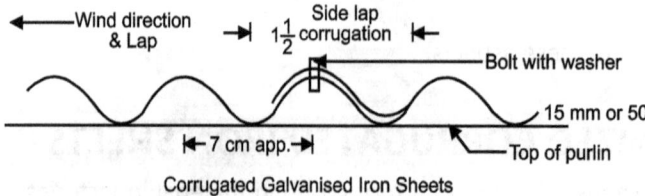

Corrugated Galvanised Iron Sheets

Fig. 7.1 : Fixing of CGI sheets

7.3 A.C. SHEETS

A.C. sheets (unreinforced corrugated and semi-corrugated A.C. sheet IS : 459 – 1970).

These sheets are light in weight, tough, durable, fire resistant, not susceptible to the attack of vermine, easy to cut, low maintenance, easy to fix, high speed of construction and cheap. On account of these advantages, A.C. sheet roof covering is adopted for workshop, factories, garages, offices, temporary sheets etc. A.C. sheets consist of Asbestos fibres (@ 15%) bonded together by cement.

Asbestos cement roof coverings are supplied in flat, corrugated and ribbed sheets in various sizes. Ribbed sections are available with ribs at a spacings of 30 to 40 cm. The A.C. sheets are fixed at a very low cost as they can be cut, sawn or screwed easily where desired A.C. sheets are obtained in the following three types, but in various lengths 1 to 3 metres, rising in 15 cm increments :

   (i) Everite big six corrugated A.C. sheets.
   (ii) Everite standard A.C. sheets.
   (iii) Turnall trafford A.C. tiles.

The particulars of these three types are given in the following Table 7.1.

Table 7.1 : Showing Particulars of Asbestos Cement Sheets

	Types of A.C. sheets	Standard lengths in metres	Laid width in metres	Thickness in mm	Side laps in cm	No. of corrugations	Pitch in cm	Depth in cm
(i)	Everite big six corrugated A.C. sheets.	1 to 3 m in 5 cm rises	1.05 m	6 mm	5 cm or 0.5 corrugation	$7\frac{1}{2}$	13 cm	5.5 cm
(ii)	Everite standard A.C. sheets	1 to 3 m	1.05 m	6 mm	10 cm or 1.5 corrugations	$10\frac{1}{2}$	5.5 cm	2.5 cm
(iii)	Turnall Trafford A.C. tiles	1.2 to 3 m, in 15 cm rises	1.09 m	6 mm	10 cm or 1 corrugation	'4' but with alternate flat portions	34 cm	5.0 cm

Table 7.2 : Dimensional tolerances for corrugated and semicorrugated sheets appear IS 459 – 1970 are as under.

(All dimensions in mm, figures in bracket indicate tolerances)

Type of sheet	Depth of corrugation	Pitch of corrugation	Overall Width	Effective Width	Thickness Nominal	Length of Sheet
Corrugated sheet	48 (+ 3)	146 + 6	1050 + 10	1010 + 10	6 mm (+) Free	1750, 2000
Semi-corrugated sheet	45 − 5	338 − 2	1100 − 2	1014 − 5	6 mm (− 0.5)	2500 or 3000

7.3.1 Laying and Fixing of A.C. Sheet

It is explained in the following steps :
   (1) Asbestos cement sheets are fixed to either timber or steel purlins directly.
   (2) A.C. sheets are laid from right to left starting at eaves.
   (3) The sheets are always fixed through the crowns of the corrugations.

(4) To connect the purlins and the sheets 8 mm diameter galvanized hook bolt is generally used. The length of this bolt is governed by the size of the purlins.
(5) The hook is engaged to the edge of the purlin and is secured by a nut. To ensure water tight joint, lead cupped and asbestos washers are also provided.
(6) The minimum overlap for lengthening is 15 cm and for widening the overlap is 60 to 100 mm or one and half corrugations.
(7) The unsupported overhang sheets should not be more than 30 cm.
(8) The ridge is formed with the aid of a pair of ridge capping. In this process, normally mitered joint is used for connection.
(9) An eaves filler piece is used to fill in the underside of the corrugations.

The details are shown in Fig. 7.2.

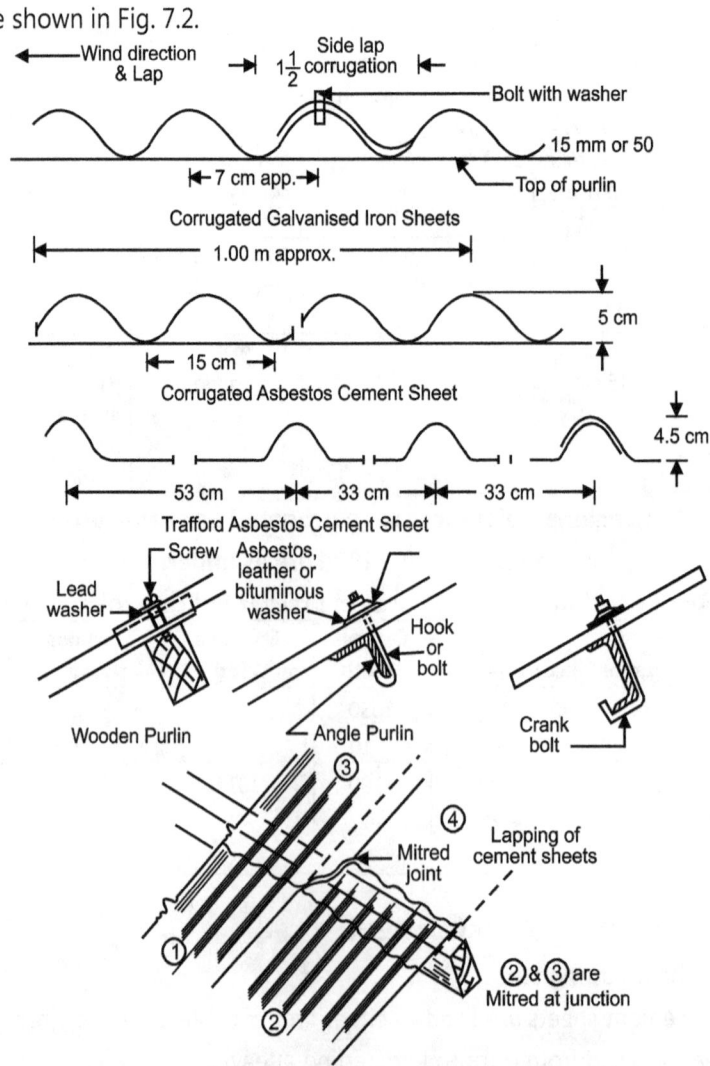

Fig. 7.2 : Details of laying and fixing of A.C. sheet

7.3.2 Asbestos Cement Products

The basic stages in the manufacture of asbestos cement are as follows :

(1) Preparation of the raw stuff consisting of several grades of fibre;
(2) Crushing of the mixture into finer fibres;
(3) Mixing with portland cement (by dry, wet, or dry/wet process);
(4) Forming and pressing (for some sheet products);
(5) Preliminary hardening;
(6) Mechanical working (cutting corrugation, etc.);
(7) Final hardening;
(8) Surface finishing (if required).

With the wet process which is most commonly used in the industry, a liquid suspension of asbestos cement is formed into a thin layer on a wire-mesh cylinder, dehydrated, and compacted.

Corrugated sheets are made by shaping a semi-finished product. Finishing sheets are additionally compressed on hydraulic presses under a pressure of 25 to 40 MPa. Formed sheets are heat treated in steam curing chambers. The combination wet/dry process and continuous rolling of large sheets can be almost completely automated (in fact, 98% of all process operations are carried out automatically) and are, therefore, the most promising technologies.

Owing to the presence of reinforcing asbestos fibres, sheets 5 to 10 mm thick can be formed to various shapes before the cement has set. Hardened asbestos cement exhibits a considerable mechanical strength (its compressive and bending strength being as high as 90 MPa and 30 MPa, respectively), weather resistance, resistance to freezing (it can sustain upto 50 cycles of alternate freezing and thawing), durability, fire resistance, impermeability to water, alkali resistance and low thermal conductivity. It has a lower density (1500 to 1950 kg m^{-3}) than plain concrete and ferrocement. On the other hand, asbestos cement has a poor impact strength (its toughness ranges between 1.5 and 2.5 kJ m^{-2}, being about 30% lower for non-compressed materials) and can readily warp in service. Fortunately, this can be rectified by using more fibre or by giving the material a water repellency treatment.

Asbestos cement products include roofing and facing tile, and sheets (plain, corrugated, or otherwise patterned), pressure and non-pressure pipes and sleeve couplings, ventilation skips, window sills, electrical insulating boards, wall cladding, special purpose products, vases, flower pots and tubes, etc.

7.4 MANGALORE TILES (IS 654-1972)

These are flat roof tiles of special pattern with suitable keys and projection for fixing to roof.

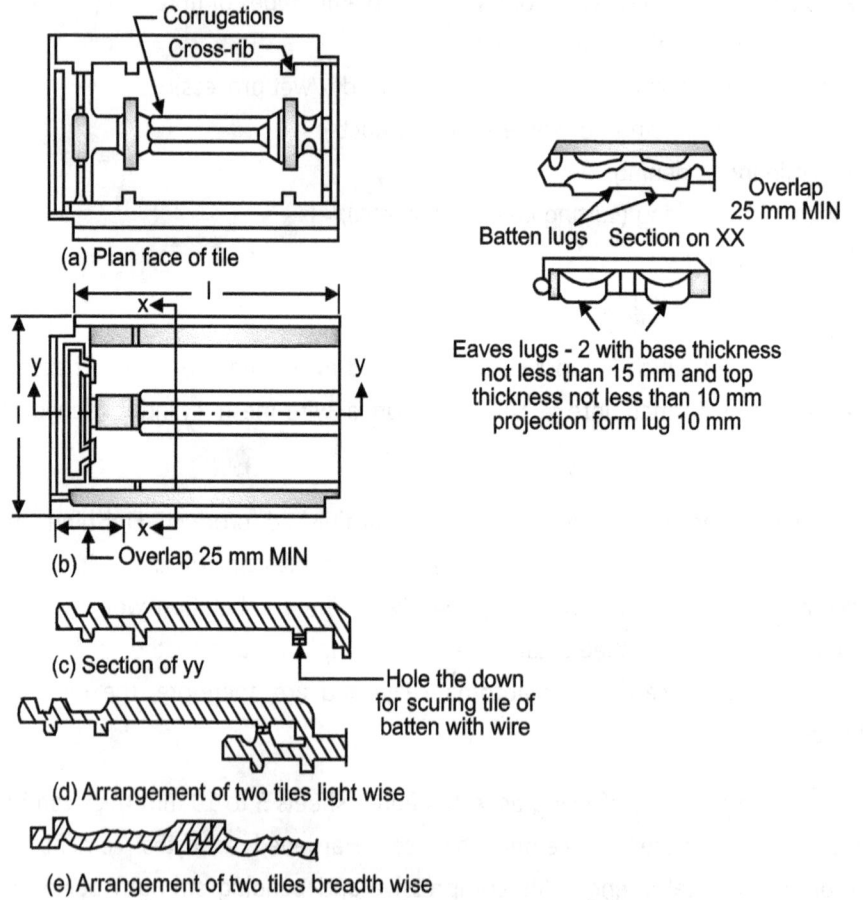

Fig. 7.3 : Mangalore tiles

On the basis of percentage of absorption, breaking load, etc. the tiles are classified as class AA and class A as detailed below :

Table 7.3

Size of Tile	Min. Breaking load kgf		Maximum water absorption %	
	Class AA	Class A	Class AA	Class A
410 × 235 mm	100	80	19	24
420 × 250	110	90	19	24
425 × 260	110	90	19	24

Minimum overlap is 60 mm lengthwise and average weight of tile should be between 2 to 3 kg, 1.6 to 2 mm diameter. Tie down holes are provided, to fix tile with galvanized wire. The tiles are well burnt and uniform in texture.

2 batten lugs and 2 eave lugs of thickness more than 15 mm are provided at bottom. The two lugs provided at top have thickness of 10 mm. The projections of batten lug shall be 7 to 17 mm and that of eave lug shall be 10 mm. For better understanding these are tabulated below.

Table 7.4

	Nos.	Thickness (mm)		Projection (mm)
		At top	At bottom	
Batten lug	2	> 10	> 15	> to 12
Eave lug	2	> 10	> 15	> 10

7.4.1 Roofing Slate Tiles : (IS 6250 – 1981)

In regions, like Himachal Pradesh slate tiles are used as roofing material.

The slate should have reasonably straight cleavage and grains should be longitudinal. The tiles should have uniform thickness, which should not be less than 15 mm. The tiles should be rectangular in shape, with reasonably full corners and edges shall be true. The standard sizes of tiles are :

600 × 300 × 15 mm thickness (minimum) or

500 × 250 × 15 mm thickness

The other physical requirements of tile are :
(i) Water absorption < to 2% by weight and should have low permeability so that, water does not ooze from the bottom.
(ii) **Sulphuric acid immersion test :** During this test, the tile should not show any sign of delamination clay, and shall not show gaseous evolution during immersion.
(iii) **Modulus of rupture :** It should not be less than 60 N/mm^2 (dry) and 40 N / mm^2 (wet).

7.4.2 Limestone Slabs and Tiles (IS 1128 - 1974)

These are used in flooring and face work. These absorb very less water, have high strength and are quite durable. The physical requirements are given in the following Table 7.5.

Table 7.5

Characteristics	Requirement
1. Water absorption	< 0.15% by weight
2. Transverse strength	> 70 kgf/cm^2
3. Durability	Should not develop signs of spalling, disintegration of cracks.

These are available in lengths and breadths ranging from 15 to 150 cm and thickness from 15 to 95 mm. Stone used for the tiles should be without soft veins, cracks, flaws, shall have uniform texture, and curvature in any direction shall not be more than 5 mm.

7.4.3 Sand Stone Slabs and Tiles (IS 3622 - 1977)

These can be used in flooring, roofing and face work. The slabs and tiles can be of (i) rough cut or (ii) machine cut. Tolerance of ± 1 mm only is allowed in length and breadth in respect of machine cut slabs and tiles.

The dimensions of slabs and tiles are :

Table 7.6

Length	Breadth	Thickness
15 to 360 cm	15 to 90 cm	15 to 100 mm
In stages of 5 cm	5 cm	5 mm
Tolerance ± 1 mm	± 1 mm	± 3 mm

7.4.4 Marble Tiles (IS 1130 – 1969)

Two classes of tiles viz white and coloured are available. The beauty of the tile can be enhanced by adopting different finishes such as :
1. Sand or Abrasive finish : A flat non-reflective finish.
2. Hone finish : Velvety finish with little or no gloss.
3. Polished finish : Highly polished glossy surface. Square tiles of size 10 × 10 cm upto 60 × 60 cm in stages of 10 cm are available. (Tolerance + 4%). Thickness ranges between 18 to 24 mm.

Other physical requirements of tile are :
1. Moisture absorption (after 24 hours) < 0.4%.
2. Hardness (Mhos Scale) 3 min.
3. Specific gravity 2.5 min.

7.4.5 Earthen Ware, Stone Ware and Glazed Wares

1. Earthen stone ware is a clay product, manufactured from clay mixed with sand, crushed pottery, and is burnt at low temperature.
2. Stone ware is also a clay product manufactured by mixing refractory clay with crushed potter and powdered stone and is heated it to high temperature.
3. Glazing is a process of formation of thin, transparent layer at the surface, which becomes integral part of the article and protects the article from corrosive sewage water, sewer gases or weathering.

Articles such as stone ware pipes, sewer pipes, sanitary appliances, in bathrooms, toilets, floor tiles etc. are examples of glazed articles.

Following two methods are used for glazing :
   (a) Opaque or slip glazing
   (b) Salt glazing.

(a) Opaque or Slip Glazing :

A thin paste materials like quartz, basic oxide, oxides of zinc, lead, tin, china clay, feldspar etc. is made.

The article to be glazed is dried, and above mentioned paste is evenly applied, and the article is heated in furnace to a high temperature of 1300°C to 1400°C when the paste gets fused with the article and forms thin, transparent protective layer at the surface. Depending upon the contents of the paste, different beautiful colours are obtained. In this process, burning and glazing of article is achieved simultaneously.

(b) Salt Glazing :

The clay product to be glazed is heated at temperature of 1300° to 1400°C in kiln and common salt (sodium chloride) is thrown on the article to be glazed 2 or 3 times at an interval of time. Sodium salt melts, and vapourises. The vapour of sodium salt combines with the clay product and forms transparent protective layer.

SWG pipes (Stone Ware Glazed pipes) are glazed in this manner. Relatively, salt glazing is inferior to opaque glazing.

7.4.6 Glazed Earthen Ware Tiles (IS 777 – 1970)

Where cleanliness is very important such as in kitchen, hospitals, bathrooms, toilets etc. glazed earthen ware tiles and its associated fittings are used. The top surface to the tiles is glazed, whereas the under surface is unglazed to facilitate fixing of the tile to wall/floor. The tiles are available in two sizes. With joint thickness of 1 mm the overall size becomes 100 × 100 mm and 150 × 150 mm. Dimensional requirements are as under :

Table 7.7

1.	Dimensional requirement tolerance	99 × 99 mm ± 0.8 mm	149 × 149 mm ± 0.8 mm
2.	Thickness tolerance	5, 6, 7 mm ± 0.8 mm	5, 6, 7 mm ± 0.8 mm
3.	Warpage	+ 0.5 mm, – 0.3 mm	+ 0.7 mm – 0.4 mm

Performance requirements are as under :

1. Water absorption < 10%.
2. Impact strength 0.02 kgf m/cm.
3. Crazing (i.e. formation of fine cracks on the surface) should not show any sign of crazing after two cycles of test in an autoclave.
4. Glazed surface should be chemical resistant i.e. should not show any deterioration.

7.4.7 Testing of Tiles

Following three tests are carried out on tiles to assess its suitability :

1. Water absorption test.
2. Efflorescence test.
3. Impact test.

Water absorption test and efflorescence test is similar to that carried for bricks. In case of efflorescence test, tile is immersed on its end, in a dish containing distilled water to a depth not less than 2.5 cm.

Impact Test :

In this test, tile to be tested with face upward is placed on 25 mm thick rubber sheet. The sheet is placed on a hard smooth and level surface such as steel plate or concrete floor.

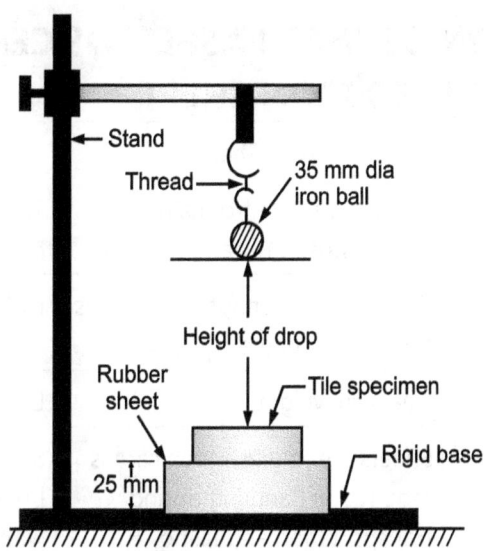

Fig. 7.4 : Impact test

A steel ball of 35 mm diameter and mass 170 gm is taken and tied to a hook by means of thread. Tile is centred, so that, on burning the thread, the ball is released and it falls exactly at the centre of the tile. The height of ball is raised from 10 cm, in steps of 5 cm, until tile specimen fractures. Average height of three specimen (taken at random from 500 tiles) is taken as resistance value of impact of tile. The specimen to be tested should be oven dried to temperature of 100 to 110°C, allowed to cool at room temperature.

By this test, toughness of tile is determined. The maximum height of drop of 53 mm diameter steel ball of mass 170 gm for class I, class II and class III tiles of different thickness shall be as under :

Table 7.8

Size of tile (mm)	Maximum height of drop of steel ball of 35 mm dia. × 170 gm (cm.)		
	Class I tile	Class II tile	Class III tile
1. 150 × 150 × 15	25	20	15
2. 150 × 150 × 20 and 200 × 200 × 20	60	50	40
3. 200 × 200 × 20	75	65	50
4. 250 × 250 × 30	80	70	60

7.5 COMPARISON BETWEEN ASBESTOS CEMENT SHEET AND GALVANISED IRON SHEET

Point of Comparison	A.C. Sheets	G.I. Sheets
1. Materials	These are made from a mixture of asbestos fibres and cement.	These are made of galvanized wrought iron.
2. Thickness	These sheets cannot be made as thin as G.I. sheets.	Light in weight.
3. Weight	Heavy in weight.	Light in weight
4. Care in handling and fixing	Sheets are fragile. Much care is required in handling during transportation and fixing.	Sheets are not liable to break and can be handled with little care.
5. Durability	Durable and do not corrode.	Durable, but gets corroded by atmospheric actions
6. Effect on acids and fumes	Not affected by acids and fumes.	Affected by acids and fumes
7. Sound insulation	More or less sound insulating and do not produce much noise during rainfall over the sheets.	Not at all sound insulating and produce noise during rainfall over the sheets.
8. Resistance to fire	These are fire resisting.	These sheets become deformed when a fire occurs.
9. Possibility of damage	There is every possibility of sheets getting damaged due to external causes.	Possibility of getting damaged due to external causes is less.
10. Workability	Care is required in working with A.C. sheets.	One can easily work with G.I. sheets.
11. Initial cost	High initial cost	Initial cost is low.
12. Maintenance	Maintenance cost is nil, if not damaged. No painting is required	Maintenance cost is due to periodic painting against corrosion.
13. Appearance	Neat and pleasing appearance can be achieved.	The appearance is not pleasing even if a neat finish is made.

7.6 TYPES OF ROOF AND THEIR SUITABILITY

7.6.1 Types of Roof

Roof types are governed by slope of the roof, material used for roof, span of it etc.

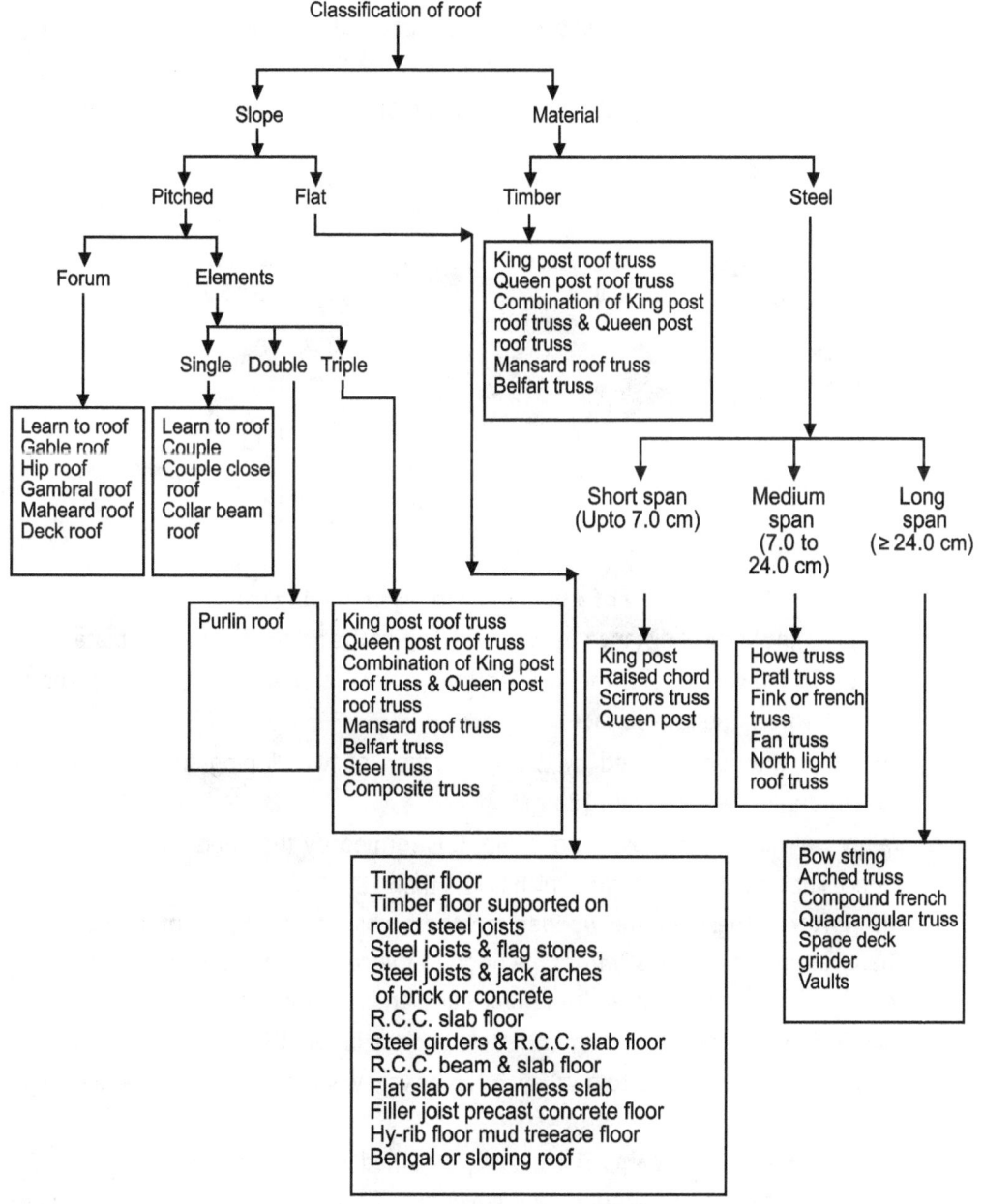

Chart : Classification of Roof

7.6.2 Technical Terms in Sloping Roof and Roof Trusses

Fig. 7.5 shows various elements of sloping roof and roof trusses. These elements are defined below.

1. **Ridge** : It is the apex line of the sloping roof.
2. **Span** : It is the clear distance between the supports of an arch, beam or roof truss.
3. **Pitch of roof** : It is the inclination of sides of a roof to the horizontal plane. The pitch of the roof is usually expressed either in terms of degrees (angle) or as a ratio of rise to span.

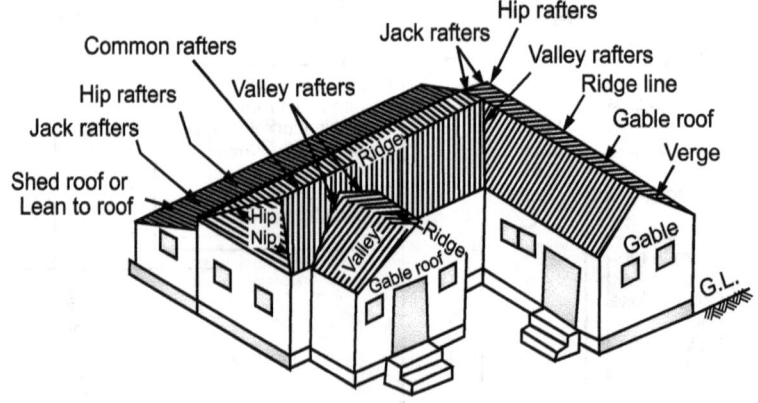

Fig. 7.5 : View of a building with basic sloping roofs.

4. **Rise** : It is the vertical distance between the top of the ridge and the wall plate.
5. **Eaves** : The lower edge of the inclined roof surface is called eaves. From eaves, the rain water from the roof surface drops down.
6. **Hip** : It is the ridge formed by the intersection of two sloping surfaces, when the exterior angle is greater than 180°.
7. **Valley** : A valley is the reverse of a hip. It is formed by the intersection of two roof surfaces having external angle, which is less than 180 degrees.
8. **Hip Rafters** : These are the wooden members which form the hip of a pitched roof. These rafters run diagonally from the ridge to the corners of the walls to support roof covering. They receive the ends of purlins and ends of jack rafters.
9. **Jack Rafters** : These are common rafters shorter in length which run from a hip to the eaves or from a ridge to a valley. A hip or valley is formed by the meeting of jack rafters.
10. **Common Rafters or Spars** : These are the inclined wooden members supporting the battens or boarding to support roof coverings. They run from a ridge to the eaves. They are normally spaced at 30 to 45 cm centre to centre, depending upon the roof covering material.

11. **Valley Rafters :** These are sloping rafters which run diagonally from the ridge to the eaves for supporting valley gutters. They receive the ends of the purlins and ends of jack rafters on both sides.
12. **Hipped End :** It is the sloped triangular surface formed at the end of a roof.
13. **Verge :** This is the edge of sheets, slates or tiles which projects beyond the gable end of the sloped roof.
14. **Ridge Piece, Ridge Beam or Ridge Board :** It is the horizontal wooden member, in the form of a beam or board, which is provided at the apex of a roof truss. It supports the common rafter fixed to it.
15. **Purlins :** These are the horizontal wooden or steel members, used to support common rafters of a roof when span is large. Purlins are supported on trusses or walls.
16. **Eaves Board or Facia Board :** It is a wooden plank or board fixed to the feet of the common rafter at the eaves. It is usually 20 - 25 mm thick and 20 - 25 cm wide. The ends of the lower most roof covering material rest upon it. The eaves gutter can also be secured against it.
17. **Barge Board :** It is the timber board used to hold the common rafter forming verge.
18. **Wall Plates :** These are long wooden members which are provided on the top of stone or brick wall, for the purpose of fixing the feet of the common rafters. These are embedded from sides and bottom in masonry of walls, almost at the centre of their thickness. Wall plates actually connect the walls to the roof.
19. **Post Plate :** This is similar to wall plate except that they run continuous, parallel to the face of wall, over the tops of the posts and support rafters at their feet.
20. **Battens :** These are thin strips of wood, called scantlings which are nailed to the rafters for lying roof materials above.
21. **Boardings, Sheeting or Sarking :** This consists of boards which are nailed to the upper edges of common rafters and to which tiles and other roofing materials are secured.
22. **Truss :** A roof truss is a frame work of triangles designed to support the roof covering or ceiling over rooms.
23. **Template :** This is a square or rectangular block, about 10 to 15 cm thick, which is placed below a beam or a truss, so as to spread the load over a larger area. It may be made of fine dressed flat stone, squared wood, concrete block or R.C.C. block.
24. **Cleats :** These are short sections of wood or steel [angle iron], which are fixed on the principal rafters or trusses to support the purlins.

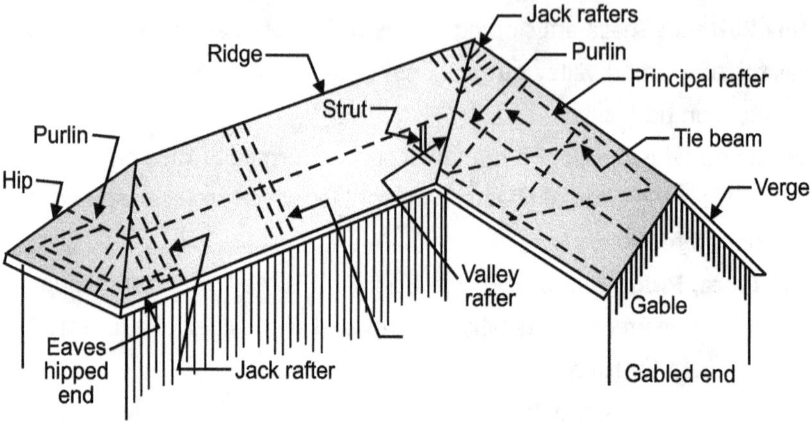

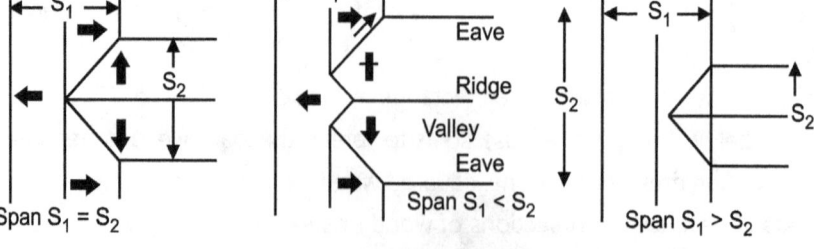

(a) Pitched roof, common terms

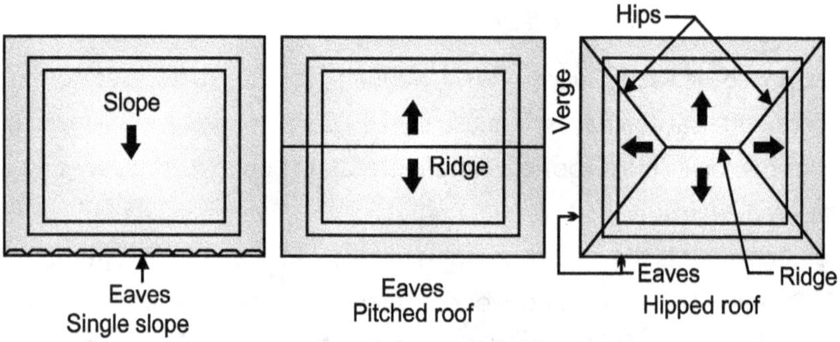

(b) Roofs of rectangular area

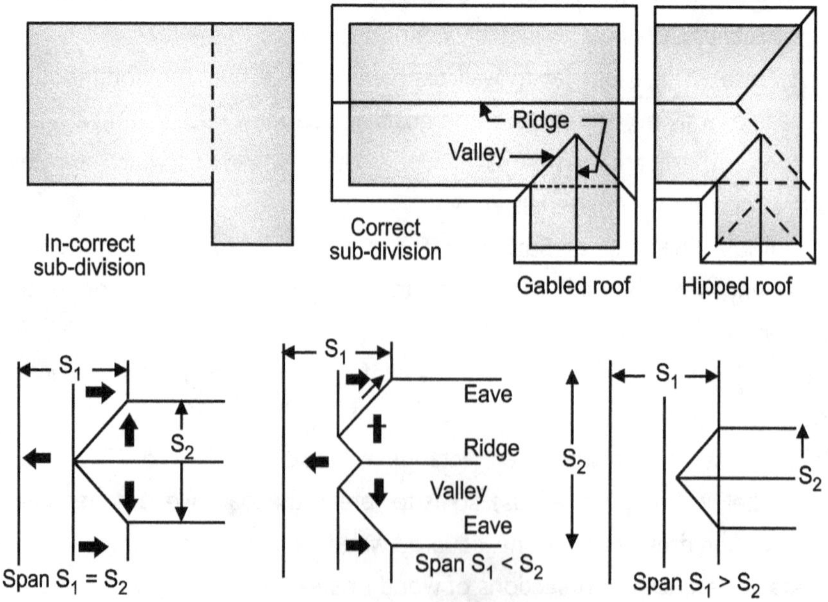

(c) Junctions of roofs of different spans

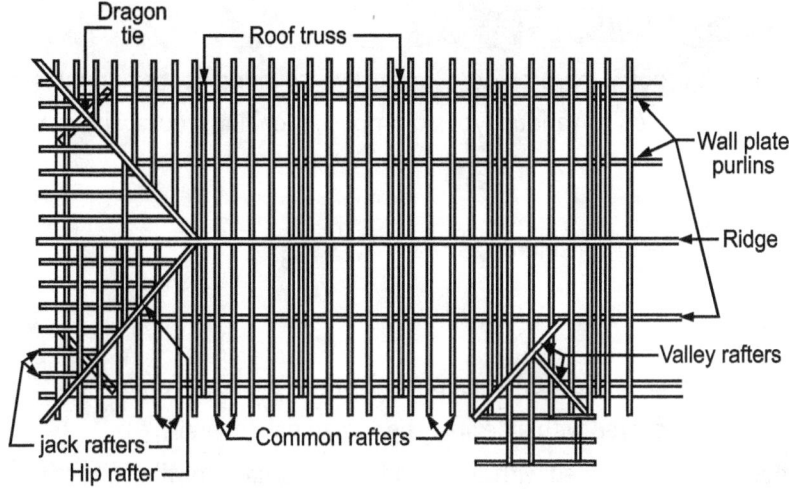

(d) Wood works for pitched roof

Fig. 7.6

7.6.3 Suitability of Roof

As per classification these are various types of roofs. Suitability of roof is governed by various factors like climatic conditions of the locality, slope of roof, durability, maintenance cost, appearance etc.

(1) **Mud Terrace Roof :** It is the cheapest and fiarly water tight. It is mainly used at places of light rainfall.

(2) **Bricks Concrete Terrace Roof :** It offers considerable water tight surface. It is mainly used in heavy rainfall region.

(3) **Madras Terrace Roof :** It is also called as "Brick Jelly or Composite Roof". It offers heat insulation and water tightness.

(4) **Jack Arch Flat Roofs :** It bears the load either from reinforcement or by arch action. It is not widely used. It does not offer pleasing appearance.

(5) **Bengal Terrace Roof :** It is mainly used in Bengal. It acts as porch. It covers verandah.

(6) **Shell :** It is three dimensional structures. It transfers the load on points of supports. It is mainly used for big area like factories, theatres, airport hangers.

(7) **Steel Structures :** It is economical. It is used from small span to large span. It offers good fire resistant. It is used for factories, sheds, etc.

(8) **Timber Roof :** It is less fire resistant. It is mainly used for small span structure. It is used in hilly and forest areas.

7.7 TYPES OF TRUSSES

The function of any roof is to provide a protective covering to the upper surface of the structure. As it is subjected to various types of imposed loadings, durability of the covering is very much important.

Based on span, roof can be considered as :

(1) Short Span :
- (a) Span is upto 7.0 m.
- (b) It is of traditional timber construction with flat or pitched profile.
- (c) Flat roofs are covered with a flexible sheet material generally.
- (d) Pitched roofs are covered with small units such as slates or tiles.

(2) Medium Span :
- (a) Span is varying from 7 m to 24 m.
- (b) The usual roof structure is a truss or lattice of standard steel sections.
- (c) Covering/sheeting may be corrugated asbestos cement or structural decking system.

(3) Long Span :

If span is greater than 24 m, it is considered as large span. Roofs for it are generally designed as girder, space deck or vaulting techniques.

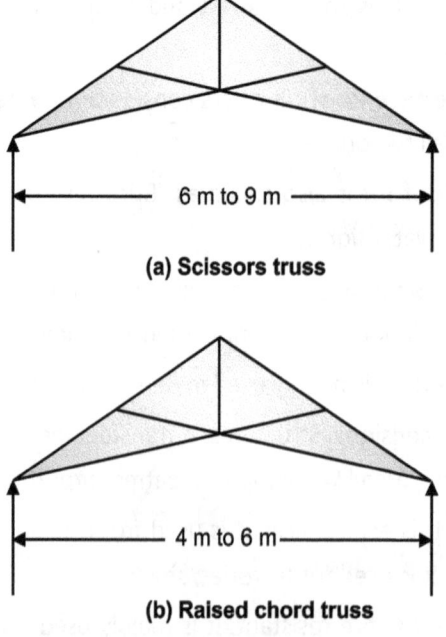

(a) Scissors truss

(b) Raised chord truss

Fig. 7.7 : Short span trusses

North light roof trusses are used for factories, workshops, etc. where natural light and ventilation are desired (Fig. 7.8 (a), (b), (c)).

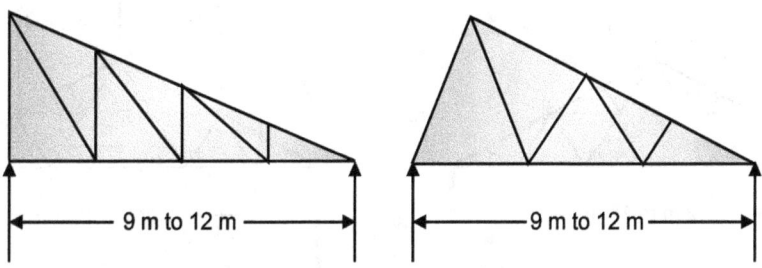

(a) North light trusses

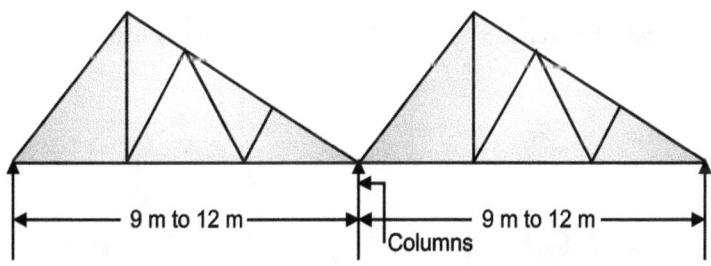

(b) North light or saw-tooth or weaving shed truss

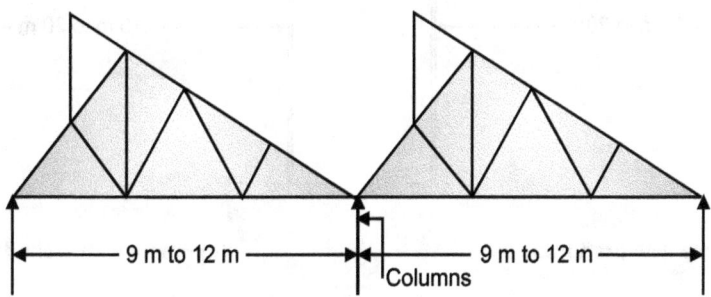

(c) Modified north light truss

Fig. 7.8 : Medium span north light steel trusses

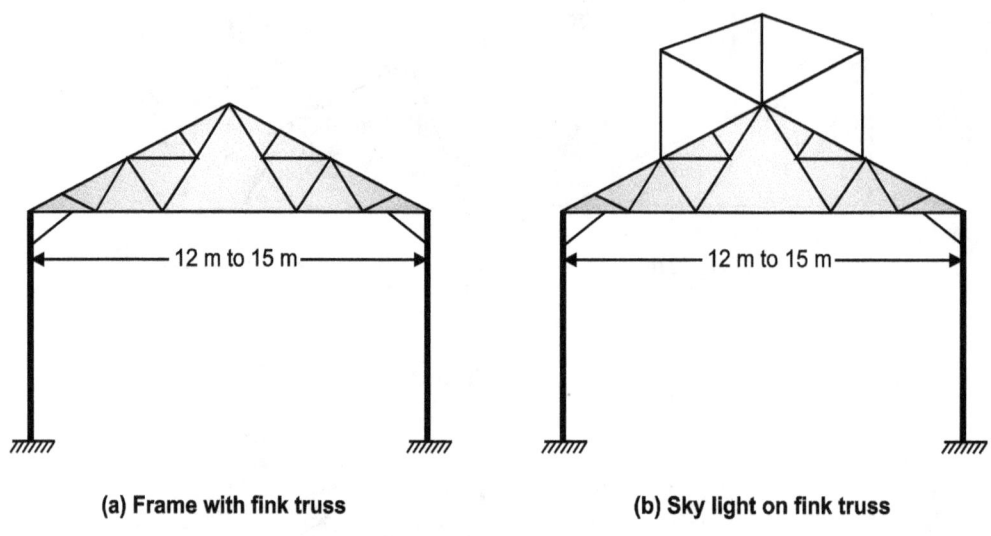

(a) Frame with fink truss

(b) Sky light on fink truss

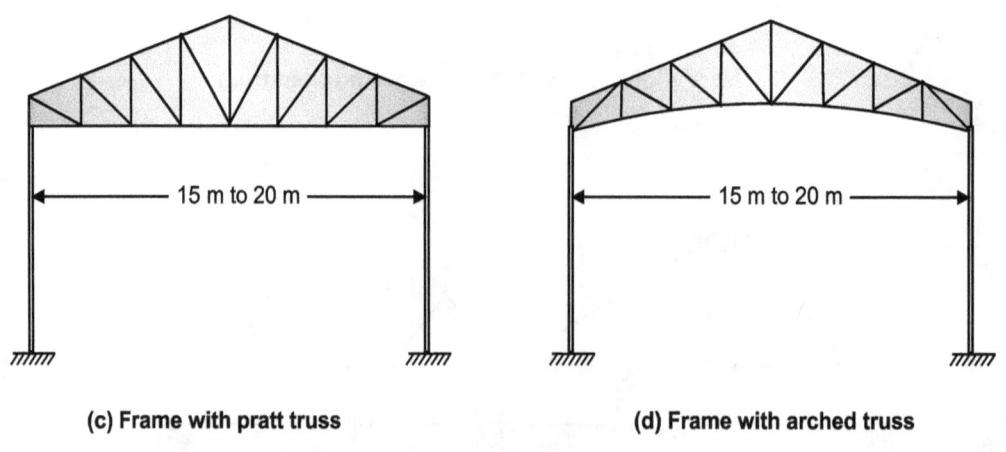

(c) Frame with pratt truss

(d) Frame with arched truss

Fig. 7.9 : Industrial building bents

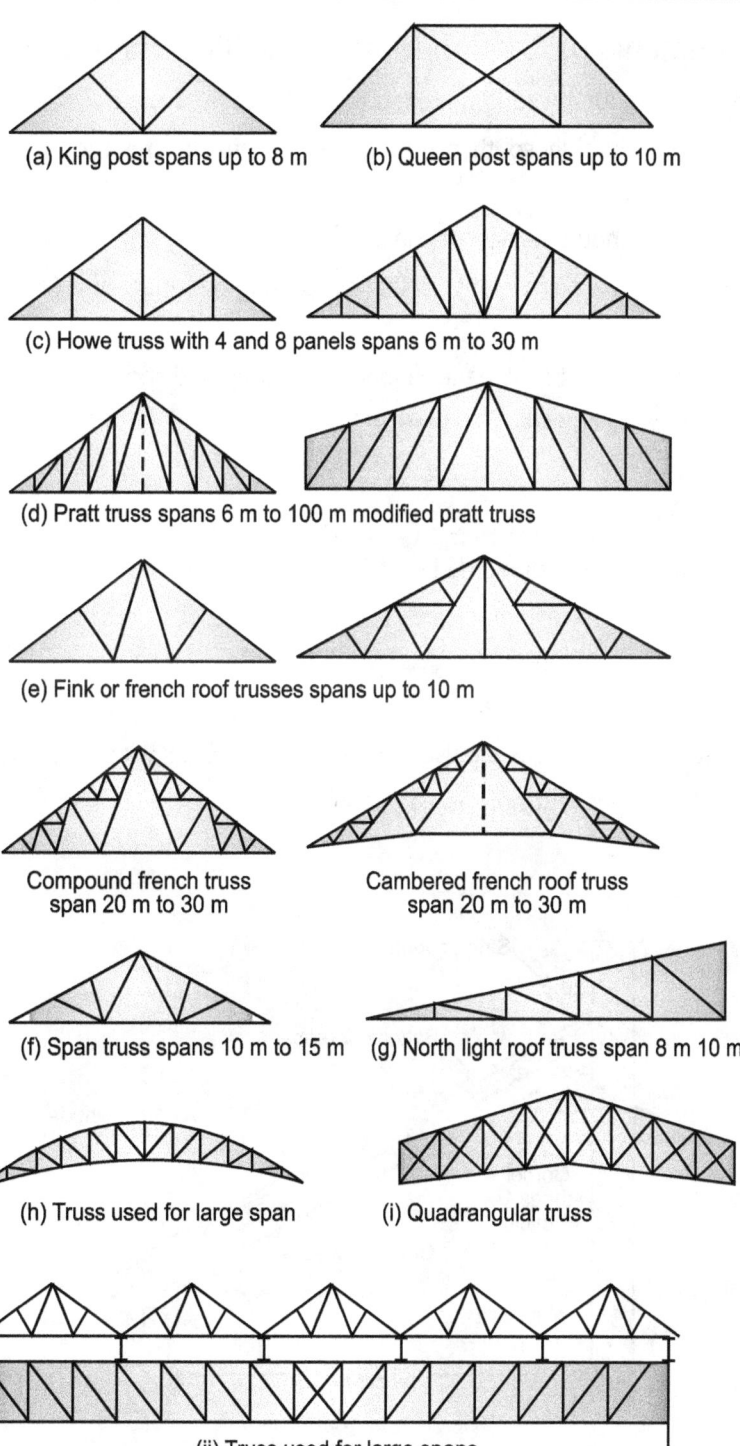

Fig. 7.10 : Various types of steel roof trusses

7.7.1 Requirements of Roofing Material for Steel Structure

The basic requirements for covering materials to steel roof trusses are :

(i) It should be durable so that throughout the life of the roof there will be less maintenance.

(ii) Fire resistance should be acceptable.

(iii) It should have less self-weight, so that supporting members of an economic size can be used.

(iv) Sufficient resistance to the penetration of rain, wind and snow.

(v) It should provide considerable thermal insulation.

7.7.2 Lean to Roof

(i) It is the simplest form of pitched roof. In this type rafters slope to one side only.

(ii) It's components are common rafters, wall plate, corbel stone, battens, roof covering, eaves board, string course etc.

(iii) Inclination of common rafter is limited to 30°.

(iv) The knee straps and bolts are used to connect the rafters with the posts.

(v) It is used for sheds, out-houses, verandah etc.

It is shown in Fig. 7.11.

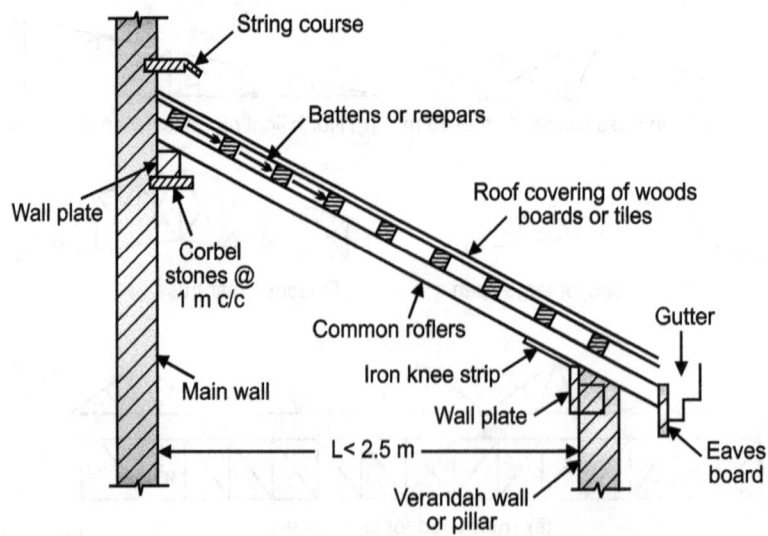

Fig. 7.11 : Lean to roof or verandah roof

7.7.3 King Post Truss Roof (Refer Fig. 7.12).

(i) It is suitable for short span.
(ii) It consists of two principal rafters or principals, a tie-beam, a king post and two struts.
(iii) It can be made sufficiently strong. Dimensions of different parts of it are defined with reference to the load they can carry.
(iv) Under various load combinations each member of this truss is subjected to the following stresses.

    Principal rafter – Compressive stress
    Struts – Compressive stress
    King post – Tensile stress
    Tie-beam – Tensile stress
    Common rafters – Transverse stress
    Purlins – Transverse stress.

(v) The functions of various elements of this truss are as given below :
    (a) Principal Rafter : It supports the framework of roof.
    (b) Tie Beam : It receives the ends of the principal rafters. It prevents the walls from being thrust outwards.
    It should be in as long length as possible.
    (c) Cleats : It is fixed on principal rafters to prevent the purlins from tilting. It is usually spiked.
    (d) Pole Plates : It is horizontal timber piece. It runs across the top of tie beam at their ends or on principal rafters near their feet.
    (e) Common Rafter : It is usually rest on the purlin. Its upper end is supported by ridge piece, its middle by the purlins and its lower ends by pole plates.
    (f) Reepers : It is nailed across the common rafter. It supports roof covering. The ends of the tie beam should not built into walls. The loads at the ends of a tie-beam should not be concentrated type. So it should be placed on bed plates.
    (g) King Post : It is a vertical member. It prevents the tie beam from sagging at its centre.
    (h) Bed Plates : It is called as bed blocks truss plates or templates. It receives ends of tie beam and principal rafter.
    (i) Struts : It supports centres of principal rafters. It prevents sagging of it.
    (j) Purlins : It is stout piece. It is usually placed over the principal rafters. It supports the common rafters.

(vi) Following joints are used at various junctions in king post truss.
    (a) Joint between principal rafter and king post – mortice and tenon joint.
    (b) Joint between principal rafter and tie beam – mortice and tenon joint or briddle joint or an oblique joint.
    (c) Joint between principal rafter and strut – an oblique mortice and tenon joint.
    (d) Joint between king post and tie beam – tenon joint. It is strengthened by a wrought iron or mild steel stirrup strap.

Joints of King post truss are shown in Fig. 7.12.

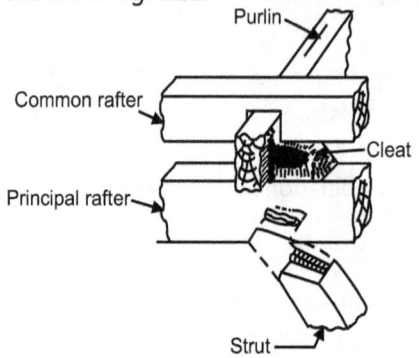

Fig. 7.12 : Joint of strut and principal rafter

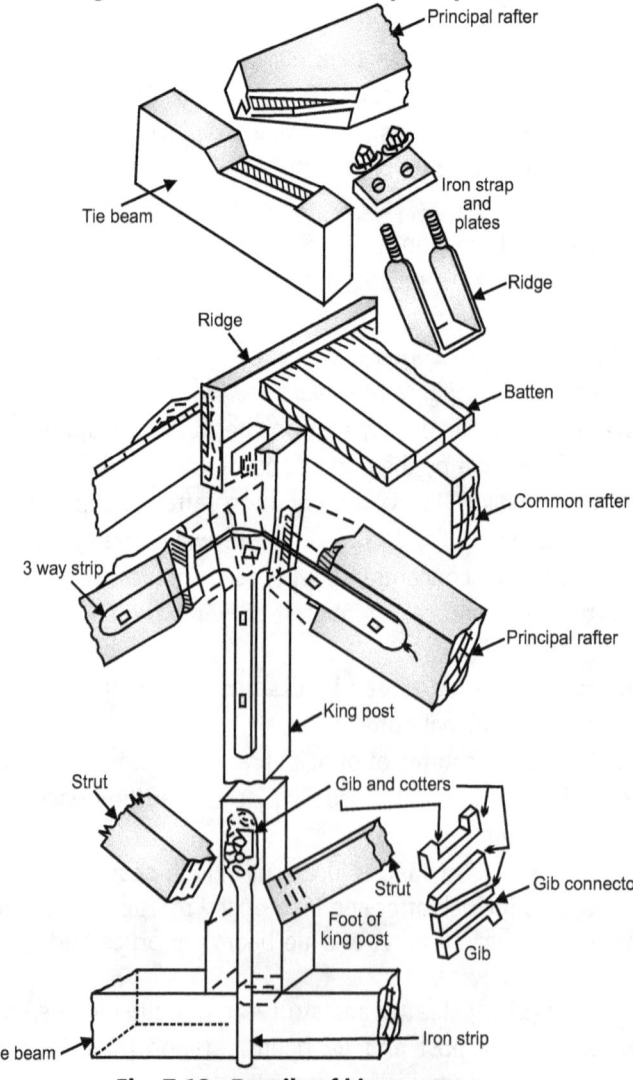

Fig. 7.13 : Details of king post truss

The ridge piece or ridge board is held in position by slotting the head of the kind post.

In combined members at a joint and that at the support it is essential to observe that the centre lines of various members intersect at the point and at the support in the joint through which the load line or reaction line passes.

7.7.4 Design and Construction of Steel Roof Trusses

The following points regarding design and construction of steel roof trusses should be noted :

(i) All the members of steel roof trusses are either designed for compression or for tension, and no bending stresses are allowed in them.

(ii) Size of various members of the truss and their arrangement depend upon the roof slope, span, loading, wind pressure and centre to centre distance of the trusses.

(iii) The compression members such as struts should be as short as possible to avoid buckling and the principal rafters subjected to transverse stresses should not be longer than 3 metres maximum. The tension members should be braced together.

(iv) Normally, angles irons or channel sections are used as struts, whereas T-sections are best suited for use as principal rafters. Round or flat section can be used for tension members. In an ideal design all the members of structure should fail simultaneously. In practice, angles less than $50 \times 50 \times 6$ mm are not used.

(v) All the members of the truss should be arranged to form triangles so that the truss will not deform to a greater extent.

(vi) The distance between the steel roof trusses should not exceed 3 metres. This distance or spacing is more for light roofs.

(vii) Small trusses are fabricated (riveted or bolted together) at the factory or workshop and transported to the working site, whereas larger trusses are usually fabricated and assembled together at the job site.

(viii) The joints or connections of members to each other are called noded or panel points are made by means of thin flat plates called gusset plates. Though the thickness of gusset plates depends upon the bearing value of the rivets employed, but usually, thickness of 6 mm and 10 mm are provided for small and large roof structures, respectively.

(ix) In riveting, the pitch of the rivets should not be less than 3 times the diameter of the rivets. The maximum pitch is 15 cm for compression members and 20 cm for tension members. Further, a minimum distance from the centre of the rivet to the edge of the member must not be less than 25 mm for 15 mm diameter rivets. Minimum two rivets should be used for all connections.

(x) For small span, the ends of the trusses are fixed. In case of long span trusses, one end should be fixed and the other end is mounted on steel rollers.

(xi) For a series of trusses, wind tie, diagonal braces between the two end trusses should be provided on either side to prevent the general distortion of the roof due to wind action.

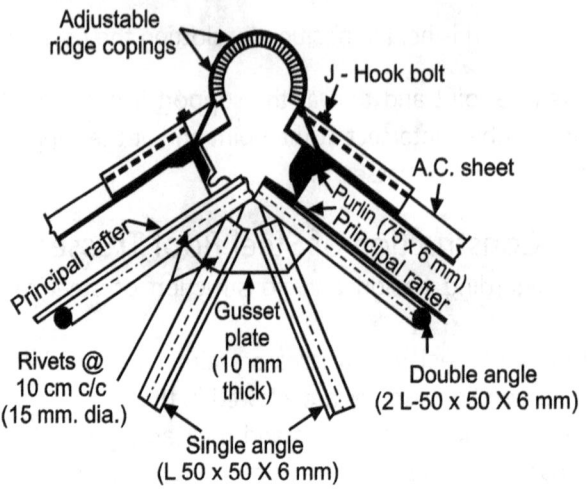

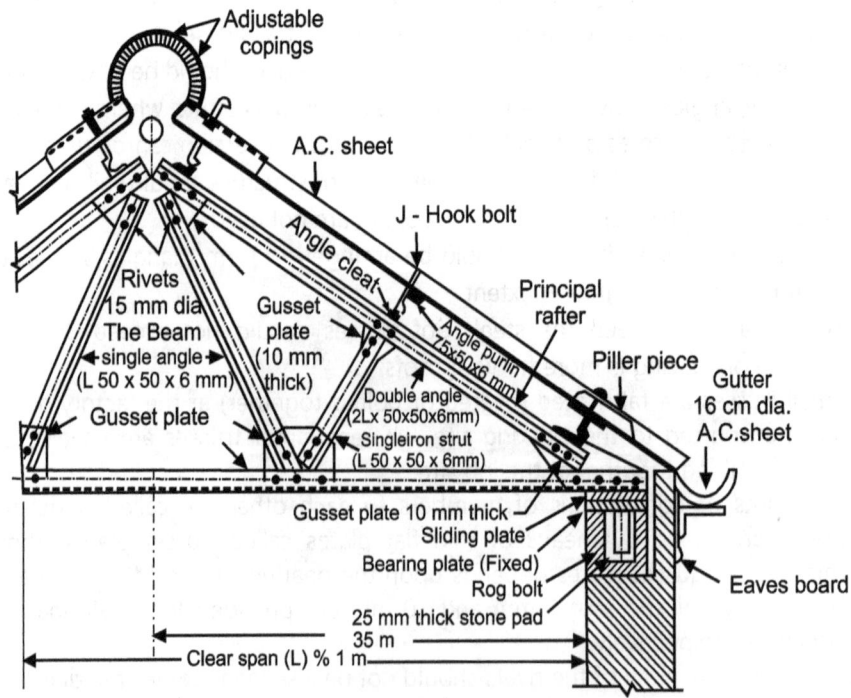

Fig. 7.14 : Simple steel fink roof trusses – details

[for span, i.e. L = 6 to 10 metres]

7.8 PROFLEX (TRUSSLESS) ROOFS

Concept of Proflex (Trussless) Roof and their Selection

The technology of trussless roof is used for last 40 years and in various countries.

The application of trussless roof are textile units, automobile units, food possessing units, sugar industry, mangal karyalaya, ware housing, parking, air plane aprons etc.

The self-supporting spans ranging from 10 to 36 meters.
The installation speed is of 900-1200 square meter in 12 hours.

Fig. 7.15

Advantages of Proflex (trussless) Roof
- It is a self-supported structure without truss purlins or ancillary support.
- The elimination of corrugation is there from a single piece raw material.
- The shell structure produces higher enclosed volumes and esthetically appealing facilities.
- Use of various coloured sheets is also possible.
- The maintenance for the structure is less, bird nuisance is less. It also provides efficient working conditions.
- The proflex roof is having the clear span due to this unobstructed air flow and superior temperature is also available.
- The temperature inside the building is maintained.

REVIEW QUESTIONS

1. State the points to be observed while providing A.C. sheet roofing to steel angle purlins.
2. A hall of size 7.50 mm and 10.0 m is to be provided with pitched roof of A.C. sheet roofing using steel trusses and angle purlins. Draw the arrangement of supporting structure, type of roof truss, purlin cleat angle junction details and fixing arrangement of A.C. sheet roofing to purlin.
3. Draw a typical arrangement for pitched roofing for L-shaped building with internal clear dimensions 7.50 m × 15.0 m for a long side and 7.50 m and 5.0 m for short side. Draw a labelled sketch and show the following :
   (a) Ridge   (b) Eaves
   (c) Valley   (d) Hip
   (e) Gable end   (f) Hip end.

State the type of truss and c/c spacing. State spacing of purlins for C.G.I. sheet roofing. Draw typical connection of fixing of C.G.I. sheet to angle purlin.
4. State the types of shell structure. What is butterfly shell ?
5. Give neat and labelled sketch of king post truss.
6. What are the advantages of constructing steel roof trusses over timber trusses ?
7. State circumstances under which each of the following is adopted :
   (a) Pitched roof, (b) Flat roof,
   (c) Dome, (d) Shell roof.
8. What are the relative advantages and disadvantages of flat roofs over other roofs ?
9. Draw neat and labelled sketch of queen post truss.
10. Name the types of roofing material available in market. State advantages and limitations of each.
11. Describe lean to roof in detail, with neat and labelled sketch.
12. Give neat and labelled sketches of the following structural steel sections. Write their minimum sections available in market :
    (a) Angle (b) Channel.
13. What are the relative advantages and disadvantages of flat roof over other types ?
14. Write short notes on :
    (a) G.I. sheets (b) A.C. sheets
    (c) Laying and fixing of G.I. sheets (d) Laying and fixing of A.C. sheets
    (e) Mangalore tiles (f) Roofing tiles
    (g) Marble tiles
15. Explain in detail testing of tiles.
16. Compare asbestos cement sheet and G.I. sheet.
17. Explain in detail fixing of A.C. sheet
18. Explain with sketches :
    (a) Ridge cover (b) Purlin
    (c) Principal rafter
19. Enlist the forms of roof trusses and explain king post roof truss.
20. Write a short note on space frame structures.
21. Define the following terms as used in pitched roof constructions :
    (a) Template (b) Post-plates
    (c) Pitch of a roof (d) Jack rafters
22. Discuss the various factors which require due consideration while selecting a roof - covering for a building.
23. Write notes on :
    (a) Shell structures (b) Folded plate structures

Chapter 8

CONCRETE FLOORING (TREMIX FLOORING)

8.0 INTRODUCTION

Floors in factories and industries have concrete being the most versatile of flooring material, has been in use for a long time. To overcome the deficiencies of concrete a system was devised to improve the properties of such concrete floors. This system is "Vacuum Dewatered Floors". (Vacuum Dewatered Concrete Flooring [TREMIX])

Process

In this system, concrete is poured in place & vibrated with a poker vibrator. Then a screed vibrator is run over the surface, supported on channel shuttering spaced 4.0 meters apart. The screed vibrator is run twice to achieve optimum compaction & leveling. After this a system of lower mats & top mat is laid on the green concrete & this is attached to a vacuum pump. This draws out excess water.

Benefits

1. Compressive strength of floor increases by upto 60%
2. Tensile strength increases by @ 70%
3. Cement consumption is reduced to the extent of 40%, no cement is required separately for finishing the surface.
4. Abrasion resistance of the floor increases by @ 60% resulting in les wear and rear of the floor surface
5. Shrinkage of concrete is reduced and floor wraps less.

8.1 FUNCTIONAL REQUIREMENTS OF FLOORING MATERIAL

The floor is intended to serve the following functions :

1. It should be strong enough to sustain safely the intended to be applied.
2. It should resist wear and tear.
3. It should sustain impact load.
4. It should be easy to clean and maintain.
5. It should have pleasing appearance.
6. It should be impermeable.
7. It should take polish.
8. It should not be slippery.
9. It should be easily available and economical.

8.2 VARIETIES OF FLOOR FINISHES AND THEIR SUITABILITY

Flooring materials can be broadly classified as :

    (i) **Hard Floor :** Natural stone, clay/ceramic tiles and cement/cement based floors.

    (ii) **Wooden Floors :** Hardwood, softwood.

    (iii) **Soft Floors :** PVC (vinyl), coir, cork, linoleum.

    (iv) **Floor Coverings :** Carpets, rugs and other floor furnishings.

    (v) **Specialised Floors :** Mild steel/iron tiles, plastics, seamless, aluminium.

Note : "All purpose" referes to the human activities confined to domestic houses, flats etc. commercial offices, shops, schools and public buildings.

Light Foot Traffic : Seldom used areas i.e. floors in houses, executive cabins etc.

Medium Foot Traffic : Moderately used areas i.e. floors in commercial establishments.

Heavy Foot Traffic : Much used areas i.e. floors in public buildings and reception room of offices.

Table 8.1 : Different types of flooring materials and their applications

Sr. No.	Material	Usage	Remarks
(1)	**Hard floors**		
1.	**Natural stone**		
	(a) Cuddapah	All purpose	Economical, available only in black. Not commonly used in bathroom, main room.
	(b) Granite	All purpose	Expensive, elegant and durable.
	(c) Marble	All purpose	Expensive, elegant and durable.
	(d) Quartzite	All purpose	Economical
	(e) Slate	All purpose	Economical
	(f) Sand stone	Light traffic areas	Economical
	(g) Shahabad	All purpose	Economical
	(h) Kotah, limestone	All purpose	Available in black colour only.
2.	**Clay/Ceramic tiles**		
	(a) Sintered clay/ceramic glazed tiles	All purpose	
	(b) Unglazed or quarry tiles	All purpose	

(Contd. ...)

Sr. No.	Material	Usage	Remarks
3.	Cement/cement based		
	(a) Cement concrete (in-situ)	All purpose includes industrial floor	End use governs mix properties.
	(b) Terrazzo floors (in-situ)	All purpose	Frequently laid where a high standard of appearance and cleanliness is required.
	(c) Mosaic tiles	All purpose	Used where high cleanliness is not required.
	(d) Other cement based tiles	All purpose	Available in various designs and shapes.
(2)	**Wooden floors (Timber flooring)**		
1.	Hard wood	Heavy foot traffic areas	It can be painted with polyurethane points. It is often covered by carpet. Durability can be improved by good seal.
2.	Parquet	Light medium foot traffic areas	It is not used in damped areas.
3.	Softwood	Light foot traffic areas	Painted with polyurethane paint. It is covered by carpet.
(3)	**Soft floors**		
1.	Coir tiles	Light medium foot traffic areas	
2.	Cork tiles	Light-heavy foot traffic areas	Avoid its use in damp areas.
3.	Linoleum	Light-heavy foot traffic areas	Available with anti-static properties.
4.	PVC (vinyl) with Asbestos	Light-heavy foot traffic areas	Available with anti-static properties.

8.3 CONSTRUCTION DETAILS OF CONCRETE FLOOR

Concrete flooring is called as artificial stone flooring. It's constructional details are explained as follows :

(i) Preparation of Ground : It should be well compacted. It should be watered properly to gain considerable strength to offer support. It should not contain pockets of loose soil.

(ii) Preparation of Sub-grade : If sub-grade is of concrete it's proportion will be 1 : 2 : 4. It should be mixed thoroughly by any means i.e. manually or mechanically. It should be provided with proper slope. It should be coated with cement slurry to get a good bond between the sub-grade and concrete floor. The surface of subgrade should be roughened with steel wire brushes without disturbing the concrete. The sub-grade may be R.C.C. slab.

(iii) Laying of Flooring : The concrete should be placed gently and evenly spread within the panel of area 2 m². The panel should be of uniform size. It's dimension should not exceed 2 m. The operation of laying of concrete for each panel should be finished within half an hour.

To ensure uniformity of colours and straightens in all the panels it should be laid in one operation using plain asbestos sheet stripes at the junction of the panels. The panels should be bounded by wooden battens. The depth of the battens should be same as that of the concrete flooring surface of the flooring which should be smoothed with wooden floats.

The battens should be removed after 24 hours once laying of concrete is finished.

If ends are damaged, it should be repaired with cement mortar 1 : 2.

(iv) Finishing of Flooring : Once moisture is varnished cement slurry should be prepared. It should spread over flooring. It should be properly pressed and finished smooth.

(v) Curing : Once the top layer has hardened, curing should be done for minimum ten days.

Casting Large Floors :

For large industrial and commercial buildings, it is not feasible to cast floor of the size required in one section. There are two methods of casting large floors to remove this difficulty.

These are explained as follows :

(1) The Chequer Board Method : In this method, floor can be subdivided into a series of sections of restricted width and length. Alternate sections of the floor can cast in a chequer board arrangement.

This method is not easy. It requires to put many structural joints running along and across the floor. It does not offer speedy construction.

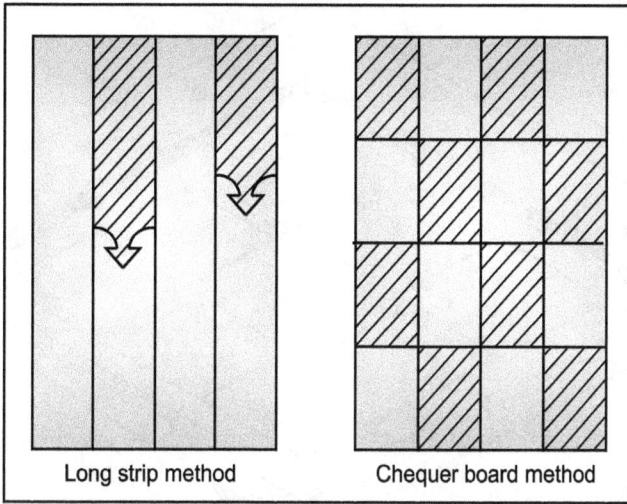

Fig. 8.1 : Long strip and chequer boad options

(2) The Long Strip Method : It is based on the division of floor into a series of long strips. It is around 4.5 m in width, running the full length of the building or upto a selected movement joint. The strips can be cast in two phases, Initially with alternate strips and the in-fill joints cast after some days.

Narrow edge strips (630 – 1000 mm wide) are formed near the walls to allow ready access for the compacting beam across full width strips. There is possibility of development of cracks. To control it strips are normally divided into bays. The need of the joints is related to the length of the strips and the presence of reinforcement.

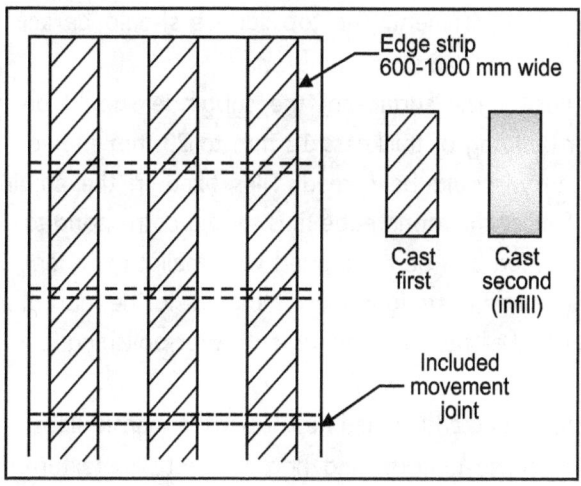

Fig. 8.2 : Long strip floor layout

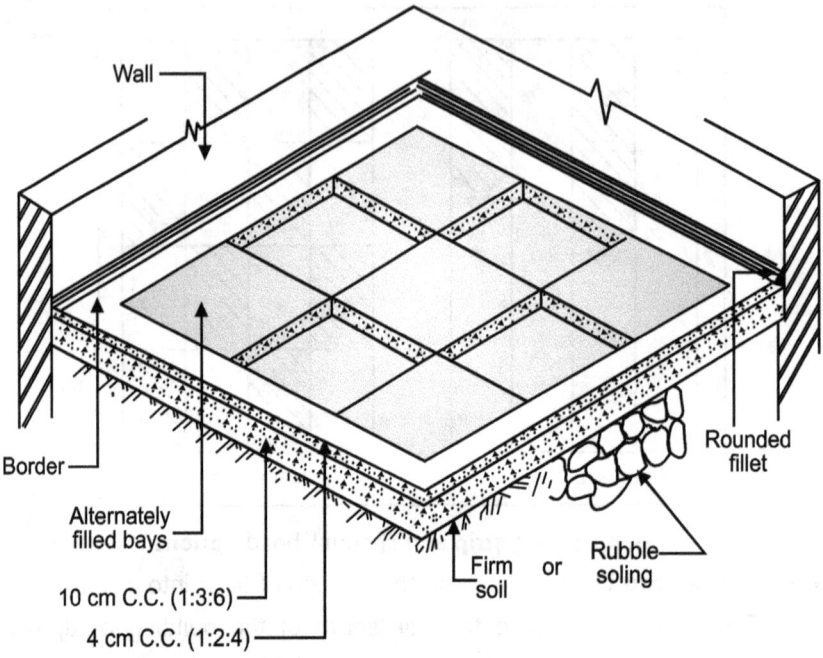

Fig. 8.3 : Laying of concrete flooring

8.4 CONSTRUCTION DETAILS FOR TILE FLOORING

It can be divided into the following types :

   (i) Levelling of ground : The ground should be levelled properly. It should be properly watered and rammed so that it can offer good base to different components.

   (ii) Preparation of subgrade : It should be of mortor cement concrete or R.C.C. of 15 to 20 cm thickness as per requirement. The top surface should be kept slightly rough. The required slope should be provided to the subgrade.

   (iii) Laying of tiles : The surface of the subgrade should be cleaned of all loose materials. The mortor bedding of thickness 12 mm to 20 mm should be placed in any one place. The cement slurry should be spread. Tiles fixed in the adjoining wall should be arranged that the surface of the round edge tiles should correspond to skirting or dado. Each tiles should be well pressed and gently tapped with mallet (wooden). The joints should be kept as close as possible and in straight lines. It should not be more than 1.5 mm. After two days it should be polished as per the requirement. After polishing it should be washed with solution.

[**Note :** For Makrana/coloured and veined Pepsu/Baroda marble slabs.

Slabs should be hard, dense uniform and homogeneous in texture. It should have even crystalline grain and free from defects and cracks. It's edges should be machine cut true and square. The rear surface should be rough enough to provide a key for the mortar.]

BUILDING CONSTRUCTION AND MATERIALS — CONCRETE FLOORING (TREMIX FLOORING)

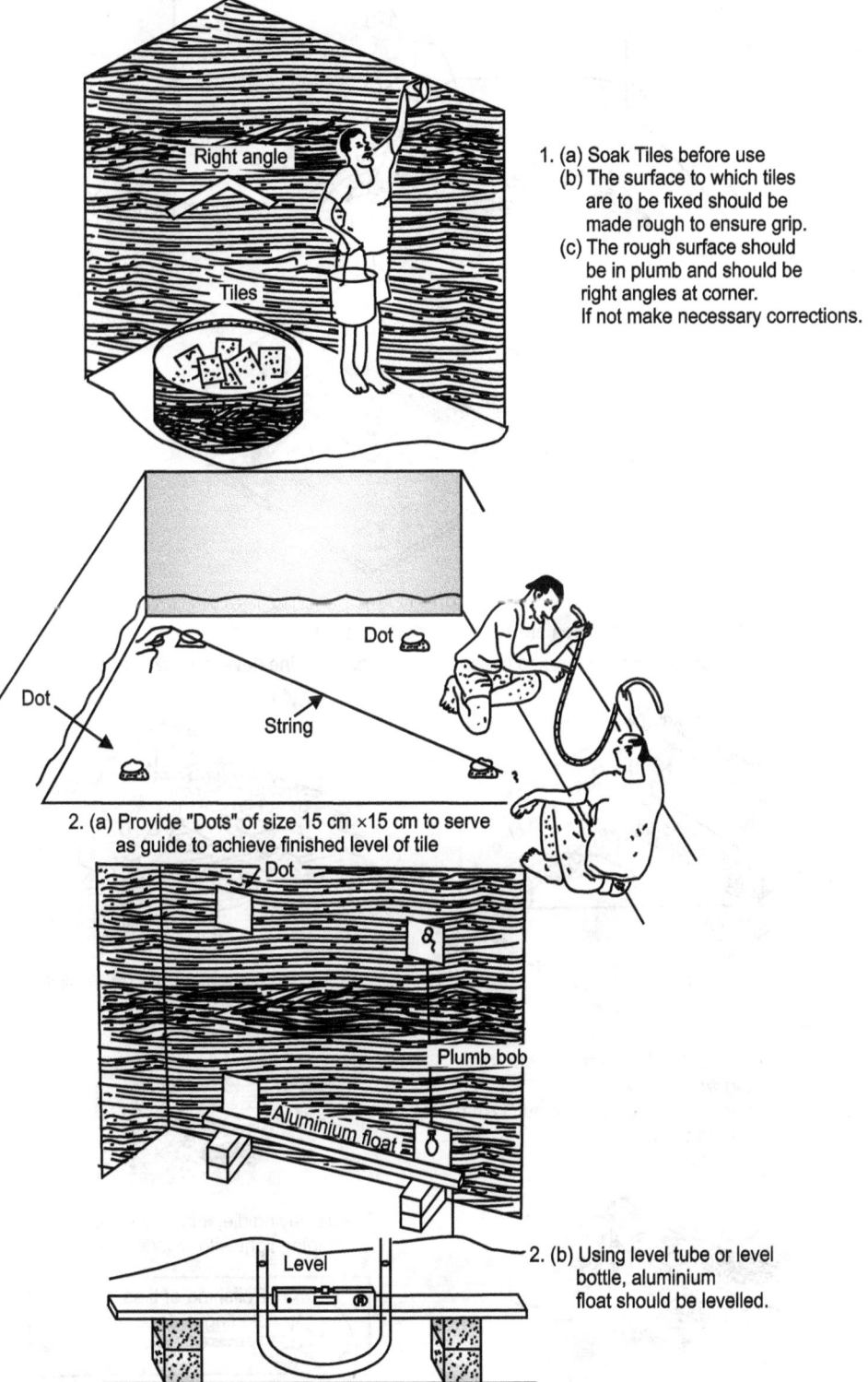

1. (a) Soak Tiles before use
   (b) The surface to which tiles are to be fixed should be made rough to ensure grip.
   (c) The rough surface should be in plumb and should be right angles at corner. If not make necessary corrections.

2. (a) Provide "Dots" of size 15 cm ×15 cm to serve as guide to achieve finished level of tile

2. (b) Using level tube or level bottle, aluminium float should be levelled.

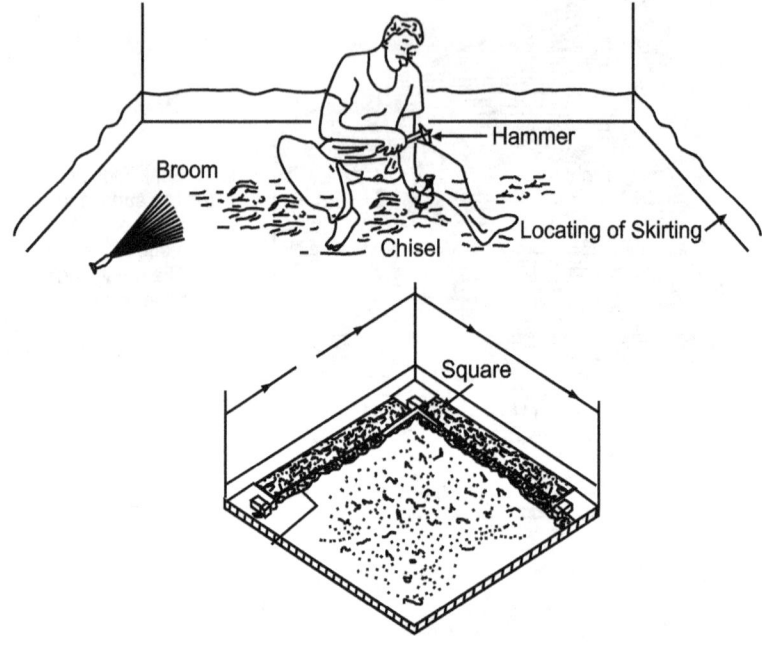

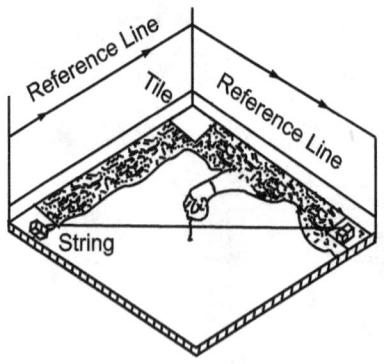

3. (a) Reference lines are set up using level tube
   (b) Using the reference lines, tiles are placed in line, level and at right angles.

5. Laying cement morter below tiles

4. (a) Using line "Dot" and tape, accuracy of tiling work is checked.
   Tiles near wall should be about 12mm away from the wall.

7. After laying tile, it is levelled by a tamping light with wooden mallet.

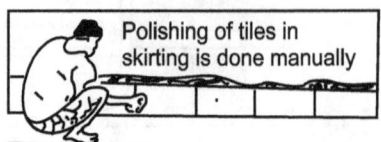

Polishing of tiles in skirting is done manually

6. Placing tile over cement morter

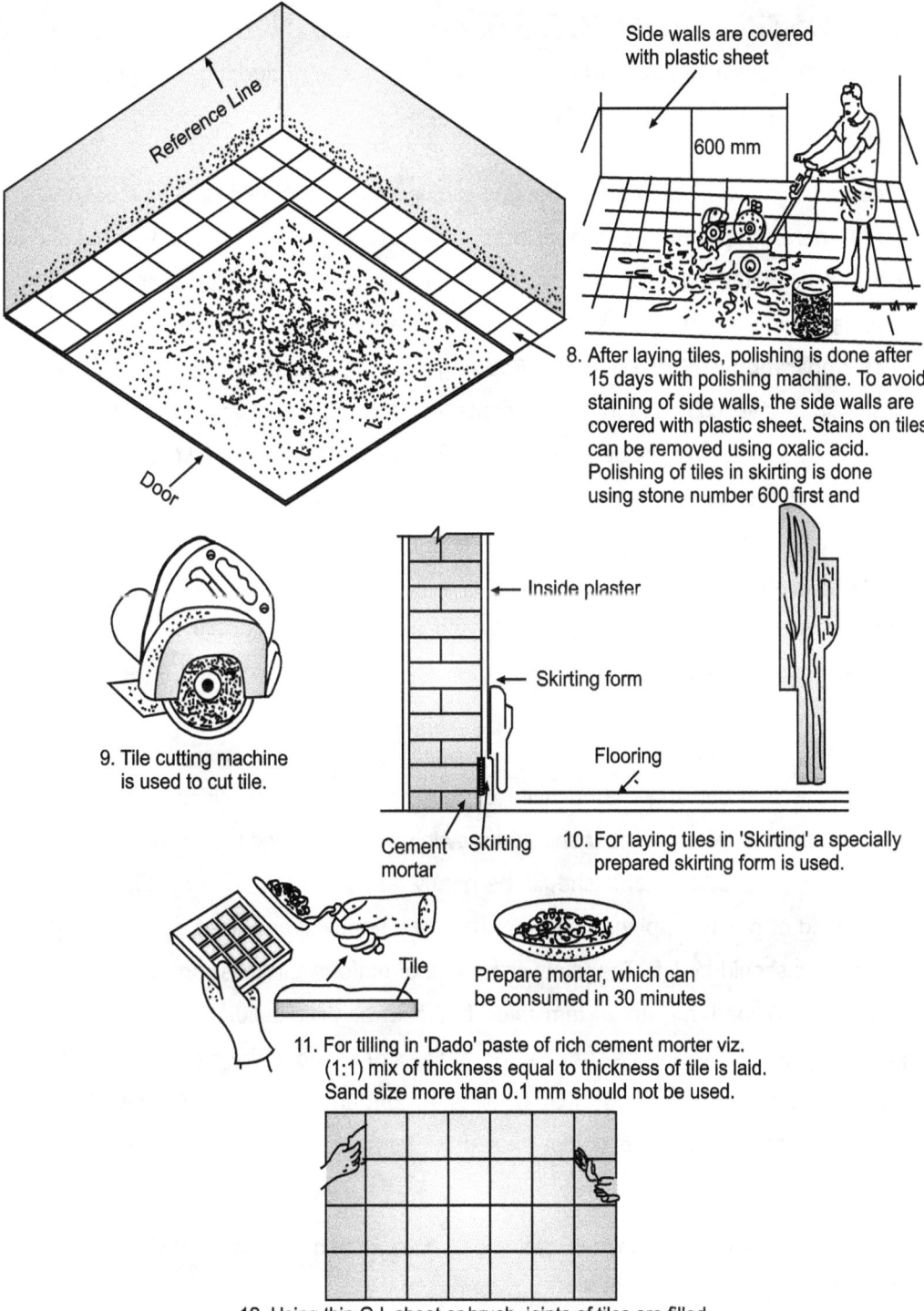

Fig. 8.4

8.5 CONSTRUCTION FOR STONE FLOORING

Stone flooring construction details are governed by purpose of flooring, thickness of stone, type of mortar specified in the defined specifications.

The method of construction of stone flooring can be divided into the following steps :

(1) General Preparation : To offer proper support to base course and wearing surface and also to distribute load evenly to the ground, it should be compacted properly. It should obtain maximum strength by reasonable spraying of water.

(2) Preparation of Bare Course or Bedding : Before spreading the mortar the floor or base should be cleaned of all dirt, scum or laitance and of loose material. It should be evenly and smoothly spread over the base by the use of screed battens. The thickness of the mortar bedding should not be less than 12 mm and not more than 25 mm. The required slope shall be given to the bed. When sand bed is provided, it shall spread upto a thickness of 12 mm. The sand shall not contain more than 10% of clay. Sand used shall be coarse.

(3) Fixing the Stones : Before placing/laying, it should be thoroughly wetted with clean water. Neat cement grout or cement slurry of required consistency should be spread on the mortar bed.

If sand bed is provided there is no need of cement grout. The specified stone should be placed on the neat cement float. It should be evenly and firmly bedded to the required level and slope in the mortar bed. It should be gently lapped with wooden mallet. If there is hollow sound or gentle tapping, the stone should be removed and reset again properly. No hollow spaces should be left. The joints should be of uniform thickness and in straight lines. The joints should be 6 mm to 10 mm thick. It should be filled solidly with mortar for their required full depth. It should be struck smooth. The stones should be placed such as to give continuous parallel long joints with cross joints at right angles to them. For polished stone flooring thickness of joints should not exceed 1.5 mm. Joints should be grouted with neat cement slurry.

The flooring joints have completely set, the surface should be machine polished to give smooth finish and pleasing appearance.

After this activity the flooring should be thoroughly cleaned and free from any mortar strains.

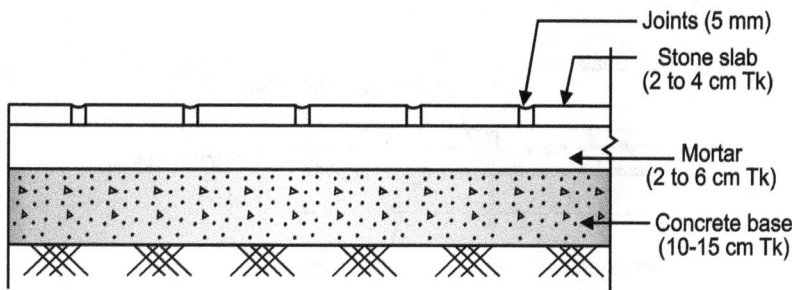

Fig. 8.5 : Cross-section of stone flooring

8.6 JOINTS IN LONG SPAN FLOORS

Large span floors are used for industrial and commercial buildings. For these floors there may be possibility of expansion and contraction process. To accommodate the movements due to these processes, there is requirement of joints. The design of joint is important to resist the vertical movement between bays.

The joints are classified into four categories as below :

(1) Longitudinal Joints : It is main construction joint in the floor. It separates the slab into the long strip pattern. It consists of tie bars. If tie bars are debonded, it will allow a degree of contraction in the slab across the joint. If tie bars are bended the contraction will be restricted. In both conditions vertical loads are transferred between adjacent bags through the bars.

If tie bars are bonded the contraction will be restricted. In both conditions vertical loads are transferred between adjacent bays through the bars.

(2) Induced Joints : These are used to control the bay length. It can be obtained through a mechanism for controlled cracking of the slab as it cures. This joint is depending upon the friction between the sides of the joint for restriction of vertical movement. It can be accomplished by sufficient interlocking of the exposed aggregate at the crack faces.

(3) Movement Joints : It is included within the slabs. Due to variation in temperature there is natural movement of the material. Due to shrinkage of concrete, contraction joint is becoming more common. Sometime expansion joint is also required.

(4) Isolation Joints : It is sub-group of movement joint. Its purpose is to allow movement of slab around fixings. In framed structures it is mainly common around the bases of columns or stanchions.

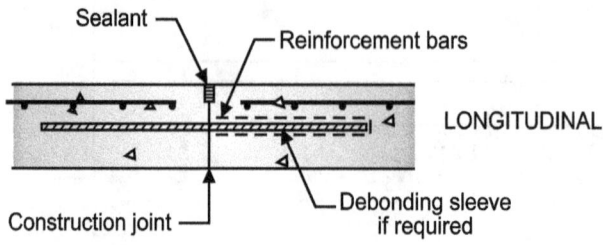

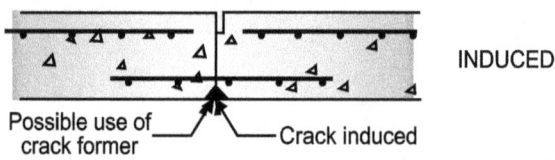

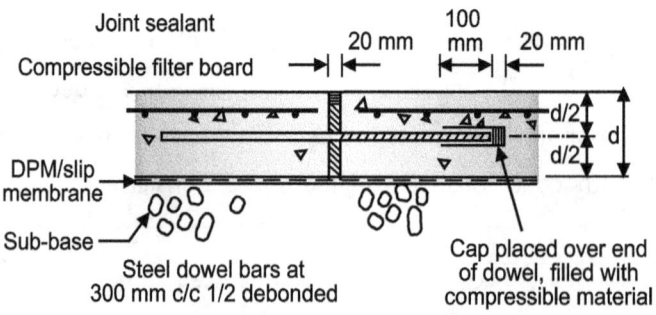

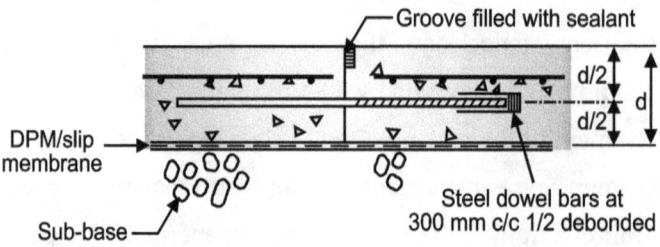

Fig. 8.6 : Joint details

8.7 TYPES OF FLOORING

(1) Filler Joist Floor :

Small sections of rolled steel joists, resting on wall or on steel beams, are placed within concrete. The centre to centre distance is 600 to 900 mm. These joists serve the purpose of reinforcement. A concrete cover of the minimum 25 mm is to be provided to avoid corrosion. Flooring is laid over concrete surface.

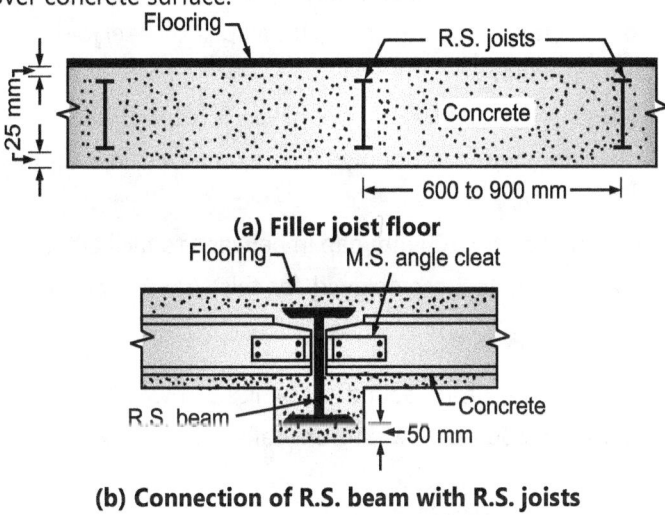

Fig. 8.7

(2) Jack Arch Floors :

Arches made up of bricks or concrete are so laid as to rest on lower flanges of M.S. joists. The joist in turn rests either on wall or a beam; with centre to centre distance ranging within 800 to 1200 mm.

1. Brick Jack Arch Flooring : Laying of bricks starts from edges of joists. Bricks to be used are well burnt and to be saturated with water. Joints are to be filled with rich mortar for proper binding and transfer of load from key brick to springer brick and finally to the support. Curing of brick work is to be carried out for 15 days minimum. On the top of concrete (above the arch) floor tiles are placed. (Shuttering – Centering can be shifted ahead to support new arch).

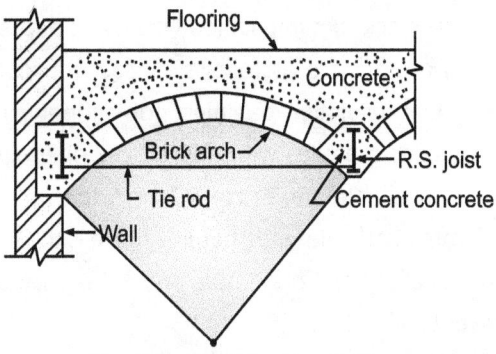

Fig. 8.8 : Brick jack arch floor

2. Concrete Jack Arch Floor : Centering : Made up of steel plate of about 3 mm thickness, hence can be moulded to take the required shape. It has pair of holes (centre to centre distance 750 mm) to hold steel bars which keep the arch at its position.

Concrete is laid to required thickness and curing for ten days is carried out. Shuttering is to be removed after concrete attains sufficient strength. Rolled steel joists are embedded within concrete if the span is more than 3.6 m for the arch. Tie rods are to be provided between the joists to resist horizontal thrust in extreme pair of steel joists.

(3) Hollow Block and Rib Floor :

As the name suggests the hollowness for the blocks is responsible for reduction in overall weight of the floor and to achieve economy. This is preferred in case of hospitals, hotels, schools, offices etc.

The blocks are placed at about 100 mm gap in between to facilitate position of M.S. bars. A cover of 80 mm or more is to be employed for this roof flooring on the top of which suitable flooring can be laid.

Advantages : Economical, fire proof, sound proof, light in weight, installation of electrical and plumbing accessories through hollow portions can be conveniently carried out.

Tiles Used : Hollow concrete or hollow clay floor tiles.

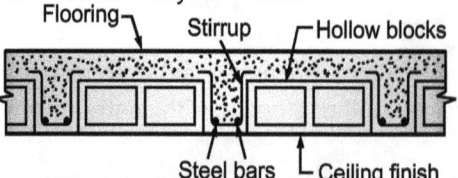

Fig. 8.9 : Hollow block and rib floor

(4) Cork :

Natural, flame retardant, made from bark of cork oak tree (bark being peeled after every 9 to 14 years with average life of 500 years). The flooring do not react to any fluid, supple under your feet but with a drawback that impact load creates a depression mark on it.

The other characteristics of cork are as follows : Insect repellent, scratch resistant, fire resistant, sound absorbent, heat insulation qualities, non-slippery. The cork tile or carpet is made by heating or baking cork granules with linseed oil, phenolic or other resin binders under pressure. Sizes of tiles available are 10 cm × 10 cm to 30 cm × 90 cm and thickness ranging between 5 to 15 mm. Cork tile with natural finish should be sanded, sealed and waxed immediately after installation. Cork floors must be maintained with sealers and protective coatings to prevent soiling.

Applications : Libraries, Theatres, Art galleries, Broadcasting stations etc.

(5) Terrazzo Flooring :

Terrazzo topping i.e. terrazzo mix of broken marble chips, stones, ceramic articles is laid on concrete sub-base. Cement and epoxy resins are used as binders. Normally, it can be used anywhere in residential, public buildings as the look is effective. It also takes high polish and seamless laying of the mix makes the layer water proof.

Normal thickness of topping PS 6 mm with marble chips 3 to 6 mm.

8.8 MATERIAL, TESTS AND IS SPECIFICATIONS

Various types of tiles are available. The following are types of tiles:
1. Clay Flooring Tiles - IS 1478 – 1969.
2. Flat Burnt Clay Tiles for Terracing – IS 2690 Part I and II.
3. Flat Burnt Clay tiles for Irrigation, Drainage Work - IS 3367 – 1975.
4. Manglore Tiles - IS 654 – 1972.
5. Roofing Slate Tiles - IS 6250 – 1981.
6. Tiles of Lime Stone - IS 1128 – 1974.
7. Tiles of Sand Stone - IS 6250 – 1981.
8. Tiles of Marble - IS 3622 – 1977.
9. Glazed Earthen Ware Tiles - IS 777 – 1970.
10. Cement Concrete Flooring Tile - IS 1237 – 1980.

8.8.1 Clay Flooring Tiles

These tiles are flat, square and are available in many colours. These should be uniform in size, shape and free from irregularities and foreign materials either on the surface or on the fractured surface.

Dimensions and permissible tolerances are :

Length	Width	Minimum thickness
150 mm	150 mm	15 / 20
200	200	20 / 25
250	250	30
Tolerances ± 5 mm	± 5 mm	± 2 mm

The tiles are classified in three classes, the physical requirements of which are as under :

Characteristics of Clay Flooring Tile	Class I	Class II	Class III
1. Water Absorption (maximum)	10%	19%	24%
2. Flexural strength kg/cm²	6	3.5	2.5
3. Impact Test : Max. height (in mm) drop of steel ball of 35 mm diameter and mass 170 gm.			
Thickness of tile 15 mm	25	20	15
20 mm	60	50	40
25 mm	75	65	50
30 mm	80	70	60

8.8.2 Flat Burnt Clay Tiles

Usually, these are available in rectangular shape in various sizes available for terracing. These may be hand made or machine made.

Burnt clay tiles are also used for lining irrigation and drainage work. However, these tiles differ from those used in roofing, as detailed in the following table.

Type of Tiles	IS No.	Dimensions with tolerances	Physical properties			
			Compressive strength kgf/cm² min	Water Absorption % (max.)	Transverse strength kgf/cm²	Wrap Max (mm)
1. Tiles for lining irrigation and drainage works.	3367 – 1975	l = 300 ± 10 mm b = 150 ± 5 mm t = 50 mm ± 1.5 mm	105 75	15% (for class 105) 20	15 12	3 mm 3
	2690 Part II (Hand made)	l = 150 to 250 in stages of 25 mm. b = 100 to 200 mm in stages of 25 mm	75	20% by weight	–	2%
2. Burnt clay flat terracing tiles.	2690 Part I (machine made)	Thickness = 25 to 50				
		l and b same as above t = 15 and 20 mm		15% by weight	15	

8.8.3 Cement Concrete Flooring Tile

According to IS : 1237 – 1980 followings are definitions of some types of tiles :

(1) **Plain Cement Tiles :** Tiles in the manufacture of which no pigments and stone chips are used in the wearing surface.

(2) **Plain Coloured Tiles :** Tiles having a plain wearing surface where pigments are used but no stone chips.

(3) **Terrazo Tiles :** Tiles at least 25% of whose wearing surface is composed of stone chips in a matrix of ordinary or coloured portland cement mixed with or without pigments and mechanically ground and filled.

Materials :

(1) **Cement :** Cement used in the manufacture of tiles shall be ordinary portland cement conforming to IS : 269 – 1976 or rapid hardening portland cement conforming to IS : 8041 – 1978 or white portland cement conforming to IS : 8041 – 1978 or Port land cement conforming to IS : 1489 – 1976.

(2) **Aggregate :** Aggregate used in the backing layer of tiles shall conform to the requirements of IS 383 – 1970.

For the wearing layer aggregates shall consist of marble chips or any other natural stone chips of singular characteristics of hardness, marble powder or dolomite powder, or mixture of two.

(3) **Pigments :** Pigments, synthetic or otherwise, used for colouring tiles shall have durable colour. It shall not contain any detrimental matter.

The pigments should not contain zinc compounds or organic dyes. Lead pigments should not be used unless otherwise specified by the purchaser.

Pigments	I.S.
(i) Black/red/brown	IS : 44 – 1969
(ii) Green	IS : 54 – 1975
(iii) Blue	IS : 55 – 1970
	IS : 56 – 1975
(iv) White	IS : 411 – 1968
(v) Yellow	IS : 50 – 1979

Dimensions :

The size of cement concrete tiles are as follows :

Length (mm)	Breadth (mm)	Thickness (mm)
200	200	20
250	250	22
300	300	25

Physical Requirements :

(i) **Flatness of the Tile Surface :** It can be tested by means of a metal ruler. The length of it is not less than the tile diagonal. The amount of concavity convexity should not exceed 1 mm.

(ii) **Perpendicularly :** It can be tested by square. The longest gap between the arm of the square and the edge of the tile shall not exceed 2% of the length of the edge.

(iii) **Wet Transverse Strength :** According to IS : 1237 – 1980, for this test the span between the supports shall be as follows :

Size of tile (mm)	Span (mm)
200 × 200	150
250 × 250	200
300 × 300	250

The load shall be applied gradually and at a uniform rate not exceeding 2000 N per minute, until the tile breaks.

The average wet transverse strength shall not be less than 3 N/mm².

(iv) **Straightness :** The gap between the fine thread and the plane of the tile cannot exceed 1% of the length of the edge.

(v) **Water absorption :** The average percentage of water absorption shall not exceed 10%.

(vi) **Resistance to Wear :** The wear shall not exceed the following value :

    (a) For general purpose tiles :
        (i) Average wear 3.5 mm
        (ii) Wear on individual specimen 4 mm.

    (b) For heavy duty floor tiles :
        (i) Average wear 2 mm
        (ii) Wear on individual specimen 2.5 mm.

Other than cement concrete flooring tiles, based upon purpose and materials, followings are types of tiles :

(i) **Common Tiles :** These are having different shapes and sizes. They are used for paving, flooring etc.

(ii) **Encaustic Tiles :** These tiles are mainly used for decorative purposes in floors, walls ceilings etc.

(iii) **Clay Flooring Tile (CBRI) :** It is based upon type of raw material used for it's preparation. It contains alluvial soil mainly. It represents high water absorption but poor impact and abrasion resistance. It possesses uniform texture and colour, a metallic sound and good finish. It is available in three sizes 15 × 15 × 1.5 cm, 20 × 20 × 2 cm, 25 × 25 × 2.5 cm etc.

(iv) **Cinder Flooring Tiles :** Cinder i.e. coal ash is an industrial waste. It is effectively used to manufacture semi-vitreous unglazed tiles. It is economical and cheaper. It can be used in school, hospital, public buildings, industrial sheds, railway platforms, roads etc.

(v) **Terracota Flooring Tiles :** It is unglazed clay flooring tiles of semi-vitreous type. It is widely used in various public buildings.

(vi) **Matt Glazed Flooring Ceramic Tiles :** It was manufactured traditionally by use of twice fired earthenware body glazed tiles. Due to advanced technology it is available in various types of shades. It has a strength of 44 N/mm^2, 0.5 – 1% water absorption.

In the market various companies like NITCO etc. offering tiles in various shapes, sizes, categories. Tiles are generally available in 30 cm × 30 cm, 40 × 40 cm, 10 × 40 cm. These are categorised as exotica, elegant, prime plus, super exclusive, rustic etc.

REVIEW QUESTIONS

1. State any four flooring materials. State the advantages and limitations of each.
2. State step-by-step procedure to construct concrete flooring for an industrial building.
3. Explain the construction of flat slab floor for commercial buildings. State the advantages of it. State recent technology used to reduce thickness of it.
4. A hall of size 7.50 m and 10.0 m is to be provided with two way ribbed floor construction. Explain process of construction with the help of neat sketches. State the grade of concrete and steel used for the construction.
5. State with reason, most suitable type of flooring material for the following situations :
   (a) A drawing room of a high specification bungalow.
   (b) Car parking of a residential flat building.
   (c) Ware house where heavy articles are stored.
   (d) Kitchen flooring for middle income group housing.
6. State step-by-step procedure of providing vacuum processed concrete flooring for industrial sheds. What type of coating is provided to make floor more resistant to abrasion and avoid dusting ?
7. Draw a labelled sketch of flat slab floor and show the following :
   (a) Capital, (b) Drop panel, (c) Flat slab.
   State two important advantages of the flat slab flooring.
8. Name the type of flooring materials available in the market. State advantages and limitations of each.
9. Write down the I.S. codes for any four tiles. Draw detailed sketch for tile impact test.
10. Describe the construction of concrete flooring.

BUILDING CONSTRUCTION AND MATERIALS — CONCRETE FLOORING (TREMIX FLOORING)

11. What do you understand by the following types of floors :
    (a) Basement floors, (b) Suspended floors ?
12. Explain the following by means of neat sketches :
    (a) Brick jack arch floor,
    (b) Hering bone strutting in timber floors.
13. What types of flooring do you recommend for the following ? Discuss justifying your selection :
    (a) Dancing hall,   (b) Public W.C. and bath rooms,
    (c) Grain storage godowns,   (d) Chemical laboratories,
    (e) Recreation hall of a high class hotel, (f) Garage
14. Explain the detailed procedure of construction of marble tiles flooring. Give sketch also.
15. State the functional requirements of flooring materials. Give the I.S. codes for any four tiles.
16. What do you understand by mosaic flooring ? Describe in detail the construction of such a floor.
17. State essential requirements of good flooring material.
18. What types of floorings would you recommend for the following :
    (a) Lecture hall of a Modern College,   (b) Drawing hall,
    (c) Laboratories,   (d) Hostels,
    (e) Dance halls.
19. Describe briefly the type of floor finishing used for different types of buildings and state the reasons for their choice.
20. What are relative advantages and disadvantages of pre-cast concrete floor ?
21. Enlist the various flooring tiles available in the market. Write advantages and disadvantages of any two.
22. What are the relative advantages and disadvantages of concrete floor ?
23. Enlist the factors to be considered for the selection of flooring and state four types of tiles based on materials and I.S. specification.
24. Explain the procedure of construction of cement concrete flooring.
25. Explain the procedure of construction of concrete floor, giving its relative merits and demerits.
26. Explain the following by means of neat sketches :
    (a) Floor ceilings   (b) Herring - bone strutting in timber floors.
27. Differentiate between the following :
    (a) Floors and Flooring   (b) Basement Floors and Suspended Floors
    (c) RCC Slab Floor and Flat Slab Floor.

www.ingramcontent.com/pod-product-compliance
Lightning Source LLC
Chambersburg PA
CBHW080242170426
43192CB00014BA/2537